Social Identity and Working Class Support for the Populist Radical Right

Social Identity and Working Class Support for the Populist Radical Right

From Economic and Political Distress to Cultural Grievances

Eric G. Castater
Kyung Joon Han

OXFORD
UNIVERSITY PRESS

Great Clarendon Street, Oxford, OX2 6DP,
United Kingdom

Oxford University Press is a department of the University of Oxford.
It furthers the University's objective of excellence in research, scholarship,
and education by publishing worldwide. Oxford is a registered trade mark of
Oxford University Press in the UK and in certain other countries

© Eric G. Castater and Kyung Joon Han 2025

The moral rights of the authors have been asserted.

All rights reserved. No part of this publication may be reproduced, stored in a retrieval system, transmitted, used for text and data mining, or used for training artificial intelligence, in any form or by any means, without the prior permission in writing of Oxford University Press, or as expressly permitted by law, by licence or under terms agreed with the appropriate reprographics rights organization. Enquiries concerning reproduction outside the scope of the above should be sent to the Rights Department, Oxford University Press, at the address above.

You must not circulate this work in any other form
and you must impose this same condition on any acquirer.

Published in the United States of America by Oxford University Press
198 Madison Avenue, New York, NY 10016, United States of America

British Library Cataloguing in Publication Data
Data available

Library of Congress Control Number: 2024946956

ISBN 9780198953074

DOI: 10.1093/9780198953104.001.0001

Printed and bound by
CPI Group (UK) Ltd, Croydon, CR0 4YY

Links to third party websites are provided by Oxford in good faith and
for information only. Oxford disclaims any responsibility for the materials
contained in any third party website referenced in this work.

The manufacturer's authorised representative in the EU for product safety is
Oxford University Press España S.A. of El Parque Empresarial San Fernando de Henares, Avenida
de Castilla, 2 – 28830 Madrid (www.oup.es/en or
product.safety@oup.com). OUP España S.A. also acts as importer into Spain
of products made by the manufacturer.

Contents

List of Figures	vi
List of Tables	vii
List of Abbreviations	ix

1. **Introduction** — 1

2. **Populist Radical Right-wing Parties and the Working Class** — 27

3. **A Social Identity Approach to Blue-Collar Worker Support for the Populist Radical Right** — 47

4. **The Policymaking Process: Economic Reforms and Support for the Populist Radical Right** — 81

5. **Policy Outputs: Labour Policies and Support for the Populist Radical Right** — 111

6. **Policy Outcomes: Economic Inequality and Support for the Populist Radical Right** — 139

7. **Concluding Remarks** — 172

Appendix A: A Multinomial Logistic Analysis of Social Identity	184
Appendix B: Robustness Checks with the International Social Survey Programme (2013)	190
Appendix C: Results of First-Stage Models in Causal Mediation Analyses	192
Appendix D: A Robustness Check with Excluding Country/Years without a PRRP	199
Appendix E: A Robustness Check with a Country Fixed-Effect Model	201
References	203
Index	231

List of Figures

1.1 A social identity approach to support for the populist radical right	10
2.1 Employment in the industrial and service sectors in Western Europe, 1971–2019	32
2.2 Union density and union composition in Western Europe	39
3.1 Blue-collar worker and party positions on the economy and culture	62
3.2 Predicted probabilities of social identity	71
4.1 Social pacts and unilaterally enacted legislation, 1980s–2010s	86
4.2 Union membership, policymaking processes, and populist radical right-wing party support	108
5.1 EPL index, 1990–2018	117
5.2 Government spending on LMPs, 1990–2018	121
5.3 Labour policies and working-class support for the populist radical right	136
5.4 Working-class support for the populist radical right, 2002–18	137
6.1 Wage inequality between white-collar and blue-collar workers, 2006–18	145
6.2 Unemployment inequality between people with tertiary education and those without it, 1989–2019	152
6.3 Wage inequality between more skilled and less skilled blue-collar workers, 2006–18	165
6.4 Unemployment inequality between people with upper-secondary education (without tertiary education) and those without upper-secondary education, 1989–2019	166
6.5 Skill level and inequality effects on party support	169

List of Tables

2.1	List of PRRPs	30
2.2	Demographics of the working class	35
2.3	Support for redistribution among the working class	37
2.4	Average vote share by decade for major party families	41
2.5	PRRP support by occupation group	44
2.6	Blue-collar workers and PRRPs	45
3.1	The macro context and social identity	69
3.2	National identity and national pride	73
3.3	National pride and issue salience	74
3.4	Issue salience and support for PRRPs	77
4.1	Social pact proposals, social pact agreements, and unilateral legislation, 1980–2018	84
4.2	Social pacts and working-class support for the populist radical right	93
4.3	Unilateral legislation and working-class support for the populist radical right	96
4.4	Failed social pact proposals and working-class support for the populist radical right (Mediation Model)	101
4.5	Unilateral legislation and working-class support for the populist radical right (Mediation Model)	102
4.6	Union membership, policymaking processes, and support for the populist radical right	106
5.1	EPL index	116
5.2	Government spending on LMPs	120
5.3	EPL and working-class support for the populist radical right	124
5.4	LMP and working-class support for the populist radical right	125
5.5	EPL and working-class support for the populist radical right (Mediation Model)	127
5.6	LMP and working-class support for the populist radical right (Mediation Model)	129
5.7	Effects of ALMPs and PLMPs	132
5.8	EPL, LMPs, and working-class support for the populist radical right (ESS)	135
6.1	Wage inequality between blue-collar and white-collar workers	144
6.2	Unemployment inequality between education groups	150

viii   List of Tables

6.3 Wage inequality and manual workers' support for the populist radical right   155

6.4 Unemployment inequality and manual workers' support for the populist radical right   157

6.5 Wage inequality and manual workers' support for the populist radical right (Mediation Model)   159

6.6 Unemployment inequality and manual workers' support for the populist radical right (Mediation Model)   161

6.7 Skill level and inequality effects on party support   168

List of Abbreviations

ACME	Average causal mediation effect
ADE	Average direct effect
ALMP	Active labour market policy
ATE	Average treatment effect
CHES	Chapel Hill Expert Survey data on party positions
CME	Coordinated market economy
EES	European Election Studies
EPL	Employment protection legislation
ESS	European Social Survey
EU	European Union
EVS	European Values Study
ICTWSS	Database on Institutional Characteristics of Trade Unions, Wage Setting, State Intervention and Social Pacts
ISSP	International Social Survey Programme
LME	Liberal market economy
LMP	Labour market policy
OECD	Organization of the Economic Cooperation and Development
PLMP	Passive labour market policy
PRLP	Populist radical left-wing party
PRRP	Populist radical right-wing party
PRT	Power resource theory
VOC	Varieties of capitalism

1
Introduction

Populist radical right-wing parties (PRRPs)[1] have been gaining strength across most Western European countries in recent decades, with support surging for long-established PRRPs like the the National Rally in France and the Sweden Democrats, as well as for more newly established parties like Alternative for Germany and Vox in Spain (Rooduijn 2015; Lees 2018; Barrio, de Oger, and Field 2021). Given that this party family is defined by its nativist nationalism,[2] anti-establishment disposition, and authoritarian inclinations (Mudde 2007; Rydgren 2008; Abedi 2014), it is unsurprising that a proliferation of research on the causes and consequences of PRRP success has emerged in recent years. One of the areas of broad consensus in this literature is that the recent growth in support for the populist radical right has been disproportionately driven by the working class,[3] a group of voters that formerly served as a key constituency of mainstream left political parties (e.g., see Salo and Rydgren 2021). The primary purpose of this book is to explain why blue-collar workers have become such strong supporters of the populist radical right, particularly given their previous support for the mainstream left (Bale et al. 2010), their generally left-leaning views on economic issues (Burgoon 2014), and the likelihood that they would be much better off in the aggregate if left-wing economic policies were adopted by their national governments (Fenger 2018).

Existing explanations for working-class support for the PRRPs can be broadly categorized into three types of interrelated theoretical arguments: those emphasizing the declining economic status of blue-collar workers in

---

[1] We use the terms 'populist radical right' and 'populist radical right-wing parties (PRRPs)' interchangeably in this book.

[2] Nativist nationalism is an ideology defined by an opposition to 'foreign' elements in one's country, believing that they pose a threat to the unity and distinctiveness of the nation-state and the general well-being of the native population (Mudde 2007).

[3] In this book, the 'working class' is used to describe 'manual workers' in 'blue-collar' jobs. Manual workers in blue-collar jobs do 'physical work' (e.g., with their hands) that typically results in the production of a tangible product of value (e.g., through manufacturing, extraction, or construction). By contrast, service work entails assisting or informing another and typically results in the production of an intangible product of value (e.g., financial planning, education, and checking out items at a grocery store) (Erikson and Goldthorpe 1992; Evans 2000).

Social Identity and Working Class Support for the Populist Radical Right. Eric G. Castater and Kyung Joon Han, Oxford University Press. © Eric G. Castater and Kyung Joon Han (2025). DOI: 10.1093/9780198953104.003.0001

2 Social Identity and Working Class Support for the Populist Radical Right

recent decades (what we refer to as the 'economic grievance theory') (e.g., see Betz 1994; Kriesi et al. 2006), the perceived cultural and societal threats posed by immigration and/or European Union membership (what we refer to as the 'cultural grievance theory') (e.g., see Oesch 2008; Han 2020a), and dissatisfaction with the existing political establishment or certain actors within it (what we refer to as the 'political discontent theory') (e.g., see Swyngedouw 2001; Werts, Scheepers, and Lubbers 2013).

We argue that each of these theories is unable to explain two interrelated and stylized facts about working-class support for PRRPs. First, why blue-collar workers increasingly find 'cultural issues' (in particular, regarding immigration) more salient than 'economic issues' (namely, regarding the welfare state) (e.g., see Oesch 2008; Rydgren 2008; Werts, Scheepers, and Lubbers. 2013; Steenvoorden and Harteveld 2018). Second, why blue-collar workers increasingly prefer to vote for a party family that they agree with more on cultural issues (the populist radical right) than economic issues (the populist radical or mainstream left), particularly when they are under adverse economic circumstances (Linos and West 2003; Burgoon 2014).

To explain this puzzle, we develop a three-stage theory utilizing the literature on social identity, which explores why individuals attach meaning to some (formal or informal) social groups they belong to more than others, and the consequences of such social group attachment (Tajfel 1982; Hornsey 2008). Based on the existing literature, the historical development of party families in Western Europe, and survey data, we argue that the two most politically relevant social identities in contemporary Western European politics are based on nation and class (Kitschelt 1994; Hooghe, Marks, and Wilson 2002). Following Easton (1965), we conceptualize macro-level economic and political factors confronted by the working class into three types: how the national government is formulating wage and welfare state policies (the *policymaking process*), the type of welfare state policies produced by the national government (*policy outputs*), and the national economic conditions shaped by such policies (*policy outcomes*). In the first stage of our theory, policy processes, outputs, and outcomes relatively unfavourable (favourable) to the working class lead them to develop a more nation-based (class-based) social identity. In the second stage, blue-collar workers with a more nation-based (class-based) identity focus primarily on cultural (economic) issues. In the third stage, blue-collar workers that focus on cultural issues (economic issues) support (oppose) PRRPs. Broadly, we find that blue-collar workers become more attracted to the populist radical right as governing parties shun a collaborative policymaking process, adopt neo-liberal welfare state reforms, and inequality grows between blue-collar workers and those with higher education and/or in white-collar professions. As will be discussed at length in

Chapter 7 and briefly at the end of this chapter, these findings have implications not only for what policies can be adopted by left-wing and mainstream right parties to reduce the support for PRRPs, but also for the 'crisis of democracy' in Western Europe, as well as labour politics, the welfare state, and the self-reinforcing nature of economic inequality in the wealthy democracies more generally.

This chapter is organized into five parts. First, we review the literature on the economic grievance theory, cultural grievance theory, and political discontent theory and discuss shortcomings of these explanations for working-class PRRP support. Second, we outline our social identity approach to blue-collar worker support for the populist radical right and briefly discuss each stage of our social identity theory. Third, we explain our empirical approach to testing each stage of our theory, including the survey data and statistical methods utilized. Fourth, we provide a summary of the real world and research implications of our analysis. Finally, we conclude the chapter by describing the plan of the book and the focus of subsequent chapters.

Blue-Collar Workers and PRRPs in Western Europe

There is a broad scholarly consensus that blue-collar workers form the core constituency of PRRPs in Western Europe (e.g., see van der Brug, Fennema, and Tillie 2000; Lubbers, Gijsberts, and Scheepers 2002; van der Brug and Fennema 2003; Norris 2005; Arzheimer 2009; Han 2016; Han and Castater 2023). However, there is much less agreement about what makes PRRPs particularly attractive to these voters. We follow previous scholarly work by consolidating the different explanations for the association between occupational type and PRRP support into three encompassing theoretical arguments: the economic grievance theory, the cultural grievance theory, and the political discontent theory.[4]

Economic Grievance Theory

Studies promoting the economic grievance theory argue that blue-collar worker support for the populist radical right is driven primarily by the (relative) decline in the economic status of these workers in recent decades

---

[4] Despite a plethora of studies examining the determinants of PRRP support in Western Europe, scholarly consensus remains elusive (e.g., see Stockemer, Lentz, and Mayer 2018; Amengay and Stockemer 2019). Nonetheless, the authors' survey of the relevant literature suggests that the cultural grievance theory has found the most empirical support (e.g., see Ivarsflaten 2005; Oesch 2008; Rydgren 2008; Gómez-Reino and Llamazares 2013; van der Brug, Fennema, de Lange, and Baller 2013; Werts, Scheepers, and Lubbers. 2013; Zhirkov 2014; Steenvoorden and Harteveld 2018; Han 2020a; Down and Han 2020).

4 Social Identity and Working Class Support for the Populist Radical Right

(e.g., see Betz 1994; Kitschelt 1995; Kriesi et al. 2006). This decline can be observed through multiple and interrelated macro-level indicators, including a reduction in available good paying blue-collar jobs (due to deindustrialization and union weakening) (Lee 2005), disproportionately high levels of (long-term) unemployment among those without a college degree (Natali et al. 2018), and, more broadly, rising levels of income inequality (Emmenegger et al. 2012). Since such economic conditions are attributed to various policies promoted and implemented by mainstream parties (more on these policies shortly), it is claimed that blue-collar workers seek out an electoral alternative that provides them with a plausible diagnosis for their economic woes and an appealing set of solutions to resolve them. Indeed, PRRPs have increasingly campaigned on the economic struggles of the working class in recent years, such as Marine Le Pen, the leader of the National Rally in France, visiting and expressing solidarity with striking workers at a Whirlpool plant in Amiens after the company threatened to offshore operations (Mosimann, Rennwald, and Zimmermann 2019); and Alternative for Germany emphasizing their climate change scepticism and concern for mining jobs in the coal-dependent state of *Brandenburg*.[5]

The literature promoting the economic grievance theory has focused primarily on three sets of interrelated factors that are argued to be indicative of blue-collar workers' economic hardships: those related to employment, globalization, and the welfare state. Most obviously, elevated levels of aggregate unemployment and/or the personal experience of being unemployed strengthen blue-collar workers' economic grievances and therefore their support for the populist radical right (Golder 2003; Kessler and Freeman 2005; Arzheimer and Carter 2006). Less obviously, so too does phenomena that blue-collar workers associate with contributing to their economic hardships. According to the economic grievance theory, the phenomena provoking the most concern among blue-collar workers relate to globalization, including immigration, international trade (particularly imports from the Global South), and European Union (EU) membership. Immigration and international trade strengthen blue-collar workers' economic grievances because they imply greater competition for blue collar jobs (either domestically in the case of immigrants[6] or via import competition and offshoring in the case of

---

[5] 'As End Looms for Coal, German Mining Region Shifts Right', *Reuters*, 11 April 2019 (https://www.reuters.com/article/us-germany-politics-coal-idUSKCN1RN0PD).

[6] Survey data generally shows that blue-collar workers have a more negative view of the economic effects of immigrants than other voters. For instance, the 2014 European Social Survey (ESS) asked whether 'immigrants take jobs away' or 'create new jobs'. Respondents were then given the option of choosing any value from zero to ten, with zero showing the strongest level of support for the belief that

trade) (Scheve and Slaughter 2001; Colantone and Stanig 2018a; Colantone and Stanig 2018b).[7] Furthermore, immigrants may be perceived as abusing the welfare state and thus placing a strain on government finances (Rydgren 2007). By contrast, EU membership strengthens blue-collar workers' economic grievances because it facilitates international trade and immigration (and thus more economic insecurity for blue-collar workers and welfare state abuse), as well as redistribution from richer to poorer regions in Europe (van Klingeren, Boomgaarden, and de Vreese 2013; Vasilopoulou 2018). Finally, welfare state policies that lessen blue-collar workers' economic hardships, such as greater spending on labour market policies and more stringent employment protection legislation, are claimed to reduce these workers' economic grievances and thus also their support for the populist radical right (Swank and Betz 2003; Rooduijn and Burgoon 2018; Vlandas and Halikiopoulou 2019).

Cultural Grievance Theory

Studies promoting the cultural grievance theory argue that blue-collar worker support for the populist radical right is driven primarily by the perceived cultural and societal threats posed by immigrants and EU membership (e.g., see Oesch 2008; van der Brug, Fennema, de Lange, and Baller 2013; and Han 2020a). Thus, while the cultural grievance theory concurs with the economic grievance theory that blue-collar workers support PRRPs because of their anti-immigrant and anti-EU sentiment, it differs on why blue-collar workers have such positions. More specifically, the cultural grievance theory claims that blue-collar workers oppose immigration because of their perception that it threatens the (ethnic, racial, and/or religious) cohesiveness of their country and results in criminality (Rydgren. 2008; Smith 2010). Relatedly, blue-collar workers are argued to oppose the EU because it reduces state sovereignty—especially as it relates to control of national borders—and facilitates immigration and therefore the creation of a more culturally diverse country (Vasilopoulou 2018).

---

immigrants take away jobs and ten showing the strongest level of support for the belief that they create them. The average responses of unskilled blue-collar workers, skilled blue-collar workers, and people in other occupation groups were 4.25, 4.36, and 4.96, respectively, with the differences between each statistically significant at the 0.05 level.

[7] There is no consensus in the existing literature regarding the aggregate effect of immigration on labour market conditions for native workers in Western Europe. Nonetheless, numerous studies have found that the influx of immigrants in Western Europe in recent decades has negatively affected the wages of less skilled blue-collar workers (e.g., see De New and Zimmermann 1994; Smith and Edmonston 1997; Card 2001).

6 Social Identity and Working Class Support for the Populist Radical Right

Cultural grievances are, of course, founded not only among blue-collar workers in Western Europe. Demographic and cultural changes that have occurred in recent decades, mostly due to immigration, have strengthened the perceived threats to national community, reinforced authoritarian attitudes, and consequently increased overall support for the populist radical right (Tillman 2021). Public responses based on cultural grievances are also understood in the framework of 'cultural backlash' by Norris and Inglehart (2019): people in industrialized democracies increasingly offer their support to the populist radical right as a hostile response to progressive social and cultural changes of the mid-to-late twentieth century.

Nonetheless, blue-collar workers' strong(er) scepticism towards cosmopolitanism and multiculturalism is argued to arise from their (more) robust nationalist and authoritarian ideologies (Burns and Gimpel 2000; Dustmann and Preston 2007; Hainmueller and Hiscox 2007; Hainmueller and Hiscox 2010).[8] These ideologies are in turn considered a product of blue-collar workers' modest levels of formal education and workplace conditions. Modest levels of formal education prohibit blue-collar workers from adequately understanding or effectively communicating with those who differ from them economically or culturally (Altemeyer 1988; Hainmueller and Hiscox 2007), while blue-collar workers' workplace provides them with little autonomy, a 'command and obedience' culture, and a general lack of personal interactions (Kitschelt 1995; Oesch 2013).

Political Discontent Theory

Studies promoting the political discontent theory argue that blue-collar worker support for the populist radical right is driven by their dissatisfaction with the political system generally and mainstream political parties in particular (e.g., see Swyngedouw 2001; Bergh 2004; Bélanger and Aarts 2006; and Werts, Scheepers, and Lubbers 2013). This claim builds off the arguments in the economic and cultural grievance theories, in that blue-collar workers' political discontent is argued to arise from their sense that mainstream political parties and the existing political establishment have been unable and/or unwilling to address their longstanding economic and/or cultural concerns. While a minority of studies portray political discontent as resulting in blue-collar workers casting a 'pure protest vote' for PRRPs (i.e., a vote

---

[8] Authoritarian ideologies indicate disapproval of individual differences and submission of such differences to authority (Sibley, Robertson, and Wilson 2006).

based on dissatisfaction with the status quo rather than for or against specific policies) (Eatwell 2018), more commonly it is described as a response to mainstream parties not appearing responsive to the policy preferences of blue-collar workers (e.g., regarding immigration or EU membership) (e.g., see Werts, Scheepers, and Lubbers 2013).[9] Indeed, there is ample evidence that blue-collar workers share many of the issue positions of PRRPs, particularly on issues relating to immigration and European integration (van der Brug, Fennema, and Tillie 2000; van der Brug and Fennema 2003).

As their party family name implies, PRRPs appeal to the politically disaffected by engaging in anti-system, anti-establishment, and/or anti-elite rhetoric, for instance by claiming that existing political leaders are uninterested in the needs of 'the people' or even actively profiting at their expense (Mudde 2004; Barr 2009; Rooduijn, de Lange, and van der Brug 2014). Thus, voters who are dissatisfied with the current political system or incumbent governments are more likely to vote for PRRPs (Canovan 1999; Bélanger and Aarts 2006).

This phenomenon of strengthening populism driven by adverse economic circumstances and political discontent actually has a long history. As Eichengreen (2018) successfully demonstrates, adverse economic conditions for workers, farmers, and miners such as high interest rates and shipping costs and monopolistic behaviours of firms reinforced populist movements in the late nineteenth century in the United States. As current populist political actors do, these movements disproved core economic and social system or policies such as the gold standard system and liberal immigration policies. On the other side of the Atlantic Ocean, tragic economic circumstances due to the Great Depression and war reparations provided fertile soil for populism and fascism in the inter-war period particularly in Germany and Italy.

According to political discontent theory, of particular concern to blue-collar workers in the late twentieth century has been the (neo)liberal policy consensus that emerged between mainstream left and right parties beginning in the 1990s (Meijers 2017). As the size of the working class shrunk, labour organizations weakened, and globalization continued apace, mainstream left parties began advocating for less generous welfare state policies and emphasizing leftwing positions on cultural and related foreign policy issues, such as support for immigration and the EU (Karreth, Polk, and Allen 2013; Carvalho and Reudin 2020). However, these economic and cultural

---

[9] Protest voting is not a new phenomenon in Western Europe. Indeed, fear of economic and social change generated strong support for anti-establishment political parties with extreme ideologies (e.g., fascist or Communist parties) in the early twentieth century (Lipset 1960).

positions, partly designed to appeal to the growing number of middle-class professionals with 'left-libertarian' values,[10] occurred at the same time as (mainstream and populist) right-wing parties were shifting leftward on economic issues (in response to the general popularity of the welfare state) and mainstream right parties were vocally supporting European integration and liberal immigration policies (Keman 2011; Gingrich and Häusermann 2015). Thus, blue-collar workers sought out a populist alternative to the mainstream parties, particularly one that shares their policy preferences on (economic and/or cultural) issues relating to immigration and the EU (Bale, Hough, and van Kessel 2013).

Shortcomings of Existing Theoretical Approaches

We argue that existing theories for blue-collar worker support for the populist radical right suffer from two main and interrelated shortcomings. First, these theories do not explain why blue-collar workers base their vote choice primarily on factors relating to globalization—such as immigration and Europeanization—rather than other issues of concern to the working class. Second, these theories do not explain why blue-collar workers choose to vote for a party that they align with on 'cultural issues' (the populist radical right) rather than a party they align with on 'economic issues' (the mainstream or populist radical left) particularly under adverse economic circumstances.

The economic grievance theory claims that blue-collar workers support PRRPs because of their (growing) economic insecurity. However, left unexplained is why this economic insecurity does not lead blue-collar workers to focus on issues with more direct relevance to their economic standing, such as specific welfare state policies (e.g., the generosity of unemployment benefits or public pensions) and government redistribution generally. This distinction is particularly important given that blue-collar workers generally have left-leaning positions on explicitly economic issues, positions that run counter to those promoted by parties of the populist radical right (Linos and West 2003; Burgoon 2014).[11]

[10] The rightward shift of mainstream left parties on economic issues has also been explained as resulting from the policy constraints associated with EU membership (including Stability and Growth Pact limits) and an increasingly globalized world economy (e.g., Garrett and Mitchell 2001; Obinger, Schmitt, and Zohlnhöfer 2014).

[11] As we will discuss further in subsequent chapters, most PRRPs have moved to the center on economic issues in recent years (Harteveld 2016). While this has resulted in many of these parties holding more centrist positions on economic issues (Mudde 2007), PRRPs still generally promote right-leaning views regarding taxation, government regulation, and egalitarianism (Norris 2005; Han 2016).

The cultural grievance theory claims that blue-collar workers support PRRPs because of their concerns about state sovereignty and rapid demographic/social change. However, left unexplained is why blue-collar workers care more about these 'cultural issues' than 'economic issues', especially given the deteriorating economic conditions confronted by blue-collar workers in recent decades (as outlined in the economic grievance theory). This, again, is critical to explaining blue-collar worker support for the populist radical right, as a focus on economic issues would instead be expected to increase blue-collar worker support for left-leaning political parties, especially those advocating leftwing positions on economic issues.

Finally, the political discontent theory claims that blue-collar workers support PRRPs because of concerns about the responsiveness of the existing political system and mainstream political parties/politicians. However, left unexplained is why this dissatisfaction appears to arise primarily in response to mainstream parties adopting liberal positions on issues relating to immigration, and thus translates into greater support for the populist radical right than support for the populist radical left. Indeed, immigration is the only globalization-related factor in which the populist radical right consistently has a more restrictive position than the populist radical left, a party family that is also critical of European integration and economic globalization generally (Vasilopoulou 2018).

A Social Identity Approach to Blue-Collar Worker Support for the Populist Radical Right

The 'social identity approach' in the social sciences broadly refers to scholarly efforts to explain the emergence and consequences of particular social identities (Hornsey 2008). A 'social identity' is a (formal or informal) social group that a person perceives themselves to belong to and that has psychological, emotional, and behavioural significance for the individual (Tajfel 1982). Thus, for a person to acquire a social identity, they must recognize themselves as a member of a social group and that membership must have enough meaning to them that it influences how they think, feel, and act.

Since people have many cross-cutting social groups that they can plausibly identify with (e.g., based on class, nation, religion, or gender), it is possible for them to embrace membership in some social groups more than others. Within the social identity approach, the desirability of a social identity is argued to be a function of the group's status that the social identity arises from. Since people tend to derive self-esteem and self-worth from the relative standing of the social group(s) they identity with, it is claimed that they are motivated to identify with available groups that compare favourably to relevant outgroups and alter or even abandon identities associated with groups that compare unfavourably to relevant outgroups (Tajfel et al. 1971; Turner 1975; Tajfel and Turner 1979; Hogg and Abrams 1988).

Following Shayo (2009), we conceptualize the Western European electoral space as consisting of two main types of social identities, those derived from economic class and nation. This is for two reasons. First, while there are many potential politically relevant social identities, class and nation are the main social identities political parties have mobilized voters on in Western Europe over the last century (Kitschelt 1994; Hooghe, Marks, and Wilson 2002).[12] Second, class- and nation-based identities approximately correspond to the two types of issues most often discussed in the literature on PRRPs, those related to the 'economy' and 'society' or 'culture' (e.g., see Bornschier 2012; Rydgren 2013; Rovny and Polk 2019).[13] In addition, as a social identity becomes more prominent in a person, it inevitably crowds out other social identities (particularly if the identities lead to perspectives that contradict those generated by the increasingly powerful identity) (Deaux et al. 1995; Cinnirella 1998). Thus, we also assume that class- and nation-based identities serve as approximate substitutes for each other.

As outlined in Figure 1.1, our social identity approach to blue-collar worker support for PRRPs consists of three sequential stages by which macro-level factors affect the vote choice of blue-collar workers. In the first stage, policy processes, outputs, and outcomes shape blue-collar workers' social identity, with economic and political conditions relatively favourable to blue-collar workers leading to a stronger class-based identity and economic and

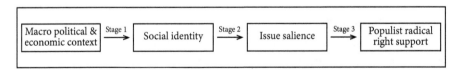

Figure 1.1 A social identity approach to support for the populist radical right

---

[12] Survey data confirms that class and nation constitute the major social identities associated with party politics in Western Europe. In 2003, the International Social Survey Programme (ISSP) asked Western European respondents the most important groups with which they identify. Only two groups were named by more than 20 per cent of respondents: class and occupation (37 per cent) and nation and ethnicity (24 per cent).

[13] While there is no consensus in the literature on what defines 'economic' or 'cultural'/'social' issues, the former generally refers to issues relating to employment, income, and/or the welfare state, while the latter generally refers to issues relating to immigration, multiculturalism, religion, and/or crime (e.g., see Rydgren 2008; Immerzeel, Jaspers, and Lubbers 2013; Han 2016; Busemeyer, Rathgeb, and Sahm 2022).

political conditions relatively unfavourable to blue-collar workers leading to a stronger nation-based identity. In the second stage, the social identity of blue-collar workers determines what issues will be most salient to them,[14] with a more class-based identity leading to a greater concern about economic issues and a more nation-based identity leading to a greater concern about cultural issues. In the third stage, blue-collar workers that care more about economic issues generally oppose the populist radical right, while blue-collar workers that care more about cultural issues generally support the populist radical right.

Stage 1: The Macro Context and Social Identity

Following Shayo (2009), Han (2016), Gidron and Hall (2017), and Engler and Weisstanner (2021), we argue that macro-level factors affect PRRP support by leading people to adopt a more class- or nation-based identity. However, our study moves beyond these analyses by considering how a broad range of economic and political factors affect social identity, not only economic inequality. More specifically, we expect the policymaking processes, policy outputs, and policy outcomes that provide a relative gain (loss) to the working class to result in blue-collar workers having a stronger (weaker) class-based identity and a weaker (stronger) nation-based identity.

When conceptualizing policy processes, outputs, and outcomes, we build off the distinctions provided by Easton (1965).[15] The *policymaking process* refers to the procedures by which a national government produces public policy; *policy outputs* refer to the specific content of any public policies produced by a national government; and *policy outcomes* refer to the socio-economic and socio-cultural contexts arising from or shaped by national government policy.

For policymaking processes, we focus on whether governments proposed or completed social pacts in the process of enacting welfare state and/or labour market reforms. Social pacts are publicly announced policy contracts between governments, labour unions, and often employers' associations that set out signatories' responsibilities regarding employment, wages, and/or fiscal policy (Avdagic, Rhodes, and Visser 2011; Colombo, Tirelli, and Visser 2014). Since labour unions have historically been dominated by blue-collar

---

[14] While 'issue salience' has multiple meanings in the social sciences, in this analysis it refers to the importance of a political issue to an individual's vote choice.

[15] While policy outputs indicate 'the binding decisions' of governments and 'certain associated kinds of behaviour', policy outcomes are 'all the consequences that flow from' policy outputs (Easton 1965, 351).

workers, blue-collar unions typically lead social pact negotiations on behalf of organized labour, and unions often market themselves as advocating for 'working people' during the social pact formation process, we argue that when labour unions successfully complete social pact agreements with the government, it signals to blue-collar workers that their social class is in a relatively advantageous economic and political position.[16] Thus, we expect the completion of social pact agreements to strengthen the class-based identity of blue-collar workers and, by consequence, to reduce their support for PRRPs. By contrast, an economic reform process that excludes labour unions—either because governing parties pursued legislation unilaterally or because they failed to convert a social pact proposal into an actual social pact agreement—suggests that working-class people are in a relatively poor economic and political position. Thus, we expect unilaterally enacted reform legislation and failed social pact proposals to result in a stronger nation-based identity for blue-collar workers and therefore increase their support for PRRPs.

For policy outputs, we focus on the degree of employment protection legislation (EPL) and government spending on labour market policies (LMPs).[17] Since EPL and spending on the labour market improve the relative economic standing of blue-collar workers (e.g., see Western 1997; Rueda and Pontusson 2000; Anderson and Pontusson 2007; Rueda 2007; Nelson 2009; Avdagic 2013), we expect higher values of these measures to translate into blue-collar workers having a stronger class-based identity and thus being less supportive of PRRPs. By contrast, since weak or non-existent EPL and modest spending on LMPs suggest that blue-collar workers are in a relatively precarious economic position, we expect such conditions to be associated with blue-collar workers having a stronger nation-based identity and thus being more supportive of PRRPs.

For policy outcomes, we focus on wage inequality between blue-collar and white-collar workers and unemployment inequality between those with and without a college degree. Since lower levels of these inequalities suggest that blue-collar workers are doing relatively well compared to other workers, we

---

[16] Furthermore, the completion of social pacts informs blue-collar workers that the government takes their economic concerns seriously and that their preferences will be reflected in any final reform package (Han and Castater 2023).

[17] The labour market spending variable includes expenditures on both active labour market policies (ALMPs) and passive labour market policies (PLMPs). ALMPs are government expenditures meant to improve the ability of someone to find employment (e.g., spending on the administration of labour market programmes, job training, employment incentives, and subsidized work or rehabilitation). By contrast, PLMPs refer to government expenditures meant to help someone stay financially solvent while unemployed (e.g., spending on unemployment benefits and early retirement schemes). In addition to examining the effect of aggregate labour market spending on blue-collar workers' support for the populist radical right, we also consider ALMPs and PLMPs separately in Chapter 5.

expect such conditions to strengthen the class-based identity of blue-collar workers and thus to reduce their support for PRRPs. By contrast, higher levels of these inequalities suggest that blue-collar workers are doing relatively poorly compared to other workers. In such a situation, we expect blue-collar workers to develop a stronger nation-based identity and thus to be more likely to support PRRPs.

Stage 2: Social Identity and Issue Salience

We argue that social identity affects a person's voting behaviour through issue salience: since voters experience the world as a member of a particular social group, they tend to focus on issues perceived to be most relevant to that group (Huici et al. 1997; Hutchings 2001; Duncan and Stewart 2007; Klar 2013). Therefore, we expect blue-collar workers with a strong class-based identity to care deeply about economic issues and blue-collar workers with a strong nation-based identity to care deeply about cultural issues (Tavits and Potter 2015). Since employment is the main source of income for the working class, we expect blue-collar workers with a strong class-based identity to place salience on policies related to maintaining a job, finding a (better compensated) job, and/or replacing income from a lost job. By contrast, blue-collar workers with a strong nation-based identity are expected to focus on cultural issues, namely those relating to nativism and immigration.[18] These issues should be of particular concern to blue-collar workers in contemporary Western Europe due to the restrictions and obligations associated with EU membership and, relatedly, growing immigrant populations and multiculturalism (Hooghe and Marks 2005; O'Rourke and Sinnott 2006; Han 2013b).

Stage 3: Issue Salience and PRRP Support

Voters in Western Europe exist in a multidimensional policy space, and therefore must consider multiple issues when determining which political party to support (Adams, Merrill, and Grofman 2005). Given the reality that people have limited time and resources and do not care about all issues equally, vote choice in such a system is substantially based on the correspondence between

[18] Although it is often difficult to determine whether those who oppose immigration do so because of economic concerns (e.g., labour market competition and the supposed burden that immigrants place on the welfare state) or cultural/societal concerns (e.g., multiculturalism and crime), those who support PRRPs have been found to be much more strongly motivated by the latter than the former (Rydgren 2008).

14 Social Identity and Working Class Support for the Populist Radical Right

a voter's position on the issue(s) most salient to them and that of the various political parties (Bélanger and Meguid 2008; Dennison 2019).

We argue that when blue-collar workers find economic issues more salient than cultural issues, they become less likely to support the populist radical right; but when blue-collar workers find cultural issues more salient than economic issues, they become more likely to support the populist radical right. This is for two reasons. First, blue-collar workers generally agree less with PRRPs on economic issues than cultural issues (Scheve and Slaughter 2001; Ireland 2004; Lahav 2004; Mayda 2006; O'Rourke and Sinnott 2006; Messina 2007; Hainmueller and Hiscox 2010). More specifically, blue-collar workers generally have more left-leaning views on the economy than PRRPs. Thus, when blue-collar workers vote for a PRRP, they do so despite differences with them on economic issues. This suggests that blue-collar workers that support the populist radical right generally do not place much salience on such issues (Bornschier and Kriesi 2013).

Second, PRRPs are generally described as having 'issue ownership' on immigration. Although PRRPs are not 'single-issue parties', opposition to immigration (and, relatedly, opposition to multiculturalism and a tough law and order stance) is the central component of their programme and the primary explanation for recent PRRP success (Mudde 1999; van der Brug, Fennema, and Tillie 2000; Lubbers, Gijsberts, and Scheepers 2002; van der Brug and Fennema 2003; Norris 2005; Ivarsflaten 2008; Rydgren 2008; van der Brug, Fennema, de Lange, and Baller 2013; Werts, Scheepers, and Lubbers 2013; Zhirkov 2014; Han 2020a). Since a political party's ownership of an issue brings electoral benefits to the party only when voters consider the issue important (Bélanger and Meguid 2008; Walgrave, Lefevere, and Tresch 2012; Klüver and Spoon 2016), we expect blue-collar workers that put salience on cultural issues to be more supportive of the populist radical right than blue-collar workers that do not. However, since there is less correspondence between the positions of blue-collar workers and PRRPs on economic issues and the populist radical right has much less 'ownership' of such issues, we expect blue-collar workers that put salience on the economy to be less supportive of the populist radical right than blue-collar workers that do not.

Political Awareness and Working-Class Support for PRRPs

We argue here that blue-collar workers' social identity is shaped by the macro-level context that they exist within, with a particular focus on policymaking processes, policy outputs, and policy outcomes. Therefore, our theory assumes that blue-collar workers are at least somewhat cognizant of their political and socio-economic environment, and that their perceptions of that environment are a reasonable approximation of reality. However, we also acknowledge the heterogeneous nature of the working class, and that some blue-collar workers have greater 'political awareness' than others, either in general terms or regarding specific matters. We incorporate political awareness in our analysis by recognizing that those who have more opportunities and incentives to be informed about politics (or certain policymaking processes, policy outputs, or policy outcomes) are more likely to have a social identity that corresponds with their social group and its objective status than those with fewer such opportunities and incentives (Claassen and Highton 2009; Jones and Brewer 2020; Jones 2023).[19]

More specifically, people's awareness is influenced by their access to information as well as their own interest in and attention to particular issues. Therefore, we consider whether blue-collar workers with different labour market and demographic characteristics are more or less likely to be politically aware and thus respond to the macro-level context in the way anticipated by our theory.

In Chapter 4, we argue that union members are more knowledgeable of policymaking processes associated with the welfare state than non-union members, as a primary function of labour unions is educating their members about national socio-economic and political conditions and labour unions are active negotiators in the social pact formation process (Regini and Colombo 2011).[20] Therefore, we hypothesize that union members are influenced by unilaterally enacted welfare state reforms, social pact agreements, and failed social pact proposals more than non-union members.

In Chapter 5, we argue that preferences regarding welfare state policies differ among 'labour market insiders' (i.e., those in secure employment) and 'labour market outsiders' (i.e., those in insecure employment), as the former desire policies that allow them to maintain their employment status, while the latter desire policies that allow them to improve their employment status (Rueda 2005, 2007). If this is the case, their interest in different types of labour policies will lead to asymmetric attention and different degrees of awareness

---

[19] Political awareness is found to strengthen the link between identity and political/policy preference. For example, people who are fully aware of politics demonstrate a preference that is expected for their own identity (e.g., libertarianism from LGBTQ+ respondents or conservatism from evangelical protestants) because they know 'which social identities go with which political views' (Jones 2023, 512).
[20] Though conversations and negotiations occur between the representatives of the government and trade unions, union leaders usually consult rank-and-file union members before finally signing a social pact agreement. Unions also often present the final draft of an agreement to their whole members for an official vote (Visser and van der Meer 2011). Union members, consequently, have opportunities of delivering their voices to union leaders as well as of getting information on a social pact from union leaders.

between the policies. Therefore, we hypothesize that the stringency of EPL (protection against dismissal) has a greater effect on blue-collar workers that are labour market insiders and spending on LMPs such as unemployment benefits and job training has a greater effect on blue-collar workers that are labour market outsiders.

In Chapter 6, we argue that less skilled blue-collar workers respond differently to growing levels of economic inequality than more highly skilled blue-collar workers, as the former has experienced particularly acute challenges in recent decades due to technological advancements and other socio-economic changes (e.g., labour union weakening and growing imports from the Global South). Therefore, we hypothesize that growing levels of economic inequality impact less skilled blue-collar workers more than highly skilled blue-collar workers.

Finally, in all our models we control for both the education level and age of blue-collar workers. People with higher education have a more sophisticated understanding of socio-economic and political outcomes than those with less formal education (Macdonald, Rabinowitz, and Listhaug 1995).[21] Younger people have grown up in the period of declining union and also been socialized in the context of substantial European integration (Lauterbach and De Vries 2020). Then, while those with more formal education may hold a higher level of awareness in general politics and/or particular policies, younger people may pay less attention to socio-economic issues, compared to other issues, than older people (Walczak, van der Brug, and de Vries 2012).[22]

Empirical Analysis

To test our social identity theory of working-class support for PRRPs, we would ideally use individual level cross-country survey data that covers a substantial time horizon and includes questions about social identity, issue salience, and political party support; and utilize a statistical model capable of

---

[21] Nonetheless, some studies disapprove the education effect on political sophistication (e.g., Luskin 1990).

[22] However, the overall roles of education and age in the link between political and economic contexts, workers' social identity, and their PRRP support are not straightforward. Though the highly educated are more aware of politics and policies, higher education tends to promote 'cosmopolitan values' that lower PRRP support (Coenders and Scheepers 2003). Blue-collar workers with more formal education are likelier to be in a stronger economic condition as well. Though older workers may pay more attention to socio-economic issues than younger workers do in general, younger workers may be concerned about policies that particularly pertain to labour markets because they need to stay in the markets longer than older workers do (Buss 2019).

testing each stage of our theory (the effect of macro-context on social identity, the effect of social identity on issue salience, and the effect of issue salience on political party support). However, the questions and potential responses in existing surveys of Western European countries preclude this possibility. Below, we discuss the limitations of this survey data and explain how we address these shortcomings by employing surveys from multiple sources, as well as a causal mediation analysis model.

Survey Data

To the best of our knowledge, there is not a single cross-country survey of Western Europeans that includes questions on social identity, issue salience, and political party support. Thus, we employ three surveys to test whether policy processes, outcomes, and outputs effect blue-collar worker support for PRRPs via a change in social identity and therefore what issues these workers find most salient: the International Social Survey Programme (ISSP) (2003); the European Election Studies (EES) (2009 and 2014); and the European Values Study (EVS) (1990, 1999, 2008, and 2017).[23]

First, the ISSP (2003) includes questions on social identity and voting behaviour, but not issue salience. Therefore, the ISSP (2003) allows us to directly test the first stage of our theory (the effect of the macro-context on social identity), while only providing an indirect test of the second and third stages of our theory (the effects of social identity on issue salience and issue salience on political party support, respectively). We construct the social identity variable based on answers to the survey question, 'We are all part of different groups. Some are more important to us than others when we think of ourselves. In general, which in the following list is most important to you in describing who you are? and the second most important? and the third most important?' In the list of potential answers provided by the ISSP, two types of social groups are related to a nation-based identity (ethnic background and nationality) and two types of social groups signify a class-based identity (social class and occupation). Based on respondents' replies, we construct an ordinal variable of social identity that indicates the relative strength of

---

[23] The ISSP, EES, and EVS surveys used here do not have questions pertaining to respondents' type of labour contract, but the ESS does. Thus, in Chapter 5, we utilize nine waves of the EES when examining the effect of labour market policies on blue-collar workers with and without secure employment (i.e., labour market 'insiders' and 'outsiders'). However, since those surveys do not include questions pertaining to social identity or issue salience, we cannot directly test the three stages of our social identity theory utilizing the ESS.

blue-collar workers' nation-based and class-based identity, with higher values indicating a more nation-based identity and lower values indicating a more class-based identity.

While two other waves of the ISSP (1995, 2013) also have questions about social identity, the wording of the questions and the possible responses differ from those provided in ISSP (2003). More specifically, the ISSP (1995, 2013) do not ask directly about what groups someone identities with, nor do they provide a response option related to economic class. Thus, our main analyses utilize the ISSP (2003) only. Nonetheless, to provide as thorough of a test as possible for our theoretical claims and ensure that our results hold with more recent data, we provide robustness checks in the appendix that include models with the ISSP (2013).

Second, the EES (2009, 2014) includes questions on issue salience and voting behaviour, but not social identity. Therefore, the EES (2009, 2014) allows us to directly test the third stage of our theory (the effect of issue salience on political party support), while providing only an indirect test of the first and second stages of our theory (the effects of the macro-context on social identity and social identity on issue salience, respectively). We construct two issue salience variables based on answers to the EES (2009, 2014) survey question, 'What do you think is the first most important issue or problem facing our country at the moment?' Using answers to this question, we make two binary variables for issue salience, one measuring the salience of economic issues and the other the salience of cultural issues. We code the economic issue salience variable as one when a blue-collar worker responded that economic conditions, creating jobs, unemployment, national employment policies, or wages and earnings is the most important issue or problem facing their country. We code the cultural issue salience variable as one when a blue-collar worker responded that immigration, labour migration, multiculturalism, national immigration policy, or ethnic minorities is the most important issue or problem facing their country.

While the EES has conducted eight waves of surveys between 1979 and 2019, only those surveys conducted in 2009 and 2014 use the same list of potential responses to the issue salience question for all countries. More specifically, the EES (1979, 1989, 1994, 1999, 2004, 2019) either uses different lists of issues for different countries or does not include a list of issues and instead ask the question in an open-ended fashion. Thus, we only utilize the EES (2009, 2014) in our empirical analysis to secure cross-country compatibility and comparability.

Finally, the EVS (1990, 1999, 2008, 2017) has questions on voting behaviour, but no explicit questions regarding social identity or issue salience.

However, the EVS does have a question regarding a topic adjacent to national identity: national pride.[24] Furthermore, the EVS covers a substantially longer time horizon (four waves between 1990 and 2017) than the other survey with a question related to social identity, the ISSP (2003). Therefore, the EVS (1990, 1999, 2008, 2017) allows us to provide another direct test of the first stage of our theory (the effect of the macro-context on social identity), as well as additional indirect tests of the second and third stages of our theory (the effects of social identity on issue salience and issue salience on political party support, respectively). We construct the EVS national pride variable based on answers to the question, 'How proud are you to be a [COUNTRY] citizen?' Respondents can then choose from four potential answers: 'very proud', 'quite proud', 'not very proud', and 'not at all proud'. Using answers to this question, we make an ordinal variable that indicates the relative strength of blue-collar workers' national pride.

Statistical Methodology

The main question of this book is not 'whether' blue-collar workers support PRRPs more strongly than others, but 'why' they do so, particularly when they go through unfavourable political and economic conditions. We theoretically suggest that workers' social identity and issue salience mediate the effects of political and economic contexts on their party support. Therefore, we need a research design and a methodological tool to examine mediation effects.

To test our three-stage social identity theory, we utilize a causal mediation analysis model. Causal mediation analysis models are designed to help researchers identify both 'indirect' and 'direct' effects. An indirect effect is when one variable (the 'treatment') affects another (the 'outcome') through its impact on an intermediate variable (the 'mediator'). A direct effect is any remaining effect the treatment has on the outcome after its impact through the mediator has been considered. Thus, causal mediation analysis models test whether an independent variable affects a dependent variable through a specific 'causal pathway' and inform us how much of the total effect of that independent variable is explained by that pathway.

In our case, we are interested in whether certain policy processes, outputs, and outcomes affect blue-collar workers' support for PRRPs by altering these workers' social identity and therefore what issues they find most salient; and the extent to which a shift in social identity and issue salience explains the

---

[24] Although national pride is conceptually distinct from a nation-based identity, the former tends to arise from and reinforce the latter (Smith 1991; Han 2013a).

overall effect that these policy processes, outputs, and outcomes have on blue-collar worker support for PRRPs. We use the causal mediation analysis model developed by Imai, Keele, Tingley, and Yamamoto (2011). A discussion of the mechanics of this model and how the results from it can be interpreted are provided prior to us first reporting the results for a causal mediation model in Chapter 4.

Contributions and Implications

PRRP Support

As outlined above, existing theories regarding PRRP support do not explain why blue-collar workers—despite relatively poor and deteriorating economic conditions—focus more on 'cultural issues' than 'economic issues' when determining their party preference or vote choice. This is of critical importance given that blue-collar workers align much more with PRRPs on cultural issues (namely, those related to immigration) than economic issues (such as those related to the welfare state). The economic grievance theory claims that blue-collar workers support the populist radical right because of their growing economic insecurity but does not explain why precarious economic conditions lead blue-collar workers to support a party that they agree with more on cultural issues than economic issues. The cultural grievance theory claims that blue-collar workers support the populist radical right because of their concerns about state sovereignty and rapid demographic/social change but does not explain why blue-collar workers care more about these issues than those of more direct relevance to the working class, such as employment protection legislation or generous unemployment insurance. Finally, the political discontent theory claims that blue-collar workers support the populist radical right because of concerns about the responsiveness of the existing political system and mainstream political parties/politicians but does not explain why this dissatisfaction arises primarily in response to mainstream parties adopting liberal positions on European integration and immigration, rather than on issues relating to organized labour, the welfare state, or other aspects of globalization, like international trade. Our social identity approach to blue-collar worker support for PRRPs addresses this shortcoming in the literature by explaining how relatively unfavourable economic and political conditions strengthen blue-collar workers' nation-based identity, leading them to focus more on cultural issues than economic issues and thus increasing their likelihood of supporting the populist radical right.

In addition, while previous scholarship on PRRP support has assumed that blue-collar workers are relatively homogenous in terms of their economic circumstances, we utilize the comparative political economy literature to argue that the effect that macro-level conditions have on blue-collar workers' social identity and thus their vote choice is a function of the extent to which they are in secure in employment, their skill level, and whether they belong to a labour union. Following the Insider–Outsider Model, we argue that blue-collar workers in secure employment are more likely to be affected by changes in EPL, while blue-collar workers without secure employment are more likely to be affected by changes in government labour market spending (Rueda 2005; Rueda 2007). Following the Varieties of Capitalism (VoC) approach, we argue that blue-collar workers with higher skill levels are less likely to respond negatively to rising economic inequality than blue-collar workers with lower skill levels (Hall and Thelen 2007; Nijhuis 2009; Iversen and Soskice 2010; Becher and Pontusson 2011; Han and Castater 2016). Finally, following Power Resource Theory (PRT), we argue that blue-collar workers that belong to a union are more likely to be knowledgeable about and responsive to the social pact formation process than blue-collar workers who are not union members.

The evidence we provide suggests that a lack of coordination with organized labour in the welfare state reform process, neoliberal economic policies, and growing economic inequality in Western Europe have led blue-collar workers in very different economic circumstances to support the populist radical right (via a change in social identity and issue salience), with union membership playing little to no role in mediating those effects. These results imply that PRRP support is likely to continue to grow unless mainstream or populist radical left-wing parties incorporate labour organizations into the welfare state reform process, enact economic policies that improve the well-being of a broad swath of the working class, and reduce economic inequality more broadly.

The Crisis of Democracy in Western Europe

Much has been written in recent years about the 'crisis of (liberal) democracy' in Western Europe (e.g., see Norris 2011; Castels 2019; Kriesi 2020). This crisis can be observed through numerous micro- and macro-level indicators, including declining satisfaction with or support for democracy generally (Cordero and Simón 2016), declining satisfaction with or trust in specific democratic institutions (e.g., the national parliament or governing political parties) (Armingeon and Guthmann 2014; Obydenkova and Arpino 2018), and decreasing political participation (Delwit 2013). Such phenomena have been explained as resulting from a plethora of factors, including high or rising levels of economic inequality (Rothstein and Uslaner 2005), perceptions of government corruption or a lack of political efficacy (Karp and Banducci 2008; Sundström and Stockemer 2015), ideological polarization (Rahn and Rudolph 2005; Catterberg and Moreno 2006), the increasingly uncivil behaviour of political elites (Mutz and Reeves 2005), a growing inability of national leaders to adopt country-specific policies in an age of Europeanization and globalization (Merkel 2014), and public policy that ignores the interests and preferences of lower income citizens (Rosset and Kurella 2021).[25]

The most obvious and worrisome consequence of this ongoing crisis in democracy is what it means for the survival of democratic political systems in Western Europe. Of particular concern here is the appeal of populist and/or radical political parties or candidates that normalize illiberal discourse regarding (ethnic) minorities (Wodak 2019), fabricate scandals about those in the existing political establishment (Weyland 2018), and embrace authoritarianism more broadly (Norris and Inglehart 2019).[26] Given that PRRPs have achieved much greater electoral success in recent decades than populist radical left parties and have a more authoritarian disposition,[27] it is the former that presents a much greater threat to democracy in contemporary Western Europe than the latter (Rooduijn et al. 2017).

Our theory and findings suggest that a decline in consultative policy-making with workers' organizations, neoliberal welfare state reforms, and growing economic inequality has contributed to the crisis in democracy in Western Europe not only by directly exacerbating blue-collar workers' grievances towards the economic and political systems in their country, but indirectly by strengthening blue-collar workers' nation-based identity

---

[25] Negative evaluations of the political system (or specific actors within it) may, at times, increase support for democracy and/or political participation. For instance, dissatisfaction with the conditionality attached to emergency loans by international organizations may lead citizens to advocate for democratic principles more strongly in their country (Cordero and Simón 2016); and a lack of trust in democratic institutions may lead to greater protest activity or voting as people seek to show their displeasure with the status quo (Kaase 1999).

[26] According to Norris and Inglehart (2019), 'authoritarian values' include three core components: an emphasis on security from instability and disorder, a desire for group conformity, and the need to demonstrate obedience to strong leaders who protect the group from instability and disorder.

[27] While PRRPs present clear and relatively consistent positions on cultural issues and 'blurry' or inconsistent positions on economic issues, populist radical left parties present clear and relatively consistent positions on economic issues and 'blurry' or inconsistent positions on cultural issues (Rovny 2013; Rooduijn et al. 2017). Although a focus on economic issues does not preclude an authoritarian disposition, contemporary populist radical left parties no longer identify with 'Communism' or 'Socialism' and are generally supportive of (liberal) democracy (Rooduijn and Akkerman 2017).

and thus also their focus on 'cultural issues' (including restrictions on the rights of ethnic minorities) and support for the populist radical right. Our analysis implies that if we desire to reverse these trends, it is insufficient to develop policies that provide an *absolute benefit* for the working class (e.g., wage increases or broad-based tax cuts), as such policies will not necessarily improve blue-collar workers' position vis-à-vis the middle and upper classes (and are therefore unlikely to affect blue-collar workers' social identity). Instead, we must focus on adopting policies that provide a *relative benefit* to the working class (e.g., labour market spending and EPL) and incorporate workers' organizations into the process of adopting those policies, as this will not only reduce blue-collar workers' economic grievances and political discontent, but also their focus on issues relating to ethnic minorities and support for the populist radical right.

Labour Politics, the Welfare State, and Economic Inequality

As will be discussed further in Chapter 6, economic inequality has been rising across nearly all Western European countries in recent decades (Hopkin and Lynch 2016). Not surprisingly, this has led to a proliferation of studies in comparative political economy examining the causes and consequences of economic inequality. A major focus of this scholarship has been the self-reinforcing nature of economic inequality: those factors or trends that mitigate inequality are themselves often undermined by higher inequality. Of relevance to us here is the two-way causality between the strength of organized labour and the design of welfare state policies on the one hand and economic inequality on the other. Labour unions are argued to decrease inequality by shrinking earning differentials among workers and between workers and owners/managers and helping to elect political parties with left-leaning economic agendas (Ahlquist 2017), while higher inequality is argued to weaken unions by shrinking the middle of the income distribution (where unionization is most common) and reducing the net benefit of union membership for those at the top and bottom of the income distribution (Checchi, Visser, and van de Werfhorst 2010).[28] Expansive and generous welfare states are argued to reduce inequality by increasing labour force participation (Huber and Stephens 2001), improving the aggregate education level of the

---

[28] Those with increasingly large incomes seek to avoid unions because of the intra-union salary compression they tend to produce, while the growing share of the population with lower or stagnating incomes seeks to avoid unions because of the relatively high cost of union dues, declining union premiums for lower-paid union workers, and, in some countries, industry- or national-level collective bargaining agreements that apply to lower-paid occupations regardless of union membership (Hassel 2009).

citizenry (Iversen and Stephens 2008), incentivizing workers' to invest in specific (and thus highly compensated) skills (Estevez-Abe, Iversen, and Soskice 2001), raising the reservation wage for workers, and through redistribution generally (Huber and Stephens 2014). However, higher inequality is argued to lead to an erosion of the welfare state through its effect on public opinion and the quality of governance. As inequality reaches higher levels, citizens increasingly perceive income differentials to be legitimate (Trump 2018; Mijs 2021), that existing welfare state policies have been ineffectual at addressing inequality (Kelly and Enns 2010), and/or that any welfare state expansion is likely to benefit others at their expense (Ove Moene and Wallerstein 2001). Furthermore, as inequality grows and public opinion shifts to the right on the economy, policymaking increasingly reflects the interests of the wealthy and/or ignores the interests of the poor (Giger, Rosset, and Bernauer 2012).

All the above explanations for the self-reinforcing nature of economic inequality assume that inequality begets inequality through a change in the cost-benefit analysis of (potential) union members, voters, or elected leaders. By contrast, our analysis suggests that inequality is self-reinforcing through a change in the social identity of blue-collar workers: as inequality rises, blue-collar workers increasingly view themselves in national rather than class terms, resulting in decreased demand to join a union and less support for parties with left-leaning economic agendas.

Plan of the Book

The book is comprised of 7 chapters. In Chapter 2, we establish the conceptual and empirical foundations for subsequent chapters of the book. Although PRRPs have received ample attention in the comparative politics literature, there remains scholarly disagreement about the exact nature of these parties and the appropriate label to apply to them. Thus, the first section of Chapter 2 explains why we have chosen the 'populist radical right' party label, identifies the key characteristics of these parties, and provides a list of those PRRPs examined in this book. The second section of the chapter discusses the economic challenges confronted by blue-collar workers in Western Europe in recent decades, as well as the shifting political landscape these workers find themselves situated within. The third section of the chapter utilizes EVS data to compare blue-collar worker support for the populist radical right to other occupational groups (small business owners and middle-class professionals).

In Chapter 3, we provide a literature review of previous scholarly work on the determinants of PRRP support and social identity, outline our social identity approach to blue-collar worker support for the populist radical right, and provide preliminary tests of our theoretical claims. In the first section of the chapter, we provide a broad overview of the literature on the determinants of PRRP support with an emphasis on the importance of policy processes, outputs, and outcomes. In the second section of the chapter, we review the literature on social identity. In the third section of the chapter, we outline our three-stage theory explaining blue-collar worker support for the populist radical right. In the fourth section of the chapter, we conduct preliminary tests of each stage in our theory (the effect of political and economic contexts on national identity; the effect of national identity on issue salience; and the effect of issue salience on PRRP support).

In Chapters 4 through 6, we examine the effects that specific policy-making processes, policy outputs, and policy outcomes have on blue-collar worker support for the populist radical right. In Chapter 4, we focus on the policymaking process. In particular, we consider whether governments adopted welfare state reforms unilaterally or in consultation with labour unions through the social pact formation process. Though we do not find strong results on the support-decreasing effect of social pact completion, results support our hypotheses on failed social pact proposals and unilateral legislation. When governments fail to convert social pact proposals into actual social pact agreements or enact reforms unilaterally, blue-collar workers become more likely to support PRRPs due to a strengthened nation-based identity and the increased salience of cultural issues. Given that union members are more likely to be informed about and actively involved in the social pact formation process than non-union members, we also consider whether unilaterally enacted reform legislation and the social pact formation process have a stronger effect on blue-collar workers that belong to a union than those who do not. Contrary to our expectations, we find that the welfare state reform process has similar effects on union and non-union members. This unexpected finding suggests that declining union membership in Western Europe in recent decades has neither strengthened nor weakened the effect that social pacts or unilaterally enacted legislation has on blue-collar workers' PRRP support.

In Chapter 5, we focus on policy outputs. In particular, we examine EPL and government spending on LMPs. Consistent with our theoretical expectations, we find that strong EPL and generous spending on LMPs decrease the likelihood that blue-collar workers will support PRRPs due to a weakened nation-based identity and the decreased salience of cultural issues. Since not all blue-collar workers are in a precarious economic position, we also examine the effect of EPL and spending on LMPs on blue-collar workers with and without secure employment, or what we refer to as 'labour market insiders' and 'labour market outsiders' (Rueda 2007; Häusermann, Kemmerling, and Rueda 2020). We find that EPL affects the PRRP support of labour market insiders, but not labour market outsiders; while government spending on LMPs affects the PRRP support of labour market outsiders, but not labour market insiders. Given that there has been a greater reduction in EPL than labour market spending in Western Europe in recent decades, these divergent effects have led to a growing share of blue-collar workers with secure employment among the ranks of PRRP supporters.

In Chapter 6, we focus on policy outcomes. We examine wage inequality between blue-collar and white-collar workers and unemployment inequality between those with and without a college degree. Consistent with our theoretical expectations, we find that high levels of these forms of inequality increase the likelihood that blue-collar workers will support PRRPs due to a strengthened nation-based identity and the increased salience of cultural issues. Given that these forms of inequality are particularly harmful for less skilled (and thus less paid) blue-collar workers, we also examine whether their effects differ based on the skill level of blue-collar workers. As anticipated, we find that higher levels of wage inequality and unemployment inequality increase PRRP support of less skilled blue-collar workers more than highly skilled blue-collar workers.

In Chapter 7, we conclude our book by summarizing our theoretical contribution and empirical results, as well as by delving deeper into the implications of our analysis for politics in the wealthy democracies and the comparative political economy literature.

2
Populist Radical Right-wing Parties and the Working Class

This chapter establishes a conceptual and empirical foundation for subsequent chapters of the book and is divided into four sections. The first section focuses on PRRPs in Western Europe. Although PRRPs have received ample attention in the comparative politics literature, there remains scholarly disagreement about the exact nature of these parties and the appropriate label to apply to them. Thus, in this section we explain why we have chosen the 'populist radical right-wing' party label, identify the key characteristics of these parties, and provide a list of those PRRPs examined in this book.

The second section—which takes up the bulk of the chapter—focuses on (White, native) blue-collar workers in Western Europe. While de-industrialization and one of its main consequences, de-unionization, have weakened the economic and political standing of the working class in general, many specific groups of blue-collar workers have been sheltered or even benefited from these phenomena. These diverging fortunes have led to deviating preferences among segments of the working class, as well as challenges and opportunities for mainstream and populist political parties. Thus, in this section we discuss the economic challenges confronted by blue-collar workers in recent decades and the shifting political landscape these workers find themselves within, as well as provide descriptive statistics on the demographic and ideological heterogeneity of the working class.

The third section of the chapter focuses on working-class support for the populist radical right. Here, we utilize EVS data to compare working-class support for the populist radical right to other occupational groups (small business owners and middle-class professionals). The evidence we provide suggests that blue-collar workers usually, although not always, disproportionately support the populist radical right, and that such class voting varies substantially across parties and over time.

Social Identity and Working Class Support for the Populist Radical Right. Eric G. Castater and Kyung Joon Han, Oxford University Press. © Eric G. Castater and Kyung Joon Han (2025). DOI: 10.1093/9780198953104.003.0002

PRRPs in Western Europe

Scholars specializing in far-right political parties in Western Europe have used various labels to describe this relatively heterogeneous party family (e.g., see Rydgren 2008; Akkerman, de Lange, and Rooduijn 2016; Sheets, Bos, and Boomgaarden 2016). Most commonly, these parties are referred to as 'radical right-wing' or 'right-wing populist' to convey the general thrust of their policy agenda and approach to politics (Mudde 2007). We have elected to refer to these parties as 'populist radical right-wing' because the broad nature of the term allows it to encapsulate not only the anti-establishment disposition of the parties (emphasized in the 'right-wing populist' party literature), but also their nativist brand of nationalism and authoritarian inclinations (emphasized in the 'radical right-wing' party literature) (more on each of these characteristics of PRRPs below).

Despite a consensus among scholars regarding the character of PRRPs, the leaders of these parties do not necessarily consider themselves 'radical' or even 'right-wing' (Mudde 2015). Indeed, despite their 'right-wing' positions on sociocultural and related foreign policy issues (e.g., their opposition to immigration and the European Union), PRRPs often support left-leaning economic policies, such as protectionism and, increasingly, government provided social insurance, although the latter is typically reserved for the 'deserving' native population (Zaslove 2008; Ketola and Nordensvard 2018; Rovny and Polk 2019). Furthermore, PRRPs often 'blur' their economic issue positions in an effort to maintain their electoral coalition, built on those sociocultural issues—such as immigration and crime—in which they have demonstrated 'ownership' (Smith 2010; Rovny 2013; Burscher, Spanje, and de Vreese 2015). In short, 'radical right' is a label given by scholars to political parties that exhibit 'far-right' views on sociocultural issues and 'extreme' approaches to politics, rather than a label provided by the parties themselves or an indicator of a consistent or coherent right-leaning policy programme.

As alluded to above, PRRPs are those parties that promote 'nativist nationalism' and exhibit an 'anti-establishment' disposition and 'authoritarian' inclinations. Nativist nationalism[1] is an ideology that opposes 'foreign' elements in one's country, believing that they pose a threat to the unity and distinctiveness of the nation-state and the overall well-being of the native

---

[1] 'Nativist nationalism' is a distinct form of nationalism that not only includes a sense that one's country is superior to other countries, but also a belief that one's country should only include those from certain 'native' groups, typically identified by their racial, ethnic, and/or religious characteristics (Mudde 2007).

population (Mudde 2007). Most obviously, this leads to a general opposition to immigration into the country and, by extension, antagonism towards certain ethnic minorities. More broadly, nativist nationalism can lead PRRPs to be sceptical of any non-native element that they determine to be corrosive to the body politic, including foreign direct investments or imports (Mudde 1999). Furthermore, nativist nationalists typically oppose their country's participation in intergovernmental or supranational organizations, believing that such organizations inherently limit the sovereignty—and therefore the power—of 'the people' of the country (Hooghe, Lenz, and Marks 2019).

PRRPs' anti-establishment (or anti-elite) disposition derives primarily from their populist rhetoric, which attacks those in the political establishment—historically dominated by mainstream political parties—as corrupt elitists who neglect the will and interests of 'the people' of the country (Betz 1993; Canovan 1999; Abedi 2014). This has most commonly resulted in attacks on liberal immigration policies and, relatedly, EU membership, both of which are portrayed by PRRPs as posing cultural, economic, and security threats to their 'nation' (Rydgren 2018). Since populism implies a desire to reduce the political power of the privileged few while expanding it for the struggling many (Jungar and Jupskås 2014), it is unsurprising that PRRPs often portray themselves as the (only) true promoters and defenders of democracy in their country (Betz 2018). Nonetheless, scholars have recognized the inherent threats to democracy posed by populism, as certain domestic populations (e.g., immigrants and leaders of mainstream political parties) are excluded from 'the people' the populists claim to represent and any lack of progress towards populist goals can be attributed to the undue influence of minority stakeholders, leading to efforts to dismantle checks on the power of the majority or top leaders in the country's government (if the populists attain such positions of power) (Jagers and Walgrave 2007; Mudde 2013).

Relatedly, scholars describe PRRPs as exhibiting 'authoritarian' inclinations due to their general antipathy towards immigrant and ethnic minority populations and their desire for order and stability over respect for individual liberty and equal treatment under the law (Rydgren 2008). Furthermore, such a preference for order and stability often translates into the promotion of strong charismatic leaders within the party and supporters who value obedience over principles better suited for democracy, such as independence, tolerance, and respect for others (Sibley, Robertson, and Wilson 2006; Dunn 2015; Eatwell 2018).

Following this literature, we identify 'PRRPs' as those parties that promote nativist nationalism and exhibit both an anti-establishment disposition

Table 2.1 List of PRRPs

Country	PRRP
Austria	Freedom Party of Austria
Austria	Alliance for the Future of Austria
Belgium	Flemish Interest
Belgium	National Front
Denmark	Danish People's Party
France	National Rally
Germany	The Republicans
Greece	Popular Orthodox Rally
Italy	Northern League
The Netherlands	Party of Freedom
Sweden	Sweden Democrats
Switzerland	Swiss People's Party
The United Kingdom	British National Party

and authoritarian inclinations. The list of PRRPs examined in this book is provided in Table 2.1.[2]

There are also parties not listed in Table 2.1 that we will include in robustness checks when data is available. These include parties for which the 'populist radical right-wing' label remains disputed among scholars (e.g., the United Kingdom Independence Party) and relatively new PRRPs that have quickly achieved electoral success (e.g., Alternative for Germany) (Ford, Goodwin, and Cutts 2012; Betz 2019).[3]

The (Native and White) Working Class in Western Europe

Throughout this book, we use the terms 'blue-collar worker' and 'manual worker' to describe a member of the 'working class'. Blue-collar/manual workers are those whose jobs require 'physical work' (most obviously, with

---

[2] The PRRPs examined in this analysis are those parties situated in Western Europe and identified as 'populist radical right-wing parties' by Mudde (2007, 2013), with the exception of those parties for which relevant data is unavailable. In general, data is unavailable for those PRRPs with a relatively brief organizational history and/or that have failed to gain substantial electoral support (e.g., the National Renewal Party—now The Rise Up—in Portugal).

[3] In addition to the United Kingdom Independence Party and Alternative for Germany, we also include the following parties in select robustness checks: the New Flemish Alliance in Belgium (McDonnell and Werner 2018; van Haute, Pauwels, and Sinardet 2018), the Finns Party (Arter 2010), the National Democratic Party of Germany (Bornschier 2012), the Pim Fortuyn List in the Netherlands (Kešić and Duyvendak 2019), the Norwegian Progress Party (Harteveld and Ivarsflaten 2018), and the Golden Dawn in Greece (Ellinas 2013).

their hands) as opposed to 'service work' (Erikson and Goldthorpe 1992; Evans 2000). Those in physical work include 'skilled' workers, such as carpenters and electricians, as well as 'semi-skilled' or 'unskilled' workers, such as assembly workers and janitors. Those in service work include 'white-collar professionals', such as accountants and attorneys, small business owners, and those in poorly compensated jobs that require relatively little formal education, such as clerical workers and retail clerks.

Our theoretical and empirical focus in this book is on the native (i.e., non-immigrant) and White working class in Western Europe. We exclude immigrant and non-White blue-collar workers for two inter-related reasons. First, PRRPs use nativist nationalism as the basis for most of their proposed policies and political appeals, such as their opposition to immigration and EU membership, as well as their tough law and order stance (Mudde 1999; Cutts, Ford, and Goodwin 2010; Golder 2016). Thus, it is natives of the country who have not recently descended from immigrants who are the main target and constituency of PRRPs. Second, the general decline of the working class in Western Europe in recent decades (discussed further below) has primarily generated (economic, cultural, and political) grievances among White, native workers, rather than non-White and/or immigrant workers (Gest 2016). This is due to the diverging historical trajectories of these two groups. In recent decades, White, native blue-collar workers have experienced a general decline in their relative economic, cultural, and political status as more-educated white-collar workers and ethnic minorities steadily grow as a share of the domestic population. At the same time, larger immigrant and ethnic minority populations have translated into greater economic, cultural, and political influence for members of these groups, as has the increasing number of white-collar workers who commonly hold 'multicultural values' (Norris 2005). Thus, the anti-establishment disposition of the populist radical right—and, relatedly, their authoritarian approach to politics—is likely to resonate much more with the White, native working class than non-White and/or immigrant workers.[4]

Since the industrial sector is dominated by blue-collar workers, Figure 2.1 displays the average share of jobs annually held by those in industry and services, respectively, in Western European countries between 1970 and 2019.[5]

---

[4] Therefore, we exclude non-native and/or non-White blue-collar workers from our analyses whenever the survey data allows. The ISSP (2003) has a question on ethnicity only, so we exclude blue-collar workers who do not belong to a Western European ethnic group. The EVS (2008, 2017) and the EES (2009) have a question on country of birth only, so we exclude blue-collar workers who were born outside Western Europe.

[5] 'Industrial' employment refers to jobs in mining and quarrying; manufacturing; electricity, gas, and water; and construction. 'Service' employment refers to jobs in whole and retail trade; transport, storage, and communication; finance and intermediation; and community, social and personal services (OECD Labour Force Statistics 2020).

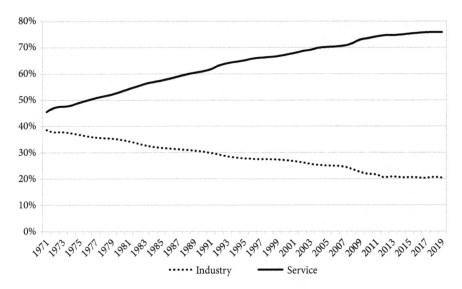

Figure 2.1 Employment in the industrial and service sectors in Western Europe, 1971–2019
Source: OECD, Annual Labour Force Statistic.

As has been well documented, the share of workers in the industrial sector of the economy has consistently declined in recent decades as the share of workers in the service sector has steadily grown. In 1971, there was a relatively equal share of industrial and service sector jobs, with 38 per cent of Western European workers in the industrial sector and 45 per cent of Western European workers in the service sector (with the remaining 17 per cent in the agricultural sector). However, by 2019, the share of employment in the industrial sector had fallen by about half, to just over 20 per cent, while the share of employment in the service sector increased by about two-thirds, to just over 75 per cent. Thus, by 2019, there were about 275 per cent more jobs in the service sector than the industrial sector in Western Europe.

The primary driver of the decline in industrial employment has been 'de-industrialization', broadly understood to mean a shift in investments (and therefore employment) from a country's manufacturing sector to its service sector (Bluestone and Harrison 1982). De-industrialization has been found to result from three main factors: changing consumer preferences, faster productivity growth in the manufacturing sector than the service sector, and greater economic linkages between the Global North and Global South (Kollmeyer 2009).

Scholars have long identified a U-shaped relationship between economic development and the preferences of a country's consumers (e.g., see Rowthorn and Wells 1987; Krugman and Lawrence 1993; and Rowthorn and

Coutts 2004). Since the poor must dedicate a substantial share of their income to basic necessities, such as food and shelter, low-income countries spend a relatively small share of national income on manufactured goods. Middle-income countries, by contrast, spend a relatively high share of national income on manufactured goods, as growing affluence translates into a greater desire and ability to purchase expensive yet durable items, such as refrigerators and automobiles, that not only increase the likelihood of survival, but also provide greater employment and/or recreational opportunities (Clark 1957). In high-income countries, however, consumers once again spend a relatively small share of national income on durable manufactured goods, as such items need to be infrequently replaced and residents are increasingly willing and able to spend money on professional and recreational services, such as those provided in the health care and restaurant industries, that further enhance their quality of life (Kollmeyer 2009). Thus, according to this explanation, the wealthy democracies are experiencing de-industrialization as a result of the natural shift in consumer preferences that occurs at high levels of economic development (Rowthorn and Ramaswamy 1999).

Productivity growth (i.e., increases in the value of goods or services produced per worker) is generally easier to achieve in the manufacturing sector than the service sector due to the unique processes required to produce manufactured goods and services, respectively (Rowthorn and Ramaswamy 1999; Rowthorn and Coutts 2004). Since manufactured goods are often mass and uniformly produced, standardization and repetition are required in their production process. By contrast, services, such as those provided in the restaurant and health care industries, often need to be produced in an ad hoc manner and on an individualized basis (Kollmeyer 2009). Thus, labour-replacing mechanization and automatization is generally easier to achieve in the manufacturing sector than the service sector, leading to declining demand for employment in the former relative to the latter.

Finally, higher volumes of trade and investment between the Global North and Global South have led to a 'new international division of labor' in which multinational corporations increasingly produce manufactured goods in countries with low labour costs (in the Global South) and import them to countries around the world, including those with high labour costs (in the Global North) (Fröbel, Heinrichs, and Kreye 1980; Wood 1995). This process reduces manufacturing employment in the Global North (directly through offshoring and indirectly through low-cost imports) and increases manufacturing employment in the Global South. Thus, greater economic linkages between the Global North and Global South produce de-industrialization in the former and industrialization in the latter (e.g., see Rowthorn and Ramaswamy 1999 and Kucera and Milberg 2003).

34 Social Identity and Working Class Support for the Populist Radical Right

As de-industrialization has diminished employment opportunities for blue-collar workers, it has also exacerbated divisions within their ranks and weakened a critical source of working class economic and political power, organized labour. While industrial employment has steadily declined as a share of total employment in recent decades, not all blue-collar workers have experienced a similar fate. Skill-biased technological change and Western Europe's comparative advantage in highly skilled labour has meant a large relative loss in demand (and therefore income) for less skilled blue-collar workers (Swank and Betz 2003; Acemoglu and Autor 2011; Goos, Manning, and Salomons 2014). Furthermore, blue-collar workers in sheltered areas of the economy, such as those in government employment or construction, have been relatively insulated from the negative consequences of de-industrialization (Iversen and Cusack 2000; Jensen 2011). So too have members of labour unions and blue-collar workers extended employment protection by the government (more on each of these below) (Rueda 2005; Lindvall and Rueda 2014). Thus, while the working class in general has experienced income losses and growing job insecurity because of de-industrialization, many specific groups of blue-collar workers have not.

Since Bourdieu (1984, 1985), the literature on economic class in the wealthy democracies has defined and categorized economic class as a multi-dimensional concept that includes components other than the type of work performed or compensation received, including 'cultural capital' and 'social capital'. Cultural capital refers to the extent to which someone is familiar with the recognized 'high culture' of their society (e.g., highly regarded literature, theatre, and music) or possesses cognitive and linguistic knowledge and skills (Andersen and Hansen 2012; Jarness, Flemmen, and Rosenlund 2019). Social capital refers to the extent to which someone is involved in personal relationships, embedded in social networks, and/or participating in social clubs.[6] The central claim here is that even if workers are in the same type of occupation and earn similar compensation, differences in cultural and social capital can result in divergent experiences, preferences, and behaviours, with those possessing greater amounts of such capital generally able to achieve more of their (economic, social, or political) goals than those with less (Siisiäinen 2003).

Given changes in employment conditions brought about by de-industrialization, welfare state development, greater female labour force participation, and longer life expectancy, scholars have also increasingly

---

[6] The term 'social capital' has a slightly different meaning in the social trust literature arising out of the work of Putnam (1993). In that research, social capital refers not only to participation in social networks and clubs, but also in general to those moral obligations, norms, and values that are conducive to positive societal outcomes (e.g., cooperation and trust).

Populist Radical Right-wing Parties and the Working Class   35

reconceptualized what is meant by 'economic class'. Within this literature, it is recognized that those in similar occupations can have very different work and life experiences based on their sector of employment, sex, and age; and that such divergent experiences often lead to dissimilar perspectives, interests, and actions (Oesch 2006; Beramendi et al. 2015; Krajnáková and Vojtovic 2017).

We incorporate the multidimensionality of economic class in numerous ways in this book. First, we consider cultural capital by controlling for the formal education level of blue-collar workers in all our models[7] and, in Chapter 6, examining the divergent effects of inequality on more and less skilled members of the working class. Second, we consider social capital in Chapter 4 by examining the effect of the welfare state reform process on union and non-union blue-collar workers, respectively, since union membership is a critical source of social capital for working-class people (Saundry, Stuart, and Antcliff 2012). Third, we consider the changing nature and experience of the working class by controlling for gender and age in all our models and, in Chapter 5, examining the effect of specific types of welfare state policies on those with and without secure employment (i.e., economic 'insiders' and 'outsiders').

Table 2.2 provides the demographic characteristics of the blue-collar workers included in two surveys utilized in this book, the ESS (2002, 2018) and the EVS (1990, 1999, 2008, 2017). The statistics on the gender, educational attainment, and skill level of blue-collar workers are from the EVS, while

Table 2.2 Demographics of the working class

Demographic characteristic	Data
Percentage men	59.1%
Percentage with post-secondary education	7.1%
Percentage economic insiders	39.7% (2002)–32.5% (2018)
Percentage highly skilled	40.8% (1990)–68.9% (2017)

Note: Data on gender and education are average statistics from four waves of the EVS (1990, 1999, 2008, 2017) and data on employment status and skill level are the average statistics from two separate waves of the ESS (2002, 2018) and EVS (1990, 2017), respectively.

Sources: EVS (gender, education, and skill level) and ESS (employment status).

---

[7] Although blue-collar workers generally have lower levels of formal education, there is substantial variation among the working class in terms of educational attainment. For example, in the EVS (2017), 14.2 per cent of blue-collar workers were not educated beyond primary school, 23.5 per cent finished lower secondary education only, 51.1 per cent of finished upper secondary education (i.e., high school) only, and 11.2 per cent attained a post-secondary education (e.g., a bachelor's degree).

the statistics on the share of the working class considered 'economic insiders' are from the ESS.[8] The provided numbers are averages across the 11 countries utilized in our analysis, with the gender and educational characteristics including all the EVS survey waves between 1990 and 2017 and the employment status and skill level of the working class including only the earliest and most recent waves of the ESS (2002, 2018) and EVS (1990, 2017), respectively. The descriptive statistics inform us that contrary to popular perceptions of the working class, women and those with post-secondary education make up a substantial portion of self-identified manual workers, with females representing more than 2 in 5 blue-collar workers and the post-secondary educated representing about 1 in 14. Furthermore, the table informs us that the share of 'economic insiders' among the working class has declined modestly (by about 18 per cent) over the last two decades, while the share of blue-collar workers who identify as 'highly skilled' has increased markedly, from less than half in 1990 to over two-thirds in 2017 (a rise of close to 69 per cent). Taken together, these latter two findings suggest that a growing share of economic outsiders are highly skilled. As we will discuss further in Chapter 7, this reality has likely contributed to working class (economic, cultural, and political) grievances and thus also blue-collar worker support for the populist radical right.

The diverging economic fortunes of blue-collar workers have, not surprisingly, resulted in deviating opinions among them on economic issues, including the desirability of specific welfare state policies and overall tolerance for inequality. In general, those workers in economically insecure labour market positions have been found to be more favourable to (private or public) policies of direct benefit to poorer workers than those in economically secure labour market positions. For instance, higher-paid workers in industries exposed to international competition are more willing to restrain their wages (to maintain their company's competitiveness) than higher-paid workers in industries sheltered from international competition (Iversen and Soskice 2010); part-time workers, temporary workers, and the unemployed are more likely to support government spending on social insurance and active labour market policies and less likely to support government provided employment protections than full-time workers in 'permanent' jobs (Rueda 2007); and less skilled workers are more supportive of government redistribution generally than highly skilled workers (Nieuwbeerta and Ultee 1999).

---

[8] The gender, educational attainment, skill level, and employment status of blue-collar workers are utilized as control variables in the models of working-class support for PRRPs reported in subsequent chapters.

One notable exception to the tendency of blue-collar workers to support those policies most directly in their economic interests is union members, who despite their status as labour market 'insiders' have a greater aversion to inequality and favour redistribution more than non-union workers. This somewhat counterintuitive yet well-established finding has been explained as result of a self-selection effect (i.e., those who favour redistributive policies are more likely to join a union) (Checchi, Visser, and van de Werfhorst 2010), union efforts to educate their members about which government policies and political parties best serve workers' economic interests, and unions nurturing a sense of worker solidarity among their members (Pontusson 2013; Mosimann and Pontusson 2017).

To examine whether support for redistribution differs among various segments of the working class in the surveys utilized here, Table 2.3 includes the 'redistribution scores' for blue-collar workers based on employment status ('economic insiders' or 'economic outsiders'), union membership, and skill level. Redistribution scores for economic insiders and outsiders are the averages from nine waves of the ESS (2002, 2004, 2006, 2008, 2010, 2012, 2014, 2016, 2018), while redistribution scores based on union membership and skill level are the averages from four waves of the EVS (1990, 1999, 2008, 2017). The ESS measure hypothetically ranges from 1 to 5, with higher values signifying greater support for government redistribution to reduce income inequality. The EVS measure hypothetically ranges from 1 to 10, with higher values signifying greater support more equal incomes in general.[9]

Table 2.3 Support for redistribution among the working class

Type of blue-collar workers		Mean score	Standard error	Difference
Employment status	Insiders	3.93	0.01	0.11***
	Outsiders	4.04	0.01	
Union membership	Non-members	5.65	0.01	0.31***
	Members	5.96	0.03	
Skill level	Highly skilled	5.77	0.02	0.23***
	Less skilled	6.00	0.02	

Note: The ESS asks whether people agree or disagree with the statement of 'the government should take measures to reduce differences in income levels'. The answer scale ranges from 1 (Disagree strongly) to 5 (Agree strongly). The EVS asks whether people think 'there should be greater incentives for individual efforts' (1) or 'incomes should be made more equal' (10). *** indicates p<.01.

Sources: ESS (employment status) and EVS (union membership and skill level).

[9] The ESS asks whether respondents agree or disagree that 'the government should take measures to reduce differences in income levels', while the EVS asks whether respondents believe that 'incomes should be made more equal'.

Consistent with expectations, we find statistically significant differences in the redistribution scores within each subgroup, with economic outsiders, union members, and those with lower skill levels more supportive of redistributive efforts (by the government) than economic insiders, non-union members, and those with higher skill levels, respectively.

In addition to influencing blue-collar workers' beliefs and opinions regarding inequality, labour unions have also been found to reduce economic inequality at the country level. Indeed, differences in union strength can account for much of the cross-national and over-time variation in economic inequality in the wealthy democracies, with stronger national union movements producing less inequality (e.g., see Wallerstein 1999; Ahlquist 2017; and Hope and Martelli 2019). This union effect on inequality is a result of unions' impact on market incomes and, less directly, government redistribution (Castater 2015; Han and Castater 2016). Unions reduce market inequality by helping workers extract greater concessions from their employers (Korpi 1985; Bradley et al. 2003), negotiating larger income gains for workers in lower-paying jobs than workers in higher-paying jobs (Hall and Thelen 2007; Iversen and Soskice 2010), and indirectly lifting the market income of lower-paid non-union workers (Rueda and Pontusson 2000; Wallerstein and Western 2000).[10] Unions increase government redistribution by instilling in their members a stronger preference for redistributive welfare state policies (Yang and Kwon 2019), increasing voter turnout disproportionately among lower income workers (who are generally more supportive of redistributive government policies and left-leaning political parties) (Pontusson 2013), and maintaining strong organizational and programmatic links with mainstream left political parties (Simoni 2013).

Although unions act as a bulwark against working-class divisions and generate greater economic equality, they too have suffered in recent decades because of de-industrialization. Since unions have historically organized most successfully in the manufacturing sector,[11] de-industrialization has directly led to a decline in 'union density' (the share of workers that belong to a union) across nearly all Western European countries in recent decades, as well as to a growing share of union members in more sheltered areas of the economy, particularly the public sector (Lee 2005; Kollmeyer and Peters 2019). Furthermore, as manufacturing employment has steadily declined,

[10] Union wage gains may lead to higher wages in the non-union sector due to 'spillover effects', which occur when non-union employers increase their employees' wages in an effort to preempt potential union organizing efforts or to entice workers away from already unionized establishments (Wallerstein and Western 2000).
[11] Union organizing has been relatively successful in the manufacturing sector due to the small number of large firms in the sector and plant employees often working in close proximity to each other (Lee 2005).

unions have become increasingly willing to trade income gains for employment guarantees in collective bargaining agreements (Glassner, Keune, and Marginson 2011). Fewer income gains for union workers relative to non-union workers have translated into less aggregate demand to join a union and thus also a further decline in union density (Visser 2002). Thus, deindustrialization has weakened unions directly through a reduction in manufacturing employment and indirectly by reducing the appeal of unions to prospective members.

Figure 2.2 displays the average level of union density and the share of union members employed in manufacturing and the public sector, respectively, in Western European countries between 1980 and 2018 (manufacturing and public sector union data are only available through 2013). In 1980, the average share of workers in Western European countries that belonged to a union was nearly 50 per cent, with slightly more union members employed in manufacturing (36.3 per cent of all union workers) than the public sector (33.4 per cent of all union workers). By 2013, however, union density had declined to about 35 per cent, with now more than twice as many union members in the public sector (40.2 per cent) than in manufacturing (19.6 per cent). By 2018, union density had fallen further, to just under 32 per cent. Given strong positive within-country correlations between union density and the

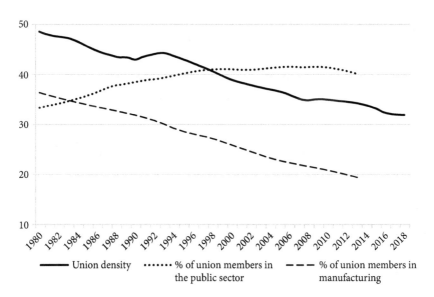

Figure 2.2 Union density and union composition in Western Europe

Source: Database on Institutional Characteristics of Trade Unions, Wage Setting, State Intervention and Social Pacts, 1960–2018 (ICTWSS, version 6.1).

40 Social Identity and Working Class Support for the Populist Radical Right

share of union workers in the manufacturing sector between 1980 and 2013, this would suggest that blue-collar workers have lost additional ground in unions in recent years.[12]

The combination of declining industrial employment, growing divisions among blue-collar workers, and weakening labour unions has created a dilemma for mainstream left parties, as their base of electoral support has historically consisted of blue-collar workers and the disproportionately working-class union organizations that represent them (Kitschelt 1999; Abou-Chadi and Wagner 2019). In the 1990s, as the size and power of this base continued to shrink, mainstream left parties began advocating for less generous welfare state policies[13] and emphasizing left-wing positions on sociocultural and related foreign policy issues, such as their support for immigration and the EU (Karreth, Polk, and Allen 2013; Carvalho and Reudin 2020). However, these economic and sociocultural positions, partly designed to appeal to the growing number of middle-class professionals with 'left-libertarian' values, occurred as (mainstream and populist) right-wing parties were tempering their opposition to the welfare state[14] and mainstream right parties were largely supportive of EU membership and liberal immigration policies (Keman 2011; Gingrich and Häusermann 2015). Thus, a general neoliberal consensus emerged among mainstream parties on both economic and sociocultural issues, providing opportunities for populist challengers on both the left and the right (Meijers 2017).

While populist radical left-wing parties (PRLPs) generally share the sociocultural issue positions of the mainstream left, it has exploited this shifting electoral landscape by emphasizing leftist positions on economic issues, such as its opposition to International Monetary Fund and EU imposed austerity and addressing the high and rising levels of economic inequality across Western Europe (March and Mudde 2005; Katsambekis and Kioupkiolis 2019). By contrast, PRRPs have done so by emphasizing far-right positions on sociocultural issues, such as the loss of sovereignty that EU membership inherently

---

[12] The average within-country correlation between union density and the share of union workers in the manufacturing sector is 0.636. The decline in the share of union workers in the manufacturing sector has been driven not only by the overall reduction in manufacturing employment, but also by fewer manufacturing workers joining a union. While data on manufacturing union density (the share of all manufacturing workers that belong to a union) are relatively scarce, the available evidence suggests that all but one Western European country (Belgium) experienced a decrease in that measure in recent decades (Visser 2019).

[13] While mainstream left parties have shifted their economic positions to the centre in recent decades, middle-class voters who support such parties are broadly supportive of the welfare state (Engler and Zohlnhöfer 2019).

[14] Right-wing parties tempered their opposition to the welfare state due to the popularity of previously established welfare state policies and the parties' growing dependence on pro-redistribution working-class voters (Gingrich and Häusermann 2015).

entails and addressing the high and rising levels of immigration that is often a consequence of it (Mudde 2013; Hooghe, Lenz, and Marks 2019). Indeed, this latter strategy has proven so electorally successful that it has motivated mainstream right parties to co-opt the sociocultural positions of PRRPs to win over (and in some cases win back) voters from these parties (Akkerman 2015). These dynamics have resulted in mainstream left parties being increasingly squeezed, as PRLPs outflank them on the (economic) left and mainstream and PRRPs outflank them on the (sociocultural) right.

Table 2.4 includes the average share of the vote by decade for PRRPs, centre-right, centre-left, and far-left political parties in the 11 Western European countries examined in our main analysis and included in Table 2.1.[15] Data on vote share are from the Comparative Political Dataset (1960–2020) and the British government (for the British National Party only). The table informs us that the share of the vote received by PRRPs and far-left political parties steadily rose from the 1990s to the 2010s, while that for centre-right and centre-left parties steadily declined, with the biggest movements observed for PRRPs and centre-left parties. Between the 1990s and 2010s, the share of the vote received by PRRPs grew by over 100 per cent (from 5.3 per cent to 10.9 per cent) and that for far-left parties grew by about 30 per cent (from 6.2 per cent to 8.1 per cent). Meanwhile, the share of the vote received by centre-left parties fell by nearly 22 per cent (from 31 per cent to 24.2 per cent) and that for centre-right parties fell by about 7 per cent (from 15.6 to 14.5 per cent). The combination of these divergent trends meant that in the 2010s, centre-left and centre-right parties had only about twice as much support as PRRPs and far-left parties, compared to more than four times as

Table 2.4 Average vote share by decade for major party families

Party Family[†]	1990–99	2000–09	2010–19
Populist Radical Right	5.3	8.2	10.9
Centre-Right	15.6	16.3	14.5
Centre-left	31.0	29.7	24.2
Far-Left	6.2	6.4	8.1

[†]The table includes only those countries and PRRPs listed in Table 2.1.
Source: Data are from the Comparative Political Dataset (1960–2020) and the British government (for the British National Party only).

[15] The table includes only those countries and PRRPs listed in Table 2.1. Party family assignment for the 'centre-right', 'centre-left', and 'far-left' are from the Comparative Political Dataset (1960–2020).

much in the 1990s.[16] The biggest change is for the PRRPs relative to centre-left parties, with the former shrinking the gap with the latter from 25.7 percentage points in the 1990s to 13.3 percentage points in the 2010s (a gain of over 50 per cent).

Working Class Support for PRRPs

The existing research on the determinants of PRRP support includes studies exploring individual level factors only (e.g., see Oesch 2008; Gest, Reny, and Meyer 2018) and a combination of individual and macro-level factors (e.g., see Lubbers, Gijsberts, and Scheepers 2002; Arzheimer 2009; Han 2016; Rooduijn and Burgoon 2018). One of the most common individual level variables in these studies is a person's occupation, typically categorized based on the type of work conducted and employer–employee status (Stockemer, Lentz, and Mayer 2018). The three occupations utilized most frequently in the literature on PRRPs are those that engage in manual work (for an employer), those that engage in professional service work (for an employer), and small business owners.

As we discussed in Chapter 1, scholars explain disproportionate blue-collar worker support for PRRPs by reference to the unique economic hardships and cultural perspectives of the working class, as well as the ensuing political dissatisfaction that arise from them. By contrast, professional service workers—those with a high level of formal education and in white collar employment—are generally anticipated to oppose PRRPs due to their relatively high levels of job security, work satisfaction, and cosmopolitan values, all of which translate into greater support for immigration, European integration, and the domestic political system more generally (Kitschelt 1994).

Small business owners, like blue-collar workers, are typically expected to support PRRPs due to economic and cultural grievances, as well as the political dissatisfaction they produce. Small business owners' economic grievances arise from increasing volumes of low-priced imports (Ivarsflaten

---

[16] While PRRPs have consistently grown their vote share and thus also their representation in national legislatures in recent decades, their progress in translating those gains into participation in governing coalitions has been less even. PRRPs participated in five governing coalitions in the 1990s, eight in the 2000s, and six in the 2010s, and did not secure the head of government (president, prime minister, or chancellor) in any of them. Furthermore, only five PRRPs in four countries participated in these governing coalitions: the Freedom Party of Austria (once in the 1990s and once in the 2010s); the Alliance for the Future of Austria (once in the 2000s); Popular Orthodox Rally in Greece (once in the 2000s); the Northern League in Italy (once in the 1990s, three times in the 2000s, and twice in the 2010s); and the Swiss People's Party (three times in the 1990s, twice in the 2000s, and three times in the 2010s).

2005), the relatively meagre government benefits they receive relative to employees (Hall and Soskice 2001), and remnants of the economic desperation that motivated many of them to initially establish their own enterprise (Thurik et al. 2008). Small business owners' cultural grievances arise from their generally low level of formal education, which often translates into nationalist and authoritarian sentiments and thus also opposition to immigration, European integration, and multiculturalism generally (Schneider 2008; Malchow-Møller et al. 2009).

Table 2.5 presents how much each of these three occupational groups are over- or under-represented among PRRP supporters in Western European countries with EVS survey data from 1990, 1999, 2008, and 2017. The numbers in the table reflect the PRRP Support Index scores for each occupational group by party. These PRRP Support Index scores are the result of the following formula:

$$\text{PRRP Support Index} = \frac{m_l/m_n}{h_l/h_n},$$

where m_l = the number of people in a particular occupation (e.g., the number of people in manual work) who vote for PRRPs, m_n = the number of all people in that occupation (e.g., the number of all people in manual work), h_l = the number of people outside the occupation under consideration (e.g., the number of people who are not in manual work) who voted for PRRPs, and h_n = the number of all people who do not belong to the occupation under consideration (e.g., the number of all people who are not in manual work).

Therefore, if an occupational group has a number larger than one, it indicates that people in that occupation are more likely to vote for PRRPs than those not in that occupation (e.g., those in other occupations, the unemployed, and the retired). By contrast, if an occupational group has a number smaller than one, it indicates people in that occupation are less likely to vote for the PRRPs than those not in that occupation.

The PRRP Support Index scores in Table 2.5 inform us that blue-collar workers are stronger and more consistent supporters of PRRPs than small business owners or middle-class professionals. While blue-collar workers disproportionately support all but one of the PRRPs included in the table (the lone exception being the Alliance for the Future of Austria), small business owners disproportionately support nine of the 13 parties, and middle-class professionals disproportionately *oppose* 11. Furthermore, blue-collar workers have the largest PRRP Support Index score for all but two of the 13 PRRPs included in the analysis, the lone exceptions being the Republicans in

44 Social Identity and Working Class Support for the Populist Radical Right

Table 2.5 PRRP support by occupation group

Country	PRRP	Blue-collar worker	Small business owners	White-collar professionals
Austria	Freedom Party of Austria	1.35	1.33	0.56
Austria	Alliance for the Future of Austria	0.91	1.34	0.30
Belgium	Flemish Interest	1.72	0.54	1.02
Belgium	National Front	3.12	2.78	0.00
Denmark	Danish People's Party	1.71	1.15	0.48
France	National Rally	1.68	1.37	0.31
Germany	The Republicans	1.53	0.44	1.56
Greece	Popular Orthodox Rally	1.73	1.66	0.29
Italy	Northern League	1.55	1.12	0.29
The Netherlands	Party of Freedom	2.05	0.83	0.54
Sweden	Sweden Democrats	3.35	1.50	0.35
Switzerland	Swiss People's Party	1.74	0.93	0.76
UK	British National Party	1.43	1.01	0.54
Average		**1.88**	**1.21**	**0.53**

Source: EVS (1990, 1999, 2008, 2017).

Germany, for which middle-class professionals have a modestly higher score, and the Alliance for the Future of Austria, for which small business owners have a higher score.[17] Nonetheless, working-class support for PRRPs does differ substantially across parties and countries. Blue-collar workers' average PRRP Support Index score for all 13 parties is 1.88 (informing us that blue-collar workers are nearly twice as likely as non-blue-collar workers to support PRRPs across these 13 countries), but rises above 3 for two of the parties (the Belgian National Front and the Sweden Democrats) and falls below 1.5 for three others (the Freedom Party of Austria, the Alliance for the Future of Austria, and the British National Party).

---

[17] One potential explanation for this finding for the German Republicans is the unique and difficult circumstances confronted by middle-class professionals in eastern Germany because of the large-scale privatization programmes implemented following German reunification in the early 1990s (Patton 2019). The relatively strong support of small business owners for the Alliance for the Future of Austria is also understandable due to its right-leaning stance on the economy relative to the other PRRP in the country, the Freedom Party of Austria. The Alliance for the Future of Austria—which splintered from the Freedom Party of Austria—maintained this position to remain a palatable coalition partner to the centre-right Austrian People's Party (Luther 2009).

Table 2.6 examines whether working-class support for the populist radical right differs across time as well as countries. Included is the PRRP Support Index score for the 13 PRRPs examined in Table 2.1 for each of the four EVS wave years between 1990 and 2017 (1990, 1999, 2008, 2017). Since some PRRPs were founded relatively recently (e.g., the Dutch Party for Freedom in 2006), have already dissolved (e.g., the Belgian National Front in 2012), and/or have had prolonged periods of political irrelevance (e.g., the British National Party), only two of the parties (the Freedom Party of Austria and the National Rally in France) have data available for all four survey years.

Since the time-series data on class voting for PRRPs is relatively scarce, it is difficult to draw strong conclusions from the figures provided in Table 2.6. Nonetheless, at least one broad stylized fact can be gleaned from the data: working-class support for PRRPs has followed different trajectories across countries and parties. Of the ten PRRPs that have at least two observations, three of them have increased their dependence on blue-collar workers (the Freedom Party of Austria, the Republicans in Germany, and the Party of Freedom in the Netherlands), two of them have decreased their dependence on

Table 2.6 Blue-collar workers and PRRPs

Country	PRRP	Class voting for the populist radical right			
		1990	1999	2008	2017
Austria	Freedom Party of Austria	1.06	1.56	1.16	1.60
Austria	Alliance for the Future of Austria			0.91	
Belgium	Flemish Interest	0.84	3.18	2.01	
Belgium	National Front		3.80	1.88	
Denmark	Danish People's Party		1.22	2.80	2.1
France	National Rally	1.68	1.58	3.65	1.53
Germany	The Republicans	0.83	2.91		
Greece	Popular Orthodox Rally			1.73	
Italy	Northern League		2.28	1.91	1.45
The Netherlands	Party for Freedom			1.64	2.77
Sweden	Sweden Democrats				3.35
Switzerland	Swiss People's Party			1.54	1.61
UK	British National Party	1.05			1.08

Source: EVS (1990, 1999, 2008, 2017).

blue-collar workers (the Northern League in Italy and the National Front in Belgium), and the remaining five have seen relatively stable levels of working-class support (the Flemish Interest in Belgium, the Danish People's Party, the National Rally in France, the Swiss People's Party, and the British National Party).

Conclusion and Discussion

In this chapter, we established the theoretical and empirical foundation for subsequent chapters of the book by defining key terms (including 'populist radical right-wing' political parties and 'blue-collar workers'); outlining which countries and PRRPs are covered in our analysis; providing a broad overview of the economic and political context confronted by blue-collar workers in recent decades in Western Europe, as well as descriptive statistics on the demographic and ideological heterogeneity of the working class; and demonstrating that working-class support for PRRPs varies substantially across parties and over time.

Why does working-class support for PRRPs differ across parties and over time? In the following chapter, we begin to answer this question. First, we consider existing research, which suggests that working-class support for PRRPs is a function of numerous 'supply side' and 'demand side' factors, including the policy positions of the PRRP, the ideological disposition of other parties in the system, and the extent of unemployment and immigration in the country. Second, we will explicate our social identity theory, which argues that working-class support for PRRPs is the result of specific national level policymaking processes, policy outputs, and policy outcomes that affect blue-collar workers' demand for PRRPs via a change in their social identity and the issues they find most salient. In Chapters 4 through 6, we delve more deeply into empirically assessing our theory by examining the effects that specific policymaking processes, policy outputs, and policy outcomes have on the PRRP party support of the working class generally, as well as specific types of blue-collar workers.

3
A Social Identity Approach to Blue-Collar Worker Support for the Populist Radical Right

This chapter outlines our social identity approach to blue-collar worker support for PRRPs and provides preliminary tests of our theoretical claims. In the first section of the chapter, we provide an overview of the literature on the determinants of PRRP support with an emphasis on the importance of policymaking processes, policy outputs, and policy outcomes. In particular, we note that previous scholarship has focused disproportionately on the influence of policy outcomes while paying much less attention to policy outputs and largely neglecting policy processes. This is despite growing evidence that inclusive and cooperative forms of decision-making can benefit incumbent parties and that elected leaders have far greater control over policy processes and outputs than they do policy outcomes.

In the second section of the chapter, we provide an overview of the literature on social identity. We begin by contrasting social identity with social group membership. We then discuss what determines the availability of specific social identities and under what conditions such identities are likely to be embraced, altered, or jettisoned entirely.

In the third section of the chapter, we outline our social identity approach to blue-collar worker support for PRRPs. While the economic grievance theory, cultural grievance theory, and theory of political discontent claim that blue-collar workers support PRRPs because of their dissatisfaction with the economic, cultural, and/or political status quo, they do not explain why blue-collar workers abandon political parties with agendas that align closely with their economic interests (but not their cultural interests) (e.g., mainstream left political parties) for political parties with agendas that align closely with their cultural interests (but not necessarily their economic interests) (i.e., PRRPs). Our social identity approach attempts to address this puzzle by outlining a three-stage theory explaining how policy processes, outputs, and

Social Identity and Working Class Support for the Populist Radical Right. Eric G. Castater and Kyung Joon Han, Oxford University Press. © Eric G. Castater and Kyung Joon Han (2025). DOI: 10.1093/9780198953104.003.0003

outcomes affect political party preferences through a change in social identity and, by consequence, what issues blue-collar workers find most salient.

In the fourth section of the chapter, we utilize survey data to conduct preliminary tests of each stage in our theory. The evidence we provide suggests that policy processes, outcomes, and outputs relatively favourable to blue-collar workers indirectly reduce these workers' support for PRRPs, while those relatively unfavourable to blue-collar workers indirectly increase these workers' support for these parties.

Policy Processes, Outputs, and Outcomes

Previous scholarship on the determinants of PRRP support has made a distinction between 'supply side' and 'demand side' factors (Giugni et al. 2005; Mudde 2010). Supply side factors refer to those attributes of the political system and political parties that inhibit or facilitate the formation of a PRRP, such as the proportionality of the electoral system and the ideological disposition of existing political parties. Demand side factors refer to those economic, socio-cultural, and political conditions that make voters more or less likely to support a party of the far-right, such as the unemployment rate, immigration level, and EU membership. Also relevant for the demand side are individual level attributes that affect the propensity of a voter to react positively to the appeals of the populist radical right, such as a person's formal education level or occupation (Stockemer, Lentz, and Mayer 2018). In short, PRRPs are strongest when supply side factors provide the electoral space for such parties to emerge, and demand side factors lead a large segment of voters to harbour those grievances that have proven fertile ground for the populist radical right (van der Brug and Fennema 2007).

While no explanation of PRRP success is complete without a comprehensive supply side component, our analysis is primarily focused on explaining variation in demand for PRRPs. At the macro level, we conceptualize the socio-economic, socio-cultural, and political context that voters are embedded within as consisting of three distinct but interrelated features of public policymaking: the policymaking process, policy outputs, and policy outcomes. The *policymaking process* refers to the procedures by which a national government produces public policy; *policy outputs* refer to the specific content of any public policies produced by a national government; and *policy outcomes* refer to the socio-economic and socio-cultural contexts arising from or shaped by national government policy. At the micro level, we focus on those voters that previous research has found to be most strongly supportive of PRRPs, blue-collar workers.

A Social Identity Approach to Blue-Collar Worker Support   **49**

Previous macro- or multi-level studies on the determinants of PRRP support have focused their attention on policy outcomes and, to a lesser extent, policy outputs. The most common policy outcomes included in this literature are those emerging from the economic and cultural grievance theories: (changes in) the unemployment rate and (changes in) the share of the population that is foreign born (e.g., see Jackman and Volpert 1996; Lubbers, Gijsberts, and Scheepers 2002; Golder 2003; Arzheimer 2009; Werts, Scheepters, and Lubbers 2013; Bustikova 2014; Down and Han 2020). Other policy outcomes arising out of the economic and cultural grievance theories but employed less commonly by scholars include the level of or changes in income inequality, gross domestic product, international trade volume, capital flows, and de-industrialization (e.g., see Swank and Betz 2003; Han 2016; Rooduijn and Burgoon 2018).

Policy outputs expected to condition the extent of economic and cultural grievances (and thus also any political dissatisfaction that arises from them), such as the level of spending on government provided social insurance, the universality of welfare state benefits, and EPL, have also been included in numerous analyses (e.g., see Swank and Betz 2003; Rooduijn and Burgoon 2018; Vlandas and Halikiopoulou 2019). While the results of these studies are far from uniform, a general consensus is that both policy outcomes and policy outputs matter for PRRP support: poor economic conditions and more foreign-born residents increase support for PRRPs by fuelling economic and/or cultural grievances (and, less directly, political discontent); but that generous and well-designed welfare state policies mitigate such effects by improving voters' economic standing, as well as their perception of elected leaders and the political system generally.

While the existing research on PRRP support has focused its attention on policy outputs and especially policy outcomes, it has neglected the influence of policy processes. We believe that the disproportionate focus on policy outcomes and the omission of policy processes is problematic for four reasons, the first three theoretical and the fourth practical. First, a large and growing body of evidence suggests that governing parties benefit electorally from inclusive and cooperative forms of decision-making, particularly on contentious issues related to the welfare state and labour market policy (Hamann and Kelly 2010; Castater and Han 2016). Given that the design and generosity of such policies has been found to matter for PRRP support, we believe it is appropriate to consider whether the process by which such policies are made is important as well.

Second, the policy options available to governing parties have declined in recent decades as a result of rules and obligations associated with EU membership and the perception that neoliberal policy prescriptions are necessary to foster competitiveness in an increasingly globalized world (Peters 2012). Indeed, mainstream party convergence on socio-economic and/or socio-cultural issues has been a prominent supply side explanation for the emergence of populist and radical parties on both the left and the right in recent decades, as it provides electoral space for issue positions that resonate with the public but are largely ignored by the dominant political parties (Rydgren and van der Meiden 2019). Thus, the policymaking process can provide an alternative method by which mainstream parties can differentiate themselves and appeal to voters in an age of relatively stringent policy constraints (Castater and Han 2018).

Third, it is often difficult for voters to identify the specific causes of economic outcomes, or to distinguish the 'signal' from the 'noise' (Sanders 1999; Ebeid and Rodden 2006; Gasper and Reeves 2011). For instance, when the unemployment rate rises, voters may be unable to confidently assess how much of it is a consequence of government policy or circumstances beyond the government's control (e.g., global economic conditions or central bank monetary policies). In such circumstances, voters evaluate governing parties and politicians based on criteria that are more easily and directly observed, such as the types of policies adopted by the government (i.e., policy outputs) and how those policies were adopted (i.e., policymaking processes) (Healy and Malhotra 2010).

Finally, and relatedly, policy outcomes are that feature of public policy that elected leaders are least able to influence (over the short- to medium-term), while the policymaking process is that feature of public policy that elected leaders are most able to control. Both these points are especially true in an age of Europeanization and globalization, which restrict the ability of governments to differentiate themselves on policy outputs and therefore indirectly, on policy outcomes as well. Thus, scholarship that focuses on policy outputs and policy outcomes and ignores policy processes has relatively little to offer governing leaders or other political actors who seek to produce or avoid certain electoral outcomes within the confines of contemporary Western European politics.

Group Membership and Social Identity

A 'social identity' refers to a (informal or formal) social group that a person perceives herself to belong to and that has psychological, emotional, and behavioural significance for the individual (Tajfel 1982).[1] Therefore, social group membership differs from social identity in that the former is an objective social fact, while the latter is a personal, subjective state of being. Given this reality, people do not necessarily hold (equally strong) social identities for all the social groups they belong to. For example, the ISSP (2003) provided survey respondents with a list of 10 social groups and asked them which of these groups they identified the most with. Western Europeans demonstrated huge variation in their social identification, with occupation, economic class, gender, age, and nationality each chosen by 10–15 per cent of respondents and ethnicity, family, religion, political party, and country region each chosen by 3–7 per cent of respondents.

In addition, just because a person identifies strongly with a particular social group, it does not mean that membership in other social groups is meaningless for that individual. When the ISSP (2003) asked Western European respondents whether there were social groups they identify with other than their top choice, 94.4 per cent named both a second and third most important social group. In short, people can and do possess multiple social identities simultaneously, but the relative importance of those identities can vary substantially. Consequently, understanding the patterns of social identity is key to understanding inter-group interactions and conflicts (Tajfel 1982), as well political behaviour, including political participation and party support (Fowler and Kam 2007).

The 'social identity approach' in social sciences broadly refers to scholarly efforts to explain the emergence and consequences of particular social identities (Hornsey 2008).[2] As part of this research tradition, scholars have sought to understand the conditions necessary for a specific social identity to plausibly emerge from membership in a particular social group and under

---

[1] According to social identity theory, people may engage in 'interpersonal relations' or 'intergroup relations' with each other. Interpersonal relations refer to those rare human interactions in which people perceive themselves and others to be unique and idiosyncratic individuals, while intergroup relations refer to those much more common human interactions in which people perceive themselves and others to be de facto representatives of the social groups they belong to (Tajfel et al. 1971).

[2] Regarding the consequences of social identity, political scientists have found that people's social identity shapes diverse political behaviours of theirs. For example, identification with a social group leads to support for a political party that is linked to, or affiliated with, the group, such as blue-collar workers' class identity enhancing their support for a social democratic party (Evans 1999). Also, when people hold a strong national identity, it weakens their partisan attachment as its rival identity and therefore lowers the level of their affective polarization by reducing both their favouritism towards their own party and their dislike to their out-group party (Levendusky 2019). In addition, people support a particular policy more strongly when they identify with a group to which the policy is unambiguously related to. For example, Cassese and Barnes (2019) find that while women are more supportive of child care subsidies than men are in the United States, the gender difference disappears when the discussion of the policy embraces race.

52 Social Identity and Working Class Support for the Populist Radical Right

what circumstances a social identity is more or less likely to be challenged or altered. We turn to each of these matters in the following two sub-sections.

Available Social Identities

A certain social identity is more likely to arise if it has a high degree of 'fit' with the social group it is associated with and is easily 'accessible' (Turner and Brown 1978; Tajfel and Turner 1979; Oakes 1987; Hogg and Abrams 1988; Oakes, Turner, and Haslam 1991). A social identity has a high degree of fit with a social group if beliefs about that social group's characteristics are consistent with the observed characteristics of the group. Two interrelated types of such fit are 'comparative fit' and 'normative fit'. A social identity's comparative fit refers to similarities between a social group's members, as well as differences between a social group's members and members of other social groups. Thus, a social identity has a strong comparative fit if a person perceives (physical and/or psycho-emotional) differences among a group's members to be smaller than differences between that group's members and members of other groups. The normative fit of a social identity indicates the match between group members' characteristics and behaviours and the stereotypical and normative content of the group. Therefore, a social identity has a strong normative fit if a person perceives themselves and others to share (physical and psycho-emotional) characteristics with prototypical members of the group the social identity arises out of.

The accessibility of a social identity refers to the extent to which social interactions reinforce a given social identity. A social identity is more accessible to an individual if current or ongoing goals and tasks require or make it highly likely that others will perceive them as a member of a particular social group and/or they will recognize themselves as a member of that group (Hornsey 2008).[3] Thus, identities that are familiar and carry emotional valence are more accessible.

In short, a social identity is more available to a person if it seems intellectually credible to them (due to its strong 'fit' with a social group they are a member of) and is frequently a fundamental feature of their public and/or private life.

---

[3] For instance, a native blue-collar worker would be more likely to experience a class-based identity when negotiating with their employer regarding compensation, but more likely to experience a nation-based identity when travelling to a foreign country.

The Dynamic Nature of Social Identity

Within the social identity literature, scholars have offered two interrelated explanations for why some social identities are challenged or altered more than others. The first focuses on the 'permeability' of the social group the social identity arises from and the second on the 'status' of the social group.

The permeability of a social group refers to the ease by which someone can credibly leave such a group (and thus diminish or completely jettison the social identity associated with it). The permeability of social group membership is determined by the inherent nature of the social group. Social identities emanating from biologically based social groups or others passed down in families through generations (i.e., 'descent identities'), such as race or nation, are more difficult to alter than social identities emanating from non-biologically based social groups and/or groups joined later in one's life (i.e., 'flexible identities'), such as political party (Huddy 2001; Kopecky, Bos, and Greenberg 2010).

Social group status refers to the relative position of a group on a certain valued dimension, such as material well-being or social/political rights. Since Tajfel (1982), social identity has been understood to consist of cognitive, evaluative, and emotional components (Ellemers, Kortekaas, and Ouwerkert 1999). While individuals must recognize that they are a member of a particular social group to identify with that group (the cognitive component), their willingness to embrace and emphasize that identity is a function of their overall assessment of the social group (the evaluative component) and their engagement with and commitment to the social group (the emotional component). Since people tend to derive self-esteem and self-worth from the relative standing of their social group(s),[4] they are motivated to suppress or attempt to eliminate those identities associated with social groups perceived to be doing poorly compared to other groups; and elevate those identities associated with social groups perceived to be doing well compared to other groups (Ellemers 1993).[5]

---

[4] The social-cognitive research tradition in social psychology emphasizes the reduction of the cost of information gathering as the chief motive of social categorization and identification. In other words, people use the characteristics of a social group to which a person belongs in order to understand and evaluate the person. However, the functional approach such as social identity theory and the social categorization theory considers social categorization and identification more as a meaning-seeking activity (Blanz and Aufderheide 1999).

[5] As a result, social identification of high-status group members is usually stronger than that of low-status group members (Ellemers, Kortekaas, and Ouwerkert 1999).

We can find a similar claim in the literature on symbolic boundaries.[6] As social identity theory suggests that people prefer a social identity that improves their sense of worth, symbolic boundary literature proposes that majority groups in society strategically choose a symbolic boundary that protects their privileges or interests. For example, Bail (2008) argues that while some countries like Germany and France emphasize language and culture in their citizenship law system to protect the privileges of natives' group status, some countries like Switzerland have taken a more integrative approach in the face of threats from their powerful neighboring countries. In both theories, people deliberately choose a criterion that separates 'us' from 'them'.

Since social identity is an intrinsic feature of the human experience, the weakening of a particular social identity necessarily means that another social identity will be strengthened. Thus, a decline in the status of a social group often results in a realignment of social identities, or people shifting their social identification towards a higher status group they are a member of (Tajfel, Billig, Bundy, and Flament 1971; Turner 1975; Tajfel and Turner 1979; Hogg and Abrams 1988). This is particularly the case when the diminished social group is considered impermeable because of its intrinsic qualities (i.e., it produces a descent identity) or a lack of opportunity to improve its standing (Ellemers 1993).

In short, a social identity is more likely to be eliminated or downgraded when membership in the social group it is arising from is (perceived to be) a personal choice rather than a matter of fate; and the social group is (perceived to be) in an unfavourable and unalterable position relative to other, related groups.

Social Identity and PRRP Support

In this section, we provide a theoretical argument explaining the process by which macro-level contexts shift party preferences of blue-collar workers via a change in social identity, with testable implications at each stage of that process. In the first stage, policy processes, outputs, and outcomes shape blue-collar workers' social identity, with economic and political conditions relatively favourable to blue-collar workers leading to a stronger class-based identity and economic and political conditions relatively unfavourable to

---

[6] Symbolic boundaries are conceptual distinctions constructed by social actors that categorize people and practices (e.g., race, ethnicity, or occupation). Symbolic boundaries differ from social boundaries that indicate objectified and institutionalized forms of differences (e.g., citizenship law) (Lamont and Molnár 2002).

blue-collar workers leading to a stronger nation-based identity. In the second stage, the social identity of blue-collar workers determines what issues will be most salient to them, with a more class-based identity leading to a greater concern about economic issues and a more nation-based identity leading to a greater concern about cultural issues. In the third stage, blue-collar workers that care more about economic issues generally oppose PRRPs, while blue-collar workers that care more about cultural issues generally support PRRPs.

Stage 1: The Macro Context and Social Identity

Following the implication of social identity theory, we argue in this book that political and economic contexts shape blue-collar workers' social identity by modifying the group status of the working class. Since the working class as a social group has been produced through the historical development of a capitalist and state-based international system, we believe that the economic and political context of blue-collar workers are relevant criteria to measure the group status of the working class.

Han (2016) and Engler and Weisstanner (2021) produce models of PRRP support utilizing the literature on social identity. Both studies argue that higher levels of income inequality lead lower income workers to eschew economic-based identities and instead seek out non-economic criteria of social status, leading to greater support for PRRPs. Han (2016), building off an economic theory of social identity provided by Shayo (2009), finds that high levels of economic inequality lead to greater support for PRRPs among the poor, but diminished support among the rich. Engler and Weisstanner (2021), building off a 'status-based theoretical perspective' provided by Gidron and Hall (2017), find that as inequality rises, so too does overall support for PRRPs, with much of the effect coming from a decline in the subjective social status of those with middle incomes.[7]

Following Shayo (2009) and Han (2016), we conceptualize the Western European electoral space as consisting of two main types of identities, those surrounding economic class and nation. While there are many other important types of social identities, including those related to gender, age, and religion, class and nation have been the major social identities that have

---

[7] Unlike Han (2016), Engler and Weistanner (2021) find no evidence that rising income inequality increases the likelihood that the lowest income voters will support the populist radical right. While the authors do not test the claim, they speculate that such voters are more likely to vote for populist radical left-wing parties than PRRPs due to the explicitly redistributive nature of the former's policy platform.

determined people's political behaviour in Western Europe over the last century. Class politics, manifesting itself in fights over the welfare state and income redistribution, has a well-known history in Western Europe. Nationalism and its related authoritarian tendencies[8] have also emerged as a major point of contention in Western Europe in recent decades as a result of increasing immigration, EU expansion, and globalization generally (Kitschelt 1994; Hooghe, Marks, and Wilson 2002).[9] While there have been ideologies and political parties that attempt to foster both class- and nation-based identities, these have primarily been in less developed countries in the Global South (e.g., Peronism in Argentina) (Lipset 1960). Thus, our model assumes that economic class and nation are the two main 'available' identities in Western European politics, with each serving as an approximate substitute for the other.

Although class and nation are the two primary social identities in Western European politics, they differ in terms of their 'permeability' and (perceived) 'status', and thus also their ability to be downgraded and/or diminished. Given that Western Europe is full of strong, well-entrenched states that grant citizenship primarily through descent, we expect blue-collar workers' national identity to be relatively impermeable. By contrast, we expect blue-collar workers' class identity to be comparatively permeable, as there is a much greater likelihood of Western Europeans changing their jobs or experiencing (upward or downward) social mobility than switching their citizenship and/or residence from their place of birth.[10] Since class-based identities are more permeable than nation-based identities, the relative salience of each is primarily determined by individuals' class position. When the working class is in a favourable position relative to other economic classes, their class-based identity strengthens, necessarily weakening the importance of their national identity. By contrast, when the working class is in an unfavourable position relative to other economic classes, their class-based

---

[8] Mudde (2007) suggests that a core goal of nationalism is creating a monocultural state through internal homogenization (i.e., assimilation) and external exclusiveness (i.e., immigration restrictions). Such homogenization and exclusiveness require an authoritarian approach that rejects the idea of equality and liberty, supports compulsory membership, and advocates a stratified ordering among communitarian units.

[9] Survey data confirm that class and nation constitute the major social identities associated with party politics in Western Europe. In 2003, the ISSP asked Western European respondents the most important groups with which they identify. Only four groups were named by more than 10 per cent of respondents: class and occupation (37 per cent), nation and ethnicity (24 per cent), gender (18 per cent), and age (13 per cent). Since not many major political parties have been formed around gender or age-related issues, we submit that class and nation are the two most important social identities that affect individuals' political opinions and behaviours in Western Europe.

[10] The evidence suggests that both inter-generational economic mobility and inter-regional migration have increased in some Western European countries in recent years (e.g., Esping-Andersen and Wagner 2012; Alvarez, Bernard, and Lieske 2021).

identity weakens, necessarily strengthening the importance of their national identity.

As we discussed in Chapter 2, the relative economic and political status of the working class has been on the decline in Western Europe in recent decades due to numerous factors, including deindustrialization, deunionization, welfare state retrenchment, and social democratic party programmatic and organizational reform. Indeed, such a reality has led blue-collar workers to be described by scholars as 'losers of globalization' and a 'stigmatized group' (Spruyt, Keppens, and Van Droogenbroeck 2016; Zagórski, Rama, and Cordero 2021).[11] While a vague perception of 'national decline' has been offered as an explanation for the rise of fascist movements in the first half of the twentieth century and PRRPs in recent decades (Jay et al. 2019), the less permeable nature of nation-based identities compared to class-based identities and the more widespread erosion of working-class power (within countries) compared to Western European state power (across countries),[12] suggest that blue-collar workers are much more likely to downgrade their class identity and elevate their national identity than vice versa.

Given the long history in Western Europe of (organized) working-class resistance (e.g., through economic or general strikes) to employers and government policies perceived as harming workers' interests, it may seem counterintuitive that a decline in blue-collar workers' status leads them to identify less with their economic class. However, the interrelated phenomena of deindustrialization, demographic change, labour union decline, neoliberal policy adoption, and rising economic inequality, have left native blue-collar workers in a particularly precarious position and a state of 'nostalgic depravation' (Gest, Reny, and Mayer 2018). As we discussed above, social identities are formed not only based on a cognitive component (or a recognition of social group membership), but evaluative and emotional components as well. If blue-collar workers no longer take pride in being a member of the 'working class' because of a decline in that group's status (an evaluative component) and have fewer opportunities to participate in labour organizations that allow them to further the interests of their class (an emotional

---

[11] In the context of the United States, Cramer (2016) argues that the diminishing status of rural communities has led to a strengthening rather than a weakening of the rural identity among people in these regions. While this appears contradictory to our claims, we believe it is a product of two unique features of the United States relative to Western European countries: very low levels of interregional mobility (resulting in a highly 'stable' regional identity) and the historical lack of robust, working-class movements (Alvarez, Bernard, and Lieske 2021).

[12] While Western European states remain among the wealthiest, most stable, and militarily strongest in the world, rising levels of economic inequality across nearly all of these states have degraded the relative class position of blue-collar workers to near its lowest level since the mid-to-late twentieth century (OECD 2019).

58   Social Identity and Working Class Support for the Populist Radical Right

component), it becomes much less likely that they will form and embrace a strong 'working-class' identity.[13]

Relatedly, the growing heterogeneity of the workforce and the weakening of organized labour in Western Europe may be diminishing the 'fit' and 'accessibility' of the working-class identity for blue-collar workers. As we have discussed and will examine further in subsequent chapters, in recent decades blue-collar workers have become increasingly diverse in terms of type of employment and skill level, implying a diminished (comparative and normative) 'fit' of the working-class identity for many of these workers. Finally, the declining membership and organizational power of labour unions suggests that economic-based identities are becoming less 'accessible' for blue-collar workers, as fewer interactions among them preclude the development of a class-based identity. In short, major socio-economic and political changes in recent decades have made a working-class identity less 'available' to blue-collar workers, reducing its importance to these individuals and its political relevance more broadly.[14]

Following Gidron and Hall (2017) and Engler and Weisstanner (2021), we argue that economic inequality and other macro-level factors matter for PRRP support through their effect on social identity, as well as on their grievances and discontent. In other words, policy processes, outputs, and outcomes affect PRRP support by leading people to adopt a more class- or nation-based identity *and* by exacerbating or mitigating the (economic, cultural, or political) grievances of people without altering their social identity. For instance, high levels of income inequality may increase support for PRRPs by moving more workers into a nation-based identity and by increasing the grievances of those with an already strong nation-based identity. Thus, we expect part but not all of PRRP support to be explained by shifts in voters' social identities.

While this study builds off Shayo (2009), Han (2016), Gidron and Hall (2017), and Engler and Weisstanner (2021), it also moves beyond them by considering how a broad range of socio-economic, socio-cultural, and political factors affect social identity, not only economic inequality. More specifically, we expect policy processes, outputs, and outcomes that provide

---

[13] Similarly, Western (1997) argues that labour movements persist when they are institutionally insulated from market forces that enhance competition between workers.

[14] Unfavourable political and economic circumstances may further diminish workers' class identity in the context of rapid demographic change brought on by immigration and the increasing complexity of modern (neoliberal) economies. In the case of the former, workers may strengthen identities (e.g., regarding race or religion) based on their status as 'natives' of their country (Winlow, Hall, and Treadwell 2017). In the case of the latter, workers may not be able to easily recognize different economic classes, including those at the top of the economic hierarchy that can serve as a focus for class antagonisms (Gest 2016).

A Social Identity Approach to Blue-Collar Worker Support   **59**

a relative gain (loss) to the working class to result in blue-collar workers having a stronger (weaker) class-based identity and a weaker (stronger) nation-based identity.

Stage 2: Social Identity and Issue Salience

Social identity affects someone's voting behaviour through issue salience, or the degree of importance that voters place on different political issues. As political scientists have long observed, 'individual voters do not perceive, and especially do not have feelings about the entire spectrum of issues. Instead, voters are characterized as being concerned with a narrow subset of issues with the content of the subset varying from voter to voter' (Davis, Hinich, and Ordeshook 1970, 440). Although the determinants of variation in issue salience remains undertheorized (Dennison 2019), numerous studies in social psychology suggest it is substantially shaped by their social identity and the self-interest that arises from it (Boninger, Krosnick, and Brent 1995).

Since people experience the world as a member of a particular social group, they tend to focus on issues perceived to be most relevant to that group and desire policies that they believe will improve the status of the group (Hutchings 2001). For instance, women with a strong gender identity care more about issues relating to women's rights (e.g., abortion) and gender equality than women with a weak gender identity (Duncan and Stewart 2007); parents who have a strong parental identity care more about issues relating to the national debt and sex offenders than parents with a weak parental identity (Klar 2013); people with a strong regional identity care more about issues related to inter-regional inequality than those with a weak regional identity (Huici et al. 1997); and those with a strong national identity care more about nativism (or multiculturalism) than those with a weak national identity (Han 2013a).

Therefore, we expect blue-collar workers with a strong class-based identity to care deeply about economic issues and blue-collar workers with a strong nation-based identity to care deeply about cultural issues (Tavits and Potter 2015). Since employment is the main source of income for the working class, we expect blue-collar workers with a strong class-based identity to place salience on policies related to maintaining a job, finding a (better compensated) job, and/or replacing income from a lost job. Indeed, according to the EES, over a third of blue-collar workers indicated an economic issue such as these as the most important in 2009 and 2014, higher than any other type of issue.

By contrast, blue-collar workers with a strong nation-based identity are expected to focus on cultural issues, namely those relating to nativism and immigration. These issues should be of particular concern to blue-collar workers in contemporary Western Europe due to the restrictions and obligations associated with EU membership and, relatedly, growing immigrant populations and multiculturalism (Hooghe and Marks 2005; O'Rourke and Sinnott 2006; Han 2013b). Indeed, according to the EES, the share of Western Europeans who indicated an immigration issue as the most important nearly doubled (from 5.3 per cent to 9.8 per cent) between 2009 and 2014.[15] While most of the existing literature suggests that the rising salience level of immigration-related issues is driven by substantial demographic and cultural changes (i.e., increasing immigration) (Camus and Lebourg 2017; Tillman 2021), we propose that the shift in people's social identity also explains the emergence of these issues as salient political issues.

Stage 3: Issue Salience and PRRP Support

In a simple unidimensional policy space, voters will generally support a political party (or candidate) that has a position on the one issue under consideration that is closest to their own. However, voters in Western Europe exist in a multidimensional policy space, and therefore must consider multiple issues when determining which political party to support (Adams, Merrill, and Grofman 2005). Given the reality that people have limited time and resources and do not care about all issues equally, vote choice in such a system is substantially based on the correspondence between a voter's position on the issue(s) most salient to them and that of the various political parties. For instance, if a voter thinks that unemployment is the most important issue, they will substantially base their vote choice on the proximity between them and the political parties on how to address unemployment. By contrast, if a voter thinks that immigration is the most important issue, they will instead base their vote choice on the proximity between them and the political parties on how to address immigration.

We expect blue-collar workers who find the economy a more salient issue to oppose PRRPs and blue-collar workers who find immigration a more salient issue to support PRRPs.[16] This is for two reasons. First, blue-collar

---

[15] By contrast, the percentage of blue-collar workers who indicated an economic issue as the most important issue slightly decreased from 37.3 per cent in 2009 to 33.7 per cent in 2014.

[16] Voters, particularly blue-collar workers, in Western Europe may be concerned about the economic impacts of immigration such as labour market competition and fiscal burden. Nonetheless, Rydgren

A Social Identity Approach to Blue-Collar Worker Support   61

workers generally agree less with PRRPs on economic issues than cultural issues (Scheve and Slaughter 2001; Ireland 2004; Lahav 2004; Mayda 2006; O'Rourke and Sinnott 2006; Messina 2007; Hainmueller and Hiscox 2010). Although many PRRPs have shifted their positions on economic issues to the centre in recent years by emphasizing protectionism and welfare policies for native people ('welfare chauvinism') (Rydgren 2013; van der Brug, Fennema, de Lange, and Baller 2013; Harteveld 2016), these parties still take centre-right (or right-wing) positions on many economic issues, such as taxes and the desirability of egalitarianism (Mudde 2007).[17]

Despite having right-leaning views on culture and society, blue-collar workers generally have left-leaning views on the economy. Utilizing data from the Chapel Hill Expert Survey (CHES) (2014) and the EVS (2017), Figure 3.1 compares blue-collar worker support for income redistribution and immigration compared to mainstream left and PRRPs, respectively.[18] While there is no statistically significant difference between the positions of blue-collar workers and mainstream left parties on income redistribution, there is a statistically significant difference between these workers and PRRPs on the issue, with blue-collar workers more supportive of income redistribution than PRRPs.[19] By contrast, blue-collar workers' stance on immigration is located between centre-left and PRRPs, with their position moderately closer to the latter than the former.[20] Thus, when blue-collar workers vote for PRRPs, they do so *despite* the distance between their positions on economic issues. This would suggest that blue-collar workers who support PRRPs generally do not put much salience on such issues (Bornschier and Kriesi 2013).[21]

(2008) finds that it is their concerns about the cultural and social impacts of immigration such as multiculturalism and crime that drive their support for the populist radical right.

[17] According to the Chapel Hill Expert Survey (CHES 2014) data on party positions, PRRPs have moved moderately to the economic centre in recent decades: their average party position score on the economy declined from 7.4 in 1999 to 6.4 in 2014 (the scale ranges from 0 to 10, with lower numbers indicating a more left-leaning position and higher numbers indicating a more right-leaning position).

[18] In the EVS, we label as 'blue-collar workers' those respondents who categorized themselves as 'skilled manual workers', 'semi-skilled manual workers', or 'unskilled manual workers'.

[19] Several criticisms have been made of measuring party positions based on expert surveys, including a lack of clarity regarding what materials are utilized when making these measurements and the (unconscious) bias of the experts completing the surveys (Volkens 2007). Nonetheless, the most available alternative measure based on text analysis (e.g., manifestoes) also has significant weaknesses, such as covering only a limited set of materials, conflating the concept of issue position and issue salience, and diverging criteria among coders (Gemenis and Dinas 2010). Given that different approaches to party position measurement have their own relative strengths and weaknesses, we believe that the CHES data are reasonably reliable and a valid sources of party positions (Hooghe et al. 2010).

[20] While the distance between blue-collar workers and the populist radical right is 2.3, that between blue-collar workers and mainstream left parties is 3.2.

[21] While some mainstream left parties have adopted more restrictive stances on immigration in recent years due to the rise of the populist radical right and the preferences of blue-collar workers (e.g., the Danish Social Democrats) (van Spanje 2010; Han 2015a; Han 2015b; Abou-Chadi 2016), there has

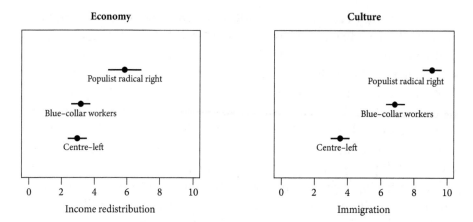

Figure 3.1 Blue-collar worker and party positions on the economy and culture

Note: Circles indicate the average blue-collar worker or party position and lines connote their 95 per cent confidence intervals. Blue-collar workers' positions are measured with their responses to the EVS (2017) question of whether they think 'there should be greater incentives for individual effort' or 'incomes should be made more equal'. Their positions on multiculturalism are measured with their responses to the EVS (2017) question of whether they think 'it is better if immigrants maintain their distinct customs and traditions' or 'it is better if immigrants do not maintain their distinct customs and traditions'. CHES (2014) variables on party position on redistribution of wealth from the rich to the poor and party position on integration of immigrants and asylum seekers are used to indicate party positions. Political parties' and blue-collar workers' positions are re-arranged to the scale of 0 (support for redistribution and more liberal immigration policies) to 10 (opposition to redistribution and support for more restrictive immigration policies).

Source: EVS (2017) and CHES (2014).

Second, PRRPs are generally described as having 'issue ownership' on immigration. Although PRRPs are not 'single-issue parties', opposition to immigration (and, relatedly, opposition to multiculturalism and a tough law and order stance) is the central component of their programme and the primary explanation for recent PRRP success (Mudde 1999; van der Brug, Fennema, and Tillie 2000; Lubbers, Gijsberts, and Scheepers 2002; van der Brug and Fennema 2003; Norris 2005; Rydgren 2008; Ivarsflaten 2008; van der Brug, Fennema, de Lange, and Baller 2013; Werts, Scheepers, and Lubbers 2013; Zhirkov 2014; Han 2020a). There are two main aspects of issue ownership, one dealing with the salience a party places on an issue (the associative aspect of issue ownership) and the other on a party's perceived competence on that issue (issue competence) (Walgrave, Lefevere, and Tresch 2012). As for the former, the CHES (2010) shows that PRRPs put significantly more

---

been little overall change in the immigration-related positions of these parties. According to the CHES data on party positions, the average centre-left party position on immigration policy shifted only by 0.3 points between 1999 and 2014, from 3.9 to 4.2 (as with the economy, the scale for immigration ranges from 0 to 10, with lower numbers indicating a more left-leaning position and higher numbers indicating a more right-leaning position).

salience on immigration-related issues (immigration policy, integration of immigrants and asylum seekers, and ethnic minorities) (8.8 on average in the 0–10 scale) than other parties (5.7 on average). As for the latter, the EES (2009) reveals that 29.4 per cent of those who indicated immigration-related issues as the most important problem in their country pointed to a PRRP as the best party to deal with the issues, compared to 21.2 for mainstream right parties and only 7.6 per cent for mainstream left parties.[22]

Since political party's ownership of an issue brings electoral benefits to the party only when voters consider the issue an important one (Bélanger and Meguid 2008; Walgrave, Lefevere, and Tresch 2012; Klüver and Spoon 2016), we expect blue-collar workers that put salience on cultural issues to be more supportive of PRRPs than blue-collar workers that do not. However, there is less correspondence between the positions of blue-collar workers and PRRPs on economic issues and PRRPs have much less 'ownership' of such issues. In recent years, PRRPs have increasingly emphasized economic issues such as protectionism and/or highlighted economic aspects of immigration such as welfare chauvinism and economic nationalism (van der Waal and de Koster 2018). Nonetheless, economic issues are still typically secondary issues to these parties (Mudde 2007).[23] In addition, when PRRPs discuss economic issues, they often do so vaguely to divert voters' attention to other issues that will be more electorally beneficial to them (Rovny 2013; Han 2020b). Therefore, blue-collar workers that care most about economic issues are less likely to be drawn to PRRPs than most other party families.

Preliminary Tests of the Social Identity Theory

In this section, we conduct preliminary tests of each stage in our theoretical argument. First, we test whether policy processes, outcomes, and outputs relatively favourable to blue-collar workers lead to a stronger class-based identity, while those that are relatively unfavourable to blue-collar workers lead to a stronger nation-based identity. Second, we test whether a more class-based identity leads to a greater concern about economic issues and a more nation-based identity leads to a greater concern about cultural issues. Third,

---

[22] Down and Han (2020) argue that mainstream parties inadvertently increase support for the populist radical right when they adopt more restrictive immigration positions, as it legitimizes positions long espoused by PRRPs and it is these parties that are perceived as most 'competent' on the issue of immigration.

[23] For example, the CHES (2010) shows that PRRPs put statistically significantly less salience on economic issues (deregulation, tax and government spending, and income redistribution) (4.7 on average in the 0–10 scale) than other parties (6.2 on average).

64 Social Identity and Working Class Support for the Populist Radical Right

we test whether blue-collar workers that care more about economic issues are less likely to support PRRPs, while blue-collar workers that care more about cultural issues are more likely to support PRRPs.

Unfortunately, to the best of our knowledge, there is not a single cross-country survey of Western Europeans that includes questions about both social identity and issue salience. Thus, we employ two surveys to test whether policy processes, outcomes, and outputs effect blue-collar worker support for PRRPs via a change in social identity and therefore what issues these workers find most salient. First, we use the ISSP (2003) because it has questions on social identity and national pride.[24] Second, we employ the EES (2009, 2014) to utilize its questions on national pride, issue salience, and party support.[25]

Stage 1: The Macro Context and Social Identity

To test whether policy processes, outputs, and outcomes matter for the class- and nation-based identities of blue-collar workers, we utilize the ISSP (2003) survey data.[26] We construct the social identity variable based on answers to the question, 'We are all part of different groups. Some are more important to us than others when we think of ourselves. In general, which in the following list is most important to you in describing who you are? and the second most important? and the third most important?' Using answers to this question, we make an ordered categorical variable of national identity that indicates the relative strength of blue-collar workers' national identity over class identity. In the ISSP dataset, there are two types of social groups that represent a national identity (ethnic background and nationality) and two types of social groups that signify a class identity (social class and occupation). A blue-collar worker's identity is coded as 5 when they name both ethnic background and nationality as the most important, second most important, or third most important social group, and do not name a social class or occupation among their choices. The variable is coded as 4 either when a blue-collar worker indicates one of the two nation-based

---

[24] While the ISSP has three waves of surveys (1995, 2003, and 2013) that cover issues related to national identity, only the 2003 wave has a question that straightforwardly asks respondents to choose a social group that they identify with.

[25] While the EES has conducted eight waves of surveys between 1979 and 2019, only those surveys conducted in 2009 and 2014 use the same list of potential responses to the issue salience question for all countries.

[26] The following countries are included in the analyses in Tables 3.1 and 3.2: Austria, Denmark, Finland, France, Germany, Ireland, the Netherlands, Norway, Portugal, Spain, Sweden, Switzerland, and the UK.

social groups and none of the class-based social groups or when they choose both the nation-based social groups and one of the class-based social groups among their three most important social groups. The variable is coded as 3 when a blue-collar worker indicates neither nation- nor class-based social groups among their responses or one nation- and one class-based social group. The variable is coded as 2 either when a blue-collar worker chooses one of the two class-based social groups and none of the nation-based social groups or when they choose both the class-based social groups and one of the nation-based social groups among their three most important social groups. Finally, a blue-collar worker's identity is coded as 1 one when they name both social class and occupation as the most important, second most important, or third most important social group, and do not name an ethnic background or nationality among their choices. Therefore, this variable indicates the strength of a person's nation-based identity relative to her class-based identity: higher values of the social identity variable indicate a more nation-based identity, while lower values indicate a more class-based identity.

We examine the following political and economic contexts that are expected to significantly affect blue-collar workers' status: the process of economic reforms (the policymaking process), labour policies (policy outputs), and economic inequality (a policy outcome). First, for policy processes, we focus on whether governments proposed or completed social pacts in the process of enacting welfare state and/or labour market reforms. There are three potential outcomes if such reforms are pursued. First, and most obviously, the government can enact the economic reforms unilaterally, or without the active participation of labour unions. Second, the government can propose and complete a social pact with labour unions that would obligate the former to follow a certain course of legislative action on the economic reforms. Third, the government can propose a social pact, but fail to convert that proposal into an actual social pact agreement (Castater and Han 2016). Previous research has found that unilaterally enacted reform legislation and failed social pact proposals depress the vote of governing parties, while social pact agreements provide an electoral boost instead (Hamann et al. 2015; Han and Castater 2023). Since labour unions have historically been dominated by blue-collar workers (Hyman 2001), blue-collar unions typically lead social pact negotiations on behalf of organized labour (Hassel 2009), and unions often market themselves as advocating for 'working people' during the social pact formation process, we argue that successful completion of a social pact strengthens the class identity of blue-collar workers and thus indirectly reduces their propensity to support PRRPs. By contrast, an economic reform process that excludes labour unions or fails to successfully convert a social pact proposal into a social pact agreement strengthens the national identity of blue-collar workers and thus indirectly increases their propensity to support PRRPs. We utilize data on social pact agreements and failed social pact proposals from the Database on Institutional Characteristics of Trade Unions, Wage Setting, State Intervention, and Social Pacts (ICTWSS). The data on unilaterally enacted reform legislation is from Hamann, Johnston, and Kelly (2013). The social pact agreements, failed social pact proposals, and unilaterally enacted reform legislation variables are all measured as the number of times each occurred in a country in the five years leading up to a particular survey wave.

Second, for policy outputs, we examine those policies that previous scholarship has found to be of most importance for PRRP support, the degree of EPL and spending on labour market policies (LMPs) (Western 1997; Rueda and Pontusson 2000; Anderson and Pontusson 2007; Rueda 2007; Nelson 2009; Avdagic 2013). Since stronger EPL and more generous spending on LMPs improve the relative economic standing of blue-collar workers, we expect higher values of these measures to increase the class-based identity of blue-collar workers and thus reduce their support for PRRPs. To measure the stringency of EPL and the generosity of LMPs, we utilize data from the OECD Indicators of Employment Protection Legislation and the OECD Social Expenditure Database, respectively. EPL is measured with an index that hypothetically ranges from zero to six, with higher values indicating greater protection for workers on temporary or fixed-term contracts from (individual or collective) dismissals. The generosity of spending on LMPs is measured by government spending on active and passive LMPs as a percentage of gross domestic product (GDP).[27]

Finally, for policy outcomes, we focus on macro-economic conditions most obviously relevant to our social identity theory of PRRP support: the relative economic standing of blue-collar workers in terms of wages and unemployment. The relative wages of blue-collar workers is measured with a 'wage inequality' variable constructed by the authors from data provided by the Eurostat Structure of Earnings Survey. It is calculated by dividing the average wages of white-collar workers by the average wages of blue-collar workers

---

[27] ALMPs refer to government expenditures meant to improve the ability of someone to find employment. By contrast, PLMPs refer to government expenditures meant to help someone stay financially solvent while unemployed (Pignatti and Van Belle 2018). ALMPs include government spending on the administration of labour market programs, job training, employment incentives, and subsidized work or rehabilitation. PLMPs include government spending on unemployment benefits and early retirement.

(thus, higher values indicate weaker relative wages for blue-collar workers).[28] The relative level of unemployment for blue-collar workers is measured with an 'unemployment inequality' variable constructed by the authors from data provided by the OECD, Education at a Glance: Educational Attainment and Labour-Force Status. Since blue-collar workers generally have a lower level of formal education than other workers, the unemployment inequality variable is calculated by dividing the unemployment rate for people without a tertiary education by the unemployment rate for people with a tertiary education (thus, higher values again indicate a weaker relative employment position for blue-collar workers).[29] Given these measures' implications for the relative standing of the working class, we expect blue-collar workers' nation-based identity and thus their support for PRRPs to be strengthened when wage inequality and unemployment inequality are high.

In addition to the variables associated with policy processes, outputs, and outcomes, we include numerous control variables in our analysis. As a macro level control, we include the share of a country's population that is immigrant, as a large foreign-born population may strengthen the nation-based identity of (native) blue-collar workers by endangering their perceived status of their nation state (Joppke 1998). As micro level controls, we include sex, age, and education. Men are more likely than women to exhibit a strong national identity due to the former's historically dominant role in politics and the military and the tendency of 'patriotism' to be equated with sacrifices more commonly associated with men, such as those relating to fighting and dying during wartime (Nagel 1998). Older people are more likely to have a strong nation-based identity than younger people, as the latter have been socialized at a time of substantial European integration and institutional efforts to foster a 'European identity' (Lauterbach and De Vries 2020). Those with a high level of formal education are less likely than those with a low level of formal education to have a strong nation-based identity, as the educational systems in Western European countries promote democratic and cosmopolitan values that reduce the appeal of exclusionary nation-based identities (Coenders and Scheepers 2003).[30]

---

[28] While there are many higher earning blue-collar workers (e.g., plumbers and electricians), the top of the income distribution is dominated by employers of large businesses and salaried white-collar professionals (Goedemé et al. 2021).

[29] We utilize the unemployment rate for those with and without a college degree for two interrelated reasons. First, the vast majority of blue-collar workers do not have a college degree. Second, deindustrialization across the wealthy democracies in recent decades has meant that blue-collar workers need to increasingly compete for jobs with non-college educated workers in the low-paid service sector (Strangleman, Rhodes, and Linkon 2013).

[30] The ISSP (2003) has the most ideal questions on social identity for our purposes, but is somewhat dated. Thus, we conduct robustness checks with the ISSP (2013), which has less appropriate questions on

68 Social Identity and Working Class Support for the Populist Radical Right

Since our analysis includes both individual- and country-level variables, we utilize an ordered logistic model with clustered standard errors to test our theoretical claims. The results are reported in Table 3.1.[31] With the exception of social pact agreements (which have no statistically significant effect on social identity in Model 1), all of the macro-level variables are found to affect social identity in the way anticipated by our theory. Failed social pact proposals and unilaterally enacted economic reform legislation ('policy processes'); weaker EPL and less generous spending on LMPs ('policy outputs'); and higher levels of wage inequality and unemployment inequality ('policy outcomes') all result in a stronger nation-based identity and a weaker class-based identity among blue-collar workers. Among the control variables, the only variable to consistently affect social identity across all our models is age, with older blue-collar workers generally having a stronger national identity than younger blue-collar workers. The education variable is also found to be significantly related to social identity in three of the six models, with less educated blue-collar workers found to have a stronger national identity than more highly educated blue-collar workers.

Results are consistent with our expectations. While variables of political and economic circumstances unfavourable for blue-collar workers (i.e., failed social pact proposals, unilaterally enacted legislation, wage inequality, and unemployment inequality) have a statistically significant positive coefficient, those of conditions favourable for the working class (i.e., strong employment protection and large spending on LMPs) have a statistically significant negative coefficient. In other words, while the former conditions strengthen blue-collar workers' nation-based identity, the latter circumstances weaken it.

Figure 3.2 utilizes the findings in Table 3.1 to graphically depict the probability that blue-collar workers will hold a strong national identity (dependent variable = 4 or 5) or strong class identity (dependent variable = 1 or 2) given changes in the measures of policy processes, outputs, and outcomes.

---

social identity, but covers a more recent period. The ISSP (2013) asks respondents whether they feel very close (4), close (3), not very close (2), or not close at all (1) to their town/city, county, country, and continent (e.g., Europe). We measure the strength of Western European blue-collar workers' national identity relative to their European identity by subtracting their response to Europe from their response to their country. We believe this is a gauge because nationalistic sentiments in Europe have largely been developed in the context of European integration and the advance of European identity (Fligstein, Polyakova, and Sandholtz 2012). While the results of these models are less strong than those reported in Table 3.1, four of the six coefficients of the policy variables are statistically significant in the expected direction. The full results for this robustness check are reported in the appendix (Table B.1).

[31] The ISSP follows the International Standard Classification of Occupations 1988 (ISCO-88) when categorizing respondents based on occupation. We label as 'blue-collar workers' those respondents who categorized themselves as 'craft and related trades workers' or 'plant and machine operators and assemblers'.

A Social Identity Approach to Blue-Collar Worker Support 69

Table 3.1 The macro context and social identity

	(1)	(2)	(3)	(4)	(5)	(6)
Policymaking process						
Social pact agreement	0.01					
	(0.02)					
Social pact failure	0.20*					
	(0.12)					
Unilateral legislation		0.20**				
		(0.10)				
Policy output						
EPL			−0.17**			
			(0.07)			
LMP				−0.35*		
				(0.19)		
Policy outcome						
Wage inequality					1.32***	
					(0.42)	
Unemployment inequality						0.28*
						(0.15)
Control variables						
Female	−0.11	−0.12	−0.12	−0.12	−0.12	−0.10
	(0.09)	(0.08)	(0.08)	(0.08)	(0.09)	(0.09)
Age	0.02***	0.02***	0.02***	0.02***	0.02***	0.02***
	(0.00)	(0.00)	(0.00)	(0.00)	(0.00)	(0.00)
Education	−0.13	−0.12	−0.15*	−0.13	−0.17**	−0.13
	(0.11)	(0.09)	(0.08)	(0.07)	(0.08)	(0.10)
Immigration	0.01	−0.01	0.04**	0.03	0.02	0.03**
	(0.02)	(0.02)	(0.02)	(0.02)	(0.02)	(0.01)
Cut point1	−1.75**	−1.49**	−1.19**	−1.30***	−0.37	−0.41
	(0.59)	(0.63)	(0.52)	(0.36)	(0.84)	(0.67)
Cut point2	−0.03	0.18	0.52	0.40	1.31	1.29*
	(0.57)	(0.61)	(0.57)	(0.41)	(0.83)	(0.68)
Cut point3	1.04***	1.23**	1.57***	1.45***	2.36***	2.34***
	(0.52)	(0.57)	(0.53)	(0.38)	(0.78)	(0.64)
Cut point4	2.23***	2.39***	2.74***	2.63***	3.52***	3.50***
	(0.53)	(0.58)	(0.57)	(0.44)	(0.77)	(0.63)
−2 x Log likelihood	6,647.8	7,216.1	7,470.8	7,463.5	7,203.8	7,479.1
Number of observations	2,172	2,348	2,443	2,443	2,348	2,443

Data: ISSP (2003)
Note: Ordered logistic regression with clustered standard errors (by country) is used. Clustered standard errors are in parentheses. ***$p < 0.01$, **$p < 0.05$, *$p < 0.1$.

Regarding policy processes, as a country's number of failed social pact proposals increases from 0 to 2 in the previous five years, the probability that a blue-collar worker has a strong national identity increases from 0.30 to 0.39 (a rise of ~30 per cent), while the probability that a blue-collar worker has a strong class identity decreases from 0.44 to 0.35 (a decline of ~20 per cent). As the number of unilateral reform efforts increases from 0 to 2 in the previous five years, the probability that a blue-collar worker has a strong national identity increases from 0.29 to 0.35 (a rise of ~20 per cent), while the probability that a blue-collar worker has a strong class identity decreases from 0.45 to 0.35 (a decline of ~22 per cent).

Regarding policy outputs, as the EPL variable increases from its 10th percentile value to its 90th percentile value, the probability of a blue-collar worker having a strong national identity decreases from 0.37 to 0.29 (a decline of ~22 per cent), while the probability of a blue-collar worker having a strong class identity increases from 0.38 to 0.46 (a rise of ~17 per cent). As the LMP spending variable increases from its 10th percentile value to its 90th percentile value, the probability of a blue-collar worker having a strong national identity decreases from 0.40 to 0.27 (a decline of ~33 per cent), while the probability of a blue-collar worker having a strong class identity increases from 0.35 to 0.48 (a rise of ~37 per cent).

Finally, regarding policy outcomes, as the wage inequality variable increases from its 10th percentile value to its 90th percentile value (indicating an increasingly large difference between the wages of white-collar and blue-collar workers), the probability that a blue-collar worker will have a strong national identity increases from 0.26 to 0.37 (a rise of ~42 per cent), while the probability of a blue-collar worker having a strong class identity decreases from 0.50 to 0.37 (a decline of ~26 per cent). As the unemployment inequality variable increases from its 10th percentile value to its 90th percentile value (indicating an increasingly large difference between the unemployment rate of those with and without a college degree), the probability that a blue-collar worker will have a strong national identity increases from 0.29 to 0.34 (a rise of ~17 per cent), while the probability that a blue-collar worker will have a strong class identity decreases from 0.46 to 0.41 (a decline of ~11 per cent).

In summary, the findings in this sub-section provide tentative support for our social identity theory. First, economic and/or political conditions unfavourable to the working class increase these workers' nation-based identity. Second, economic and/or political conditions favourable to the working class increase these workers' class-based identity. The most substantive results are for failed social pact proposals, labour market spending, and wage

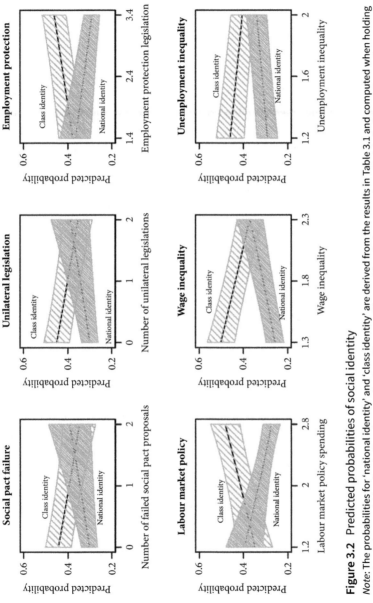

Figure 3.2 Predicted probabilities of social identity

Note: The probabilities for 'national identity' and 'class identity' are derived from the results in Table 3.1 and computed when holding all independent variables (excluding the one displayed in a specific graph) at their mean values. We label a blue-collar worker as having a 'national identity' when his/her social identity score is either 4 or 5 and a blue-collar worker as having a 'class identity' when his/her social identity score is either 1 or 2.

72   Social Identity and Working Class Support for the Populist Radical Right

inequality, suggesting that policymaking processes, policy outputs, and policy outcomes all play major roles in shaping the social identity of blue-collar workers.[32]

Stage 2: Social Identity and Issue Salience

Since the ISSP (2003) data does not include a question on issue salience, we are unable to utilize it directly to test whether social identity affects issue salience in the way anticipated by our theory. Indeed, to the best of these authors' knowledge, there is not a single cross-country survey of Western Europeans that includes questions about both social identity and issue salience. Fortunately, however, the ISSP (2003) has questions about social identity and national pride, while the EES (1994) has questions about national pride and issue salience. Thus, if the ISSP (2003) data informs us that national pride is an approximate substitute for a nation-based identity, we can test the second stage of our theory with the EES (1994) data.[33] While national pride and a nation-based identity are distinct conceptually, the former tends to arise from and reinforce the latter (Smith 1991; Han 2013a).[34] In an effort to confirm this association empirically, we utilize an ordered logistic regression model to test whether a nation-based identity can predict national pride

---

[32] We also utilize a multinomial logistic regression model to examine how the macro context affects blue-collar workers' social identity among all the identities presented in the ISSP (2003) (gender, age, political party, family, religion, and region). The findings indicate that relatively poor political and economic circumstances for the working class (i.e., failed social pact proposals, unilaterally enacted legislation, wage inequality, and unemployment inequality) weaken the class identity and strengthen the non-class-based identities (including the national identity) of blue-collar workers. By contrast, relatively favourable conditions (i.e., strong employment protection and large spending on LMPs) for the working class strengthen the class identity and weaken the non-class-based identities of blue-collar workers. The full results are reported in the appendix.

[33] We use the EES (1994) because it is the only cross-country survey that has both a question on national pride and issue salience. The wording of the EES (1994) question on national pride is nearly identical with that of the ISSP: 'Would you say that you are very proud, fairly proud, not very proud or not at all proud to be [nationality]?'. Nonetheless, we acknowledge two limitations of this analysis. First, both the ISSP (2003) and EES (1994) are relatively dated. Second, there is a nine-year gap between the survey data used to examine the link between social identity and national pride (ISSP 2003) and the relationship between national pride and issue salience (EES 1994), respectively. The following 11 countries are included in these models: Belgium, Denmark, France, Germany, Greece, Ireland, Italy, the Netherlands, Portugal, Spain, and the UK.

[34] There are numerous terms related to nationalistic sentiments, such as national identity, national pride, and nationalism. Someone with a national identity considers themselves a member of a 'nation' with a particular territory and certain collective historical memories (Smith 1991). Someone with national pride feels positively about their country (Smith and Kim 2006). And someone with nationalistic sentiments perceives their own country or nation to be (inherently) superior to other countries or nations (Kosterman and Feshbach 1989). Thus, national identity can be described as a prerequisite for national pride and nationalism, as one cannot feel positively about their country or believe their country is superior to other countries if they do not identify as a member of a country (Han 2013a).

among blue-collar workers in the ISSP (2003).[35] The results are reported in Table 3.2.[36] As anticipated, in both of the models (the first including only our main variables of interest and the second including a set of micro-level controls), a nation-based identity is a strong predictor of national pride, with the former found to be statistically significant at the 99 per cent confidence level. As a blue-collar worker moves from a strong class identity (the social identity variable = 1) to a strong national identity (the social identity variable = 5), the predicted probability of being 'very proud' of their nation (the national pride variable = 4) increases from 0.38 to 0.54 (a rise of ~30 per cent), while the predicted probability of them being 'somewhat proud', 'not very proud', or 'not proud at all' of their nation (the national pride variable = 3, 2, or 1) decreases from 0.62 to 0.46 (a decline of ~26 per cent).

Table 3.2 National identity and national pride

	(1)	(2)
Social identity (National identity)	0.16*** (0.05)	0.12** (0.05)
Female		0.05 (0.10)
Age		0.02*** (0.00)
Education		−0.11 (0.09)
Cut point 1	−3.68*** (0.36)	−3.18*** (0.57)
Cut point 2	−1.39*** (0.44)	−0.89 (0.65)
Cut point 3	0.64 (0.35)	1.18 (0.50)
−2 x Log likelihood	4,837.7	4,726.2
Number of observations	2,328	2,302

Data: ISSP (2003).
Note: Ordered logistic regression is used. Standard errors are in parentheses. ***$p < 0.01$, **$p < 0.05$, *$p < 0.1$.

[35] The same variable of the relative strength of national identity over class identity utilized in Table 3.1 is used here. Blue-collar workers' responses to the question of 'How proud are you of being [country nationality]?' are used to indicate their national pride.

[36] As with the models in Table 3.1, we ran robustness checks for the models in Table 3.2 with the ISSP (2013). The main findings were confirmed. The full results of these models are reported in the appendix (Table B.2).

74 Social Identity and Working Class Support for the Populist Radical Right

Given the findings in Table 3.2, we examine the relationship between blue-collar workers' national pride and issue salience in Table 3.3 using the EES (1994). The cultural issue salience variable is coded as one when a blue-collar worker indicates immigration as the most important issue and the economic issue salience variable is coded as one when a blue-collar worker indicates unemployment as the most important issue.[37] In addition to blue-collar workers' demographic characteristics (their gender, age, and education level), we also add two macro-level controls to our models that have been found to be relevant for the salience of economic and cultural issues, the unemployment rate and immigration level (Wlezien 2005). The results are reported in Table 3.3.[38]

Table 3.3 National pride and issue salience

Most important problem	(1)	(2)	(3)	(4)	(5)	(6)
	Culture (Immigration)			Economy (Unemployment)		
National pride	0.39**	0.42***	0.36**	−0.13*	−0.13**	−0.17***
	(0.16)	(0.16)	(0.15)	(0.07)	(0.07)	(0.06)
Female		0.50***	0.53***		−0.14	−0.12
		(0.19)	(0.18)		(0.20)	(0.19)
Age		0.01	0.01		0.00	0.00
		(0.02)	(0.02)		(0.01)	(0.01)
Education		0.11***	0.10***		−0.00	−0.00
		(0.03)	(0.03)		(0.03)	(0.03)
Unemployment rate			−0.03			−0.02
			(0.07)			(0.02)
Migration			0.07			0.03
			(0.07)			(0.02)
Constant	−3.92***	−6.24***	−6.35***	−0.12	−0.15	−0.09
	(0.54)	(1.46)	(1.64)	(0.15)	(0.52)	(0.43)
−2 x Log likelihood	286.6	280.3	279.1	1,125.1	1,124.1	1,121.8
Number of observations	833	833	833	833	833	833

Data: EES (1994).
Note: Logistic regression is used in Models 1, 2, 4, and 5. Logistic regression with clustered standard errors (by country) is used in Models 3 and 6. Standard errors are in parentheses in Models 1, 2, 4, and 5 and clustered standard errors are in parentheses in Models 3 and 6. ***p < 0.01, **p < 0.05, *p < 0.1.

---

[37] 42.1 per cent of blue-collar workers indicated unemployment as the most important problem, while 3.3 per cent of blue-collar workers indicated immigration as the most important problem. Other issues in the most important issue question include crime, European integration, stable prices, and agricultural surpluses.
[38] As with the EVS, we label 'blue-collar workers' in the EES as those respondents who categorized themselves as 'skilled manual workers', 'semi-skilled manual workers', or 'unskilled manual workers'.

As anticipated by our theory, national pride is found to increase the salience of immigration-related issues (Models 1, 2, and 3) and decrease the salience of economic issues (Models 4, 5, and 6) among blue-collar workers. As a blue-collar worker's national pride is strengthened from being 'not at all proud' of their nation (the national pride variable = 1) to being 'very proud' of their nation (the national pride variable = 4), their predicted probability of indicating immigration as the most important issue increases from 0.03 to 0.07 (a rise of ~133 per cent), while their predicted probability of indicating unemployment as the most important issue decreases from 0.45 to 0.33 (a decline of ~27 per cent).

Stage 3: Issue Salience and PRRP Support

To test whether issue salience affects blue-collar worker support for PRRPs as outlined in our theory, we utilize the EES (2009, 2014) survey data.[39] We construct our main independent variables based on answers to the question, 'What do you think is the first most important issue or problem facing our country at the moment?' The economic issue salience variable is coded as one when a blue-collar worker indicated economic conditions, creating jobs, unemployment, national employment policies, or wages and earnings as the most important issue or problem facing their country. The culture issue salience variable is coded as one when a blue-collar worker indicated immigration, labour migration, multiculturalism, national immigration policy, or ethnic minorities as the most important issue or problem facing their country.

We construct an ordered categorical variable of PRRP support as the dependent variable. The variable is based on a respondent's answer to the question, 'How probable is it that you will ever vote for (the PRRP in your country)? Please specify your views on a scale where 0 means "not at all probable" and 10 means "very probable". Thus, higher scores of the ordered categorical variable indicate a greater probability of supporting a PRRP in an upcoming election.

The choice of control variables follows the previous literature on the determinants of PRRP support. Basic demographic characteristics of individual respondents are included in the models: gender, age, education level, and left/right political ideology (Lubbers, Gijsberts, and Scheepers 2002). We also include macro-level factors in our models, including the effective number of political parties, the unemployment rate, and the levels of immigration and

---

[39] The following countries are included: Austria, Belgium, Denmark, Finland, France, Germany, Greece, Ireland, Italy, the Netherlands, Portugal, Spain, Sweden, and the UK.

government social spending. The level of immigration is included because the economic and cultural grievance theories claim that higher levels of immigration lead to greater support for PRRPs. The unemployment rate is included because the economic grievance theory claims that higher levels of unemployment lead to greater support for PRRPs. Electoral disproportionality is included because electoral systems with lower (higher) thresholds to attain office facilitate (inhibit) the electoral success of minor parties, which PRRPs have historically been. Finally, we include government spending on social policies, although we have no clear expectation for this measure. On the one hand, generous welfare state policies may reduce blue-collar workers' economic grievances and thus also their support for PRRPs (Swank and Betz 2003). On the other hand, welfare state generosity may enhance the ability of PRRPs to exploit working-class (economic, cultural, and political) grievances by focusing on the supposed abuse by immigrants and ethnic minorities of their country's generous welfare system (i.e., through their promotion of 'welfare chauvinism') (Kitschelt 1995). In addition, the moral economy literature suggests that people's attitudes towards welfare derive not only from their self-interest but also from their ethical principles, social norms, and moral values (Hootegem, Abts, and Meuleman 2024). In particular, people's perception on the deservingness of welfare recipients matters in their political behaviour such as party support (Attewell 2021) as well as their preferences on income redistribution (Petersen et al. 2011). Blue-collar workers are inclined not to endorse the deservingness of welfare recipients when their income level is considered.[40] This may be because of their low education level that is associated with the perception of deservingness (Attewell 2022). Then, generous welfare spending will enhance blue-collar workers' PRRP support by reinforcing their perception of the 'undeservingness' of migrants' welfare receipt and making PRRPs' welfare chauvinism rhetoric more attractive. The results are reported in Table 3.4.

As anticipated by our theory, we find that when blue-collar workers care more about immigration-related issues, they become more likely to support PRRPs, but when they care more about economic issues, they become less likely to support PRRPs. When a respondent indicated that an immigration-related issue was the biggest issue or problem facing their

---

[40] We made a deservingness score using the same survey data (ESS 2016), survey questions, and a method (principal component analysis) that Attewell (2021, 2022) used. When we regress the score on a binary variable of blue-collar workers with controlling for income level, the coefficient of the blue-collar worker variable is statistically significant at the 0.05 level with a negative coefficient.

Table 3.4 Issue salience and support for PRRPs

	(1)
Issue salience (culture)	0.82***
	(0.22)
Issue salience (economy)	−0.26**
	(0.13)
Female	−0.31**
	(0.12)
Age	−0.02***
	(0.01)
Education	−0.37***
	(0.11)
Political ideology (right)	0.27***
	(0.04)
Effective number of political parties	0.01
	(0.07)
Unemployment rate	−0.25***
	(0.09)
Immigration	−0.06
	(0.05)
Social spending	0.07***
	(0.03)
−2 x Log likelihood	5,504.1
Number of observations	1,722

Data: EES (2009, 2014).
Note: Ordered logistic regression with clustered standard errors (by country/years) is used. Clustered standard errors are in parentheses. Results on the cut points are not reported.
***p < 0.01, **p < 0.05, *p < 0.1.

country, the probability that they provided a score of zero for a PRRP (indicating that it was 'not at all probable' that they would vote for them in a future election) decreased from 0.57 to 0.37 (a decline of ~35 per cent), while the probability that they provided a score of 10 (indicating that it was 'very probable' that they would vote for a PRRP in a future election) increased from 0.05 to 0.10 (a rise of 100 per cent). However, when a respondent indicated that an economic issue was the biggest issue or problem facing their country, the probability that they provided a score of zero for PRRPs increased from 0.53 to 0.59 (a rise of ~11 per cent), while the probability that they provided a score of 10 decreased from 0.06 to 0.04 (a decline of 33 per cent).

78   Social Identity and Working Class Support for the Populist Radical Right

After accounting for the salience of economic and cultural issues among blue-collar workers, numerous micro- and macro-level control variables are found to have a significant effect on working-class support for PRRPs. Regarding the micro-level variables, men, younger people, those with a low level of formal education, and people with a right-wing political ideology are more likely to support PRRPs than women, older people, people with a high level of formal education, and those with a left-wing ideology. These results are largely consistent with previous research on PRRP support. Men are more likely than women to support PRRPs due to the former's lower levels of altruism (translating into less care for immigrants) and greater risk of job loss due to imports and immigrant labour, as well as the more traditionally 'masculine' approach to politics promoted by PRRPs (Ralph-Morrow 2022). Younger people are more likely to support PRRPs due to their lack of attachment to long-established mainstream political parties and their greater attraction to the 'anti-establishment' disposition of PRRPs (Miller-Idriss 2018). More formally educated people are consistently found to be less likely to vote for PRRPs than less educated people because higher levels of formal education weaken authoritarian attitudes and strengthen multicultural and cosmopolitan dispositions (Hainmueller and Hiscox 2010).

Regarding macro-level control variables, only the unemployment rate and social spending are found to have statistically significant coefficients in the model: higher unemployment decreases working-class support for PRRPs, while greater social spending increases working class support for PRRPs. While these findings appear to contradict our claim that blue-collar workers are more likely to support PRRPs when they are in a relatively poor economic and/or political position, the nature of the unemployment and social spending variables used in Table 3.4 suggest that is not necessarily the case. First, the unemployment rate measure captures aggregate unemployment, not unemployment inequality between blue-collar and white-collar workers, as the variable that we construct and employ in Chapter 6 attempts to do. Some previous studies have similarly found that higher aggregate unemployment depresses support for PRRPs, with scholars typically claiming it is the result of mainstream parties having greater 'ownership' of economic issues than traditionally smaller party families (Coenders and Scheepers 1998; Knigge 1998; Arzheimer and Carter 2006).

Second, the social spending measure captures a broad range of spending programmes that are not directly relevant for the status of blue-collar workers, including old-age pension, childcare, and aid to single-parent households. A substantial welfare state may strengthen the position of PRRPs because these parties can claim that generous benefits for the (deserving) native population are being threatened by aid to (non-deserving) immigrants (Veugelers and Magnan 2005). By contrast, we focus exclusively on labour market spending in our analysis in Chapter 5, which we argue provides a substantial relative benefit to the working class.[41]

Conclusion and Discussion

In this chapter, we outlined our social identity approach to working class support for PRRPs and provided preliminary tests of our theoretical claims. We argued that policymaking processes, policy outputs, and policy outcomes affect working class support for PRRPs through a three-stage process. In the first stage, those policymaking processes, policy outputs, and policy outcomes relatively favourable to blue-collar workers' lead them to have a stronger class-based identity, while those relatively unfavourable lead them to have a stronger nation-based identity. In the second stage, blue-collar workers with a stronger class-based identity have a greater concern for economic issues, while those with a stronger nation-based identity have a greater concern for cultural issues. In the third stage, blue-collar workers that care more about economic issues are much more likely to oppose PRRPs, while blue-collar workers that care more about cultural issues are much more likely to support PRRPs.

Our empirical analysis provided preliminary tests of each of these three stages utilizing logistic regression, multiple surveys, and macro-level data. Consistent with our expectations, we found that failed social pact proposals, unilaterally enacted welfare state reform legislation, weak or non-existent EPL, meager spending on LMPs, wage inequality between blue-collar and white-collar workers, and unemployment inequality between the more and less educated increase the nation-based identity of blue-collar workers; that blue-collar workers with a stronger nation-based identity find cultural issues more salient; and that blue-collar workers that find cultural issues more salient are much more likely to support PRRPs.

In the following three chapters, we examine in more depth how certain policymaking processes, policy outputs, and policy outcomes affect blue-collar workers' social identity and issue salience and thus also their support

---

[41] Empirically, the correlation between spending on LMPs and spending on overall social spending is positive, but somewhat weak, ranging from 0.196 (ISSP) to 0.293 (EES) in the surveys used here.

for PRRPs: In Chapter 4, we consider the economic reform process (social pact proposals, social pact agreements, and unilaterally enacted legislation); in Chapter 5, we consider EPL, active LMPs, and passive LMPs; and in Chapter 6, we consider wage inequality between blue-collar and white-collar workers and differences in unemployment between the more and less educated.

4
The Policymaking Process

Economic Reforms and Support for the Populist
Radical Right

Over the next three chapters, we examine the effects that policymaking processes, policy outputs, and policy outcomes have on blue-collar support for the populist radical right. In this chapter, we focus on policymaking processes, or the procedures by which national governments produce public policy. More specifically, we consider whether governments adopt wage and welfare state reforms unilaterally or in consultation with labour unions through the social pact formation process.

Our central claim is that if governing parties successfully engage with organized labour when formulating and implementing (controversial) wage and welfare state policies, it signals to blue-collar workers that they are in a relatively strong political position and that economic improvements are forthcoming. By contrast, if governing parties enact such economic reforms unilaterally or are unable to convert a social pact proposal into a completed social pact agreement, it signals to blue-collar workers that they are in a relatively weak political position and that economic conditions are unlikely to improve (and may even worsen) in the near- to medium-term. Thus, we expect successfully completed social pact agreements to strengthen the class identity of blue-collar workers and the salience of economic issues among the working class, leading these workers to be less supportive of the populist radical right. However, if the government enacts economic reforms without the input and support of organized labour (reflected in unilaterally enacted reform legislation or a failed social pact proposal), we expect it to strengthen the national identity of blue-collar workers and the salience of cultural issues among the working class, leading these workers to be more supportive of the populist radical right.

This chapter is divided into four sections. In the first section, we provide a broad overview of the literature on policymaking processes and political efficacy, examine the main policymaking processes utilized by governments in Western Europe when they attempt to enact (neoliberal) economic reforms,

Social Identity and Working Class Support for the Populist Radical Right. Eric G. Castater and Kyung Joon Han,
Oxford University Press. © Eric G. Castater and Kyung Joon Han (2025). DOI: 10.1093/9780198953104.003.0004

outline the history of social pacts, and discuss the overall electoral consequences of social pacts and unilaterally enacted reform legislation. In the second section, we outline our main theoretical arguments of the chapter and test these claims by utilizing macro-level and survey data and employing logistic and mediation regression models. In the third section, we consider whether policymaking processes utilized during economic reform efforts have a greater effect on the social identity and PRRP support of blue-collar workers that belong to a union than those that do not, as the former are much likelier to be actively involved in and knowledgeable about such reform efforts. In the fourth section, we summarize the main arguments and findings in the chapter.

Policymaking Processes, Political Efficacy, and Economic Reforms in Western Europe

When citizens are engaged in the policymaking process, it affects their sense of 'political efficacy', or belief that they can effectively participate in the political system and thus produce positive changes within it (Kahne and Westheimer 2006). Scholars have conceptualized political efficacy as consisting of two broad and interrelated types, 'internal political efficacy' and 'external political efficacy' (Balch 1974; Morrell 2003; Esaiasson, Gilljam, and Persson 2017; Knobloch, Barthel, and Gastil 2020). Internal political efficacy refers to whether citizens believe they have the necessary knowledge and skills to successfully understand politics and participate in the political system, while external political efficacy refers to whether citizens believe governing authorities and institutions are or will be adequately responsive when they do participate. Thus, for political efficacy to be fully realized, citizens must have a generally positive impression of their own political capabilities, as well as governing authorities' ability/willingness to engage with citizens and incorporate their preferences into government policy.

Researchers have found that political efficacy produces a positive feedback loop for democracy: a sense of political efficacy increases public trust (or the trust citizens have in governing authorities and institutions) and political participation (Karp and Banducci 2008); and public trust and political participation increase a sense of political efficacy (Pateman 1970; Finkel 1985; Morrell 2003; Boulianne 2019; Knobloch, Barthel, and Gastil 2020). More specifically, citizens are likelier to participate in the political process if they believe such engagement will be successful; and participating in the

The Policymaking Process   **83**

political process enables citizens to develop political skills and perceptions of self-competence, leading to greater acceptance of and support for the existing political system (Pateman 1970).

In addition to reinforcing each other, greater political efficacy, public trust, and political participation increase the likelihood that citizens will find common ground, have their policy preferences reflected in public policy, and even accept—if not explicitly support—government decisions that are inconsistent with their ideal policies (Gastil, Black, and Moscovitz 2008). Such outcomes are the result of government leaders taking the time to listen to and seriously consider citizens' concerns and providing citizens with the reasoning behind their policy positions (Pitkin 1967; Schmidt 2002; Öhberg and Naurin 2016; Esaiasson, Gilljam, and Persson 2017). As we will discuss further below, such dynamics have been particularly important in the 'age of austerity' in Western Europe, whereby national governments have enacted relatively unpopular neoliberal welfare state reforms out of a sense of economic necessity and European Union budgetary rules.

Social Pacts and Unilaterally Enacted Reform Legislation

Since the 1960s, there have been two broad policymaking processes by which national governments in Western Europe have enacted substantial economic reforms. The first is a unilateral approach in which governing parties enact economic reform legislation without first consulting the 'social partners' (i.e., labour unions and potentially employers' associations). The second is a collaborative approach in which governing parties propose a 'social pact' to the social partners.

A social pact is a policy contract between a national government, labour unions, and sometimes employer associations that lays out their responsibilities regarding employment, wages, and/or the welfare state (Visser and Rhodes 2011; Colombo, Tirelli, and Visser 2014; Han and Castater 2023). To begin the social pact formation process, governing parties must first decide to relinquish their policymaking autonomy and propose a social pact to the social partners. Once a social pact proposal is offered, the potential signatories determine through negotiations whether that proposal is ultimately converted into an actual agreement (Castater and Han 2016).

Table 4.1 includes the number of times national governments offered social pact proposals, completed social pact agreements, and enacted economic reform legislation unilaterally across sixteen Western European countries since 1980. The social pact data covers the 1980 to 2018 period and is

84 Social Identity and Working Class Support for the Populist Radical Right

Table 4.1 Social pact proposals, social pact agreements, and unilateral legislation, 1980–2018

Country	Social pact proposals	Social pact agreements	Unilateral legislation	Coordination score
Austria	3	2	6	−4
Belgium	8	1	6	−5
Denmark	4	2	8	−6
Finland	18	13	1	12
France	1	0	9	−9
Germany	2	1	13	−12
Greece	3	1	21	−20
Ireland	11	9	4	5
Italy	14	11	10	1
The Netherlands	9	9	6	3
Norway	3	3	1	2
Portugal	17	15	10	5
Spain	11	6	8	−2
Sweden	1	0	8	−8
Switzerland	0	0	N/A	N/A
UK	0	0	18	−18
Total	105	73	129	−56
Average	6.6	4.6	8.1	−3.5

Note: The figures in the table represent the number of social pact proposals, social pact agreements, and unilaterally enacted reform legislation, respectively, in the countries and periods analyzed. The social pact proposal and agreement data covers the 1980–2018 period and the unilateral legislation data covers the 1980–2016 period. A 'coordination score' is computed by subtracting the number of unilaterally enacted legislation from the number of social pact agreements (in a particular country).

Sources: ICTWSS (2019), Hamann, Johnston, and Kelly (2013), Hamann et al. (2015), and authors' data from Eurofound reports.

provided by the Database on Institutional Characteristics of Trade Unions, Wage Setting, State Intervention and Social Pacts, 1960–2018 (ICTWSS, version 6.1). The unilateral legislation data covers the 1980–2016 period. Hamann, Johnston, and Kelly (2013) and Hamann et al. (2015) provide data from 1980 to 2012, and we extend that data to 2016 by utilizing Eurofound reports on industrial relations (Eurofound 2015a; Eurofound 2015b; Eurofound 2016; Eurofound 2017; Eurofound 2020).

There are at least three important stylized facts that can be gleaned from the table. First, both social pact agreements and unilaterally enacted legislation have been commonly utilized by Western European governments

The Policymaking Process 85

in recent decades. In the periods analysed, there were a total of 73 social pact agreements and 129 instances of governments enacting economic reforms unilaterally, with the average national government completing 4.6 social pacts and enacting reform legislation unilaterally on 8.1 occasions. Second, a large minority of social pact proposals never result in a social pact agreement. Between 1980 and 2018, nearly one-third of all governing parties' social pact proposals experienced such a fate. Finally, substantial variation exists between countries in terms of the number of social pact agreements and unilaterally enacted reform legislation, as well as the share of social pact proposals that were ultimately converted into social pact agreements. During the periods covered in the table, the total number of social pact agreements and unilaterally enacted reform legislation in a country ranges from 0 (in France) to 21 (in Greece),[1] while the difference between the number of social pact agreements and unilaterally enacted reform legislation in a country ranges from −20 (in Greece) to +12 (in Finland). In addition, in two countries (the Netherlands and Norway), every social pact proposal offered by the government was successfully converted into a social pact agreement, while in two countries (Belgium and Greece), less than half of such proposals ultimately became social pact agreements. In short, while nearly all Western European countries have adopted substantial economic reforms in recent decades, the number of such reforms and the process by which they were formulated have differed markedly across these countries.

The data presented in Table 4.1 also informs us that 6 of the 16 countries included in it account for over 85 per cent of the social pacts that were completed between 1980 and 2018 (the number of social pact agreements is in parentheses): Portugal (15), Finland (13), Italy (11), Ireland (9), the Netherlands (9), and Spain (6). Interestingly, many of the most 'neo-corporatist'[2] countries in Western Europe, including Austria, Belgium, Norway, and Sweden, have completed relatively few social pacts during the period. Existing scholarship on the determinants of social pacts explains this counterintuitive result by reference to the supposedly superior macro-economic results generated by neo-corporatist arrangements compared to those produced

---

[1] Switzerland had no social pact agreements during the period analyzed, but is excluded from the unilateral legislation dataset provided by Hamann, Johnston, and Kelly (2013).

[2] While there is no universally recognized definition of 'neo-corporatism', it typically refers to an institutionalized form of policymaking in which large interest organizations—including those representing workers and employers, respectively—engage with each other and government leaders to set private policies regarding compensation and employment; and public policies pertaining to the welfare state (Lehmbruch 1979; Williamson 1985). The collaborative approach of neo-corporatism can be contrasted with 'state corporatism' (or 'statism'), a system that concentrates economic decision-making in a powerful state that imposes its will on existing workers' and employers' organizations, and that is more commonly found in non-democratic regimes (Molina and Rhodes 2002).

in countries with relatively strong, but organizationally fragmented labour organizations (as observed in most of the high social pact countries listed above). While the (nearly) all-encompassing nature of neo-corporatist institutions facilitates participants' ability to 'internalize externalities' and thus effectively manage the macro economy, the existence of powerful but organizationally divided labour organizations results in excessive compensation packages for those benefiting from collective bargaining agreements, leading to suboptimal economic outcomes, such as elevated levels of unemployment and inflation. Thus, social pacts are claimed to arise most in those countries in which labour unions are robust enough to effectively participate in the social pact formation process, but fragmented enough to (inadvertently) create the poor economic conditions that make a social pact more likely (Baccaro and Simoni 2008; Traxler and Brandl 2010; Castater and Han 2016).

In an effort to determine whether there is substantial over-time variation in policymaking processes relating to economic reform efforts across the 16 Western European countries included in Table 4.1, Figure 4.1 graphically depicts the total number of social pact proposals, social pact agreements, and unilaterally enacted reform legislation in these countries per decade between the 1980s and 2010s. As with the table above, there are at least three important stylized facts that can be gathered from the figure. First, the total number of social pact agreements has steadily declined since the 1990s. In that decade,

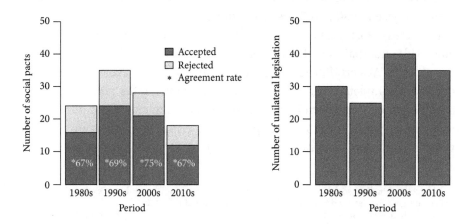

Figure 4.1 Social pacts and unilaterally enacted legislation, 1980s–2010s

Note: The social pact data covers the 1980 to 2018 period and the unilateral legislation data covers the 1980–2016 period.

Sources: ICTWSS (2019), Hamann, Johnston, and Kelly (2013), Hamann et al. (2015), and authors' data from Eurofound reports.

there were a total of 23 social pact agreements (2.3 per year), which declined to 19 in the 2000s (1.9 per year) and 12 in the first nine years of the 2010s (or 1.3 per year). Second, the decline in social pact agreements in recent decades is primarily a product of governments offering fewer social pact proposals rather than fewer proposals resulting in social pact agreements. The share of social pact proposals that resulted in social pact agreements during the period never falls below 67 per cent (in the 1980s and 2010s) or rises above 75 per cent (in the 2000s). Finally, compared to social pact proposals and agreements, the number of unilaterally enacted legislation had remained relatively constant over time until 2000, but increased in the 2000s due to, at least partially, economic crises.[3] National governments enacted economic reforms unilaterally 30 times (or three times per year) in the 1980s, 25 times (or 2.5 times per year) in the 1990s, 39 times (or 3.9 times per year) in the 2000s, and 35 times (or 5.8 times per year) in the 2010s. In short, the available data suggests that in recent decades, Western European governments are increasingly choosing to implement substantial economic reforms unilaterally, or without first engaging the social partners in the social pact formation process.

Social Pacts: A Brief History and Their Electoral Consequences

While social pacts have been present in Western Europe since the mid-twentieth century, the socio-economic context in which they have been proposed, their content, and the relative participation of different actors in the social pact formation process has changed substantially in recent decades (Avdagic, Rhodes, and Visser 2011). In the 1960s and 1970s, social pact negotiations were primarily between elected governments, strong national-level union organizations, and employers' associations with the aim of achieving wage restraint in a generally strong economic environment for workers that included robust economic growth, tight labour markets, and significant restrictions on the cross-national flow of capital and labour. Governing parties sought to facilitate the completion of a social pact during this period by offering labour unions additional union or employee rights, generous social insurance policies, and/or tax reductions in exchange for their willingness to restrain wages (with governing parties sometimes threatening organized labour with tax penalties if wage restraint was not achieved)

[3] Almost half (25 out of 55) of unilateral legislation after 2007 occurred in three Southern European countries (Portugal, Spain, and Greece).

88 Social Identity and Working Class Support for the Populist Radical Right

(Visser and Rhodes 2011). In addition, governing parties often attempted to increase employment opportunities (for younger workers) through these agreements by adopting early retirement schemes and/or expanding public sector employment.

Since the 1980s, social pacts have more commonly been the result of negotiations between elected governments and weaker, more fragmented union organizations, with employers' associations participating less frequently. Unlike the 'first generation' social pacts of earlier decades, 'second generation' pacts have been proposed in a generally sluggish economic environment for workers that included modest economic growth, monetary union, European Union budgetary rules, and in more recent decades, the free flow of capital and labour over most of the European continent. These social pacts have sought to increase 'international competitiveness' through greater labour market flexibility as well as wage restraint. They also re-oriented welfare state spending away from 'demand side' measures that provide direct aid to (potential) workers and retirees (e.g., unemployment benefits and public pensions), towards 'supply side' investments in 'active labour market policies' meant to increase labour force participation (e.g., vocational training for young adults and older workers) (Hassel 2009; Natali and Pochet 2009). Thus, instead of joining social pact negotiations expecting to gain substantial concessions from the government and/or employers, labour unions have often entered these talks with the modest hope of minimizing losses and maintaining institutional relevance (Regini 2000).[4]

For instance, amid the European Debt Crisis, the Dutch government sought to address rising unemployment and growing government deficits and debt through a series of neoliberal reforms. After several of these reforms were instituted unilaterally and proved unpopular, the cabinet of Prime Minister Mark Rutte proposed a social pact in 2012 in the hopes of preserving his fractured governing coalition and gaining greater support among the social partners. Organized labour, despite their general opposition to austerity, agreed to negotiations to gain greater influence over reforms than they had previously and improve social relations following controversial government bailouts of the financial sector and the collapse of the first Rutte government.[5]

---

[4] For example, the Federation of Dutch Trade Unions (FNV) agreed with the Confederation of Netherlands Industry and Employers (VNO-NCW) on wages, but the agreement was rejected by a part of the union in the early 1980s. As a result, the Dutch government imposed a moratorium on wage increases and then a partial wage freeze. Later, FNV leaders thought that it was their 'mistake' to reject the agreement with employers and believed that the only way of avoiding such a suffering outcome is making a deal with employers (Visser and van der Meer 2011).

[5] The first Rutte government was a minority government consisting of two centre-right parties, the People's Party for Freedom and Democracy and the Christian Democratic Appeal, with the support of an opposition populist radical right party, the Party of Freedom. The government fell in 2012 after Geert Wilders, the leader of Party of Freedom, withdrew his party's support for the government in opposition to its newly drafted austerity measures (van Kessel and Castelein 2016).

The result was the Mondriaan Pact, a social pact that offered modest concessions to organized labour, but that also included a new tax on rents, a freeze on most social insurance and labour market spending, and a sharp reduction in health care expenditures (Hemerijck, Karremans, and van der Meer 2023).

Although second-generation social pacts are less palatable to workers and organized labour than their first-generation predecessors, multiple studies have found an electoral benefit for governing parties that adopt them rather than institute economic reforms unilaterally (Hamann et al. 2015; Han and Castater 2023). At least three explanations have been offered for these findings. First, the completion of a social pact allows governing parties to avoid a portion of the blame for painful and unpopular economic reforms, as such agreements require the active consent of the social partners (Balbona and Begega 2015; Hamann et al. 2015). For example, the Austrian grand coalition government of the Social Democratic Party and Austrian People's Party attempted to pass a pension reform bill twice in the mid-1990s but encountered a huge backlash from the Austrian Trade Union Federation as well as union members in parliament. To avoid blame, the government eventually pursued consensus with unions (Hamann and Kelly 2010). Thus, social pact agreements help governing parties minimize or avoid negative electoral consequences arising from their economic reform efforts (Castater and Han 2018).

Second, the completion of a social pact signals to voters that economic improvements are forthcoming. Such positive signals may generate optimistic prospects among people and a virtuous cycle in the economy. Indeed, despite the substantial sacrifices that 'second-generation' social pacts often entail, research has shown them to produce lower inflation and unemployment than the alternative (Brandl and Traxler 2005; Brandl 2012).

Third, the completion of a social pact indicates that governing parties are competent and sincere negotiators and managers, as they were able to successfully govern in an inclusive manner and generate broad consensus on contentious policy matters (Hamann et al. 2015; Castater and Han 2018). Governments, therefore, sometimes attempt to reach consensus with social partners, particularly unions, though they control the majority in the parliament. For instance, the majority Socialist government in Portugal sought for unions' support for labour reforms in 2010 despite its parliamentary domination in order to legitimize the contentious reforms (Campos Lima and Naumann 2011).

In addition to the positive electoral consequences for governing parties of completing social pact agreements rather than implementing economic reform legislation unilaterally, at least two studies have found that failed social pact proposals (i.e., proposals that are not converted into social pact agreements) harm governing parties at the ballot box (Castater and Han 2018; Han and Castater 2023). Two reasons have been provided for this finding. First, since voters' evaluation of government performance is partly a function of how well that performance met previously existing expectations (Malhotra and Margalit 2014), a failed social pact proposal harms governing parties by inflating and then puncturing voters' optimism that a social pact agreement—and therefore economic improvement—is forthcoming. Second, a failed social pact proposal suggests that governing parties did not have the skills or wherewithal necessary to complete an actual agreement.

Economic Reforms, Social Pacts, and Working-class Support for the Populist Radical Right

Most of the existing literature on the electoral consequences of the social pact formation process and unilaterally enacted reform legislation focuses on their effects on voters generally. While we recognize that a broad swath of voters are likely to be affected by policymaking processes relating to economic reforms in the ways outlined in the previous sub-section, we argue here that such expectations are likely to apply to blue-collar workers in particular. This is for two interrelated reasons. First, blue-collar workers are more likely to sympathize with labour unions and their issue positions in negotiations with the government and/or employers than other members of the electorate: not only do blue-collar unions in the exporting sector of the economy lead most social pact negotiations (Hassel 2009),[6] but labour unions' history as working-class organizations give them a unique credibility with blue-collar workers (Hyman 2001). Indeed, unions—clearly recognizing this fact—frequently portray themselves as representing 'working people' during the social pact formation process (Culpepper and Regan 2014). Relatedly, there are many other voters—such as small business owners and middle-class professionals—that are likely to actively oppose incorporating unions into the policymaking process regarding economic reforms, as well as the issue positions advocated by unions in any such process (Hamann and Kelly 2007).

Second, since blue-collar workers are disproportionately in a precarious economic position, the issues discussed in economic reform efforts, such as wage levels, employment protections, unemployment benefits, and public

---

[6] Unions in the exporting sector tend to lead wage and social pact negotiations because exposure to the global economy means their members' jobs are particularly vulnerable to the higher business costs associated with generous worker compensation.

pensions, are especially relevant to them. Although blue-collar workers typically do not have the political knowledge of those in professions requiring higher levels of formal education, the highly contentious nature of economic reforms, public relations campaigns by governments and labour unions during the economic reform process, and union mobilization—including through (general) strikes if union demands are not being met—can be expected to generate the news media attention necessary to overcome any information deficit (Graziano and Jessoula 2011; Hamann, Johnston, and Kelly 2013).

Given that working-class organizations play a leading role in the social pact formation process and blue-collar workers are much likelier to identify with organized labour and approve of union positions on welfare state reforms than those with a different socio-economic status, we expect the completion of a social pact agreement to signal to the working class that they are in a relatively strong political (and, by extension, economic) position. Thus, we expect blue-collar workers to have a stronger class identity, focus primarily on economic issues, and therefore be less likely to support the populist radical right when governing parties propose and successfully complete a social pact in the recent past.

By contrast, when governing parties enact economic reforms unilaterally and/or unions and governing parties are unable to convert a social pact proposal into a completed agreement, it signals to the working class that they are in a relatively weak political (and, by extension economic) position compared to those with a different socio-economic status. Thus, we expect blue-collar workers to have a stronger national identity, focus primarily on cultural issues, and therefore be more likely to support the populist radical right when governing parties enact economic reform legislation unilaterally and/or a social pact proposal fails to be converted into an actual social pact agreement in the recent past.

In this section, we test these hypotheses with data on the social pact formation process contained within the ICTWSS (2019) and data on unilaterally enacted economic reform legislation provided by Hamann, Johnston, and Kelly (2013), Hamann et al. (2015), and our own data from various Eurofound reports. The social pact agreements, failed social pact proposals, and unilaterally enacted reform legislation variables are measured as the number of times each occurred in a country in the five years leading up to a particular survey wave.[7]

---

[7] We focused on the five years leading up to a particular election survey because all the Western European countries examined in this analysis have four- or five-year election cycles.

92 Social Identity and Working Class Support for the Populist Radical Right

As was discussed in the previous chapter, the ISSP includes questions on social identity and voting behaviour, but not issue salience. By contrast, the EES includes questions on issue salience and voting behaviour, but not social identity. Therefore, we test the mediation effect of national identity using the ISSP and test the mediation effect of issue salience with the EES. In addition, though the EVS (1990, 1999, 2008, 2017) does not have any explicit questions about social identity or issue salience, it does have a question regarding a topic adjacent to nation-based identity, national pride.[8] Furthermore, the EVS covers a substantially longer time horizon (four waves between 1990 and 2017) than the other survey with a question related to social identity, the ISSP (a wave in 2003 only). Thus, the EVS data allows us to test causal mediation effects through an aspect of nationalistic sentiments (national pride) over a much longer time horizon than the ISSP.

We include control variables discussed and included in Table 3.4 in the previous chapter, but also add one variable in this chapter. The link between policy process on economic reform and party support may differ between countries because they have different institutions that provide blue-collar workers opportunities to participate in the overall policymaking process. Therefore, we add a variable on corporatism to models in this chapter.[9]

First, we test the direct effects of the social pact formation process and unilaterally enacted reform legislation on PRRP support by utilizing logistic and ordered logistic regression models.[10] Results on the effects of social pact agreements and failed social pact proposals are reported in Table 4.2. Models 1 and 2 employ the ISSP, Models 3 and 4 employ the EVS, and Models 5 and 6 employ the EES. Models 1, 3, and 5 include the basic list of PRRPs and Models 2, 4, and 6 add 'borderline' PRRPs.[11]

---

[8] Although national pride is conceptually distinct from a nation-based identity, the former tends to arise from and reinforce the latter (Smith 1991; Han 2013a).

[9] The data is from Jahn (2016). We, however, do not add the corporatism variable in models with the ISSP because of the degree of freedom issue.

[10] The party support variable from the ISSP is coded as 1 if a blue-collar worker indicates that she intends to vote for a PRRP in the next national election in her country. The EVS variable is coded as 1 if a blue-collar worker indicates that he currently supports a PRRP. The party support variable from the EES is ordinal and based on a blue-collar worker's answer to the question, 'How probable is it that you will ever vote for (the PRRP in your country)? Please specify your views on a scale where 0 means "not at all probable" and 10 means "very probable". Thus, higher scores of the ordinal variable indicate a greater probability of supporting the populist radical right in an upcoming election.

[11] The list of basic and 'borderline' PRRPs was discussed in Chapter 2. We also run two sets of robustness checks for models on the direct effects of the policymaking process (Chapter 4), policy outputs (Chapter 5), and policy outcomes (Chapter 6). First, while excluding country/years without a PRRP may bring in a selection bias (Golder 2003), including them may also be problematic because prospective PRRP supporters in the country/years do not have a chance to cast their vote to a PRRP due to the absence of the party (or its candidates) in electoral ballots (Arzheimer and Carter 2006). Therefore, we add robustness checks with excluding these country/years. Second, we use (country) fixed-effect model in another set of robustness checks. However, we run these robustness check models only with the EVS due to the degree of freedom problem. In addition, models with the EES already exclude country/years without a PRRP. The results, which are quite similar with original ones, are presented in the appendix.

The Policymaking Process 93

Table 4.2 Social pacts and working-class support for the populist radical right

	(1)	(2)	(3)	(4)	(5)	(6)
Data	ISSP		EVS		EES	
PRRPs	Basic	All	Basic	All	Basic	All
Social pact agreement	0.18	0.08	0.07	0.06	0.01	−0.02
	(0.49)	(0.82)	(0.05)	(0.05)	(0.02)	(0.02)
Failed social pact proposal	2.10**	0.35	0.95**	0.61*	0.38**	0.28
	(0.86)	(0.93)	(0.40)	(0.37)	(0.19)	(0.23)
Female	−0.08	−0.17	−0.30***	−0.47***	−0.26**	−0.35***
	(0.25)	(0.21)	(0.11)	(0.12)	(0.13)	(0.09)
Age	−0.01	−0.02**	−0.01**	−0.01***	−0.02***	−0.01***
	(0.01)	(0.01)	(0.00)	(0.00)	(0.00)	(0.00)
Education	−0.38***	−0.31***	−0.93***	−0.34*	−0.34***	−0.25***
	(0.15)	(0.10)	(0.21)	(0.20)	(0.09)	(0.08)
Political ideology (right)	2.88**	2.94***	0.30***	0.32***	0.27***	0.25***
	(1.46)	(0.99)	(0.05)	(0.04)	(0.04)	(0.03)
Number of political parties	0.10	2.31***	−0.01	0.03	−0.07	0.11
	(0.57)	(0.86)	(0.10)	(0.09)	(0.07)	(0.09)
Unemployment rate	−0.17	−1.44	−0.19***	−0.18***	−0.24**	−0.10**
	(0.29)	(1.64)	(0.07)	(0.06)	(0.12)	(0.05)
Immigration	0.45***	0.41	0.17***	0.11***	0.06	−0.02
	(0.14)	(0.37)	(0.04)	(0.03)	(0.08)	(0.06)
Social spending	0.31**	0.82	0.06	0.02	0.04	0.04
	(0.12)	(0.68)	(0.05)	(0.05)	(0.05)	(0.04)
Corporatism			−0.05	0.21	0.25	−0.16
			(0.53)	(0.43)	(0.19)	(0.17)
Constant	−24.56***	−38.70**	−5.72***	−4.42***		
	(9.43)	(18.17)	(1.74)	(1.39)		
−2 x Log likelihood	202.8	280.8	11,194.4	14,273.7	5,091.4	7,966.7
Number of observations	1,430	1,430	34,054	34,054	1,796	2,377

Note: Logistic regression with clustered standard errors (by country/year) is used in Models 1 to 4. Ordered logistic regression with clustered standard errors (by country/year) is used in Models 5 and 6. Clustered standard errors are in parentheses. Results on cut-points are not reported in Models 5 and 6. ***p < 0.01, **p < 0.05, *p < 0.1.

Source: ISSP (2003), EVS (1990, 1999, 2008, 2017), and EES (2009, 2014).

The results indicate that social pact agreements have no effect on PRRP support, but that failed social pact proposals increase blue-collar workers' support for the populist radical right. While the coefficient of the social pact

94 Social Identity and Working Class Support for the Populist Radical Right

agreement variable is not statistically significant in any model, the coefficient of the failed social pact proposals variable has a positive sign across all models and is statistically significant in four out of six models. In Models 1 and 3, the failed social pact proposal coefficients inform us that as the number of failed social pact proposals increases from 0 to 1 in the previous five years (the number of failed social pact proposals in the five years before a survey wave in most our cases), blue-collar workers' probability of voting for a PRRP increases tenfold, from 0.01 to 0.10. In Model 5, the failed social pact proposal coefficient informs us that as the number of failed social pact proposals increases from 0 to 1 in the previous five years, the probability that blue-collar workers are 'not at all' likely to vote for the populist radical right (i.e., the dependent variable = 0) declines by almost one-third, from 0.60 to 0.41, while the probability that they are 'very' likely to vote for the populist radial right (the dependent variable = 10) increases by 80 per cent, from 0.05 to 0.09.[12] In short, failed social pact proposals are found to substantially increase the probability that a blue-collar worker will support (or at least consider supporting) a PRRP.

Why do social pact agreements not reduce working-class support for the populist radical right? We offer two preliminary explanations, the first relating to the content of second-generation social pacts and thus also labour unions' motivation for signing on to them; and the second relating to the (increasingly) fragmented nature of organized labour. First, as was noted above, second-generation pacts often contain neoliberal reforms—such as reductions in employment protections, unemployment benefits, and pensions—that are anathema to unions. Nonetheless, unions willingly engage in social pact negotiations out of fear of the alternative: with economic reforms seemingly inevitable, the absence of a social pact is likely to mean an even less desirable legislative outcome for organized labour than would otherwise be the case, as well as further erosion in unions' political influence. Second, the existence of numerous peak-level union organizations in many Western European countries means that a social pact agreement may be agreed to by one segment of organized labour while being opposed by another. For instance, amid worsening economic conditions, the Portuguese government was able to complete five social pacts between 2006 and 2008, all of which were supported by the union confederation with longstanding ties to the Socialist Party, the General Workers' Union (UGT). By contrast, only one of those agreements included the union confederation with longstanding ties to the Portuguese Communist Party, the General Confederation of Portuguese Workers (CGTP). Indeed, on one occasion during this period, the

---

[12] All the other variables are fixed at their mean values when a predicted probability is calculated.

CGTP even mobilized a general strike while the UGT was engaged in social pact negotiations with the government (Campos Lima and Artiles 2011). Given that blue-collar workers are unlikely to be enthusiastic about the content of social pact agreements and may, at times, receive conflicting signals from unions regarding their desirability, social pact agreements are unable to provide governing parties with consistent electoral gains (even if they are able to help governing parties avoid electoral losses that would arise from failed social pact proposals and/or unilateral reform efforts).

Results on the effects of unilaterally enacted reform legislation are reported in Table 4.3. As with Table 4.2, Models 1 and 2 employ the ISSP, Models 3 and 4 employ the EVS, and Models 5 and 6 employ the EES. The results indicate that unilateral reform legislation increases blue-collar workers' support for the populist radical right. The coefficient of the unilateral legislation variable has a positive sign across all models and is statistically significant in five out of six models. In Models 1 and 3, the unilateral legislation coefficients inform us that as the number of unilaterally enacted economic reform legislation increases from 0 to 2 in the previous five years (the number of unilaterally enacted reform legislation in the five years before a survey wave in many cases), blue-collar workers' probability of voting for a PRRP increases more than sevenfold, from 0.02 to 0.15 (Model 1), or sixfold, from 0.01 to 0.06 (Model 3). In Model 5, the unilateral legislation coefficient informs us that as the number of unilaterally enacted economic reform legislation increases from 0 to 2 in the previous five years, the probability that blue-collar workers are 'not at all' likely to vote for the populist radical right (i.e., the dependent variable = 0) declines by about 30 per cent, from 0.64 to 0.44, while the probability that they are 'very' likely to vote for the populist radial right (the dependent variable = 10) increases by more than 100 per cent, from 0.03 to 0.07. In short, unilaterally enacted economic reform legislation is found to substantially increase the probability that a blue-collar worker will support (or at least consider supporting) a PRRP.

Taken together, the above analyses suggest that blue-collar workers become more likely to support the populist radical right when the government enacts economic reform legislation without consulting the social partners or governing parties and labour unions are unable to convert a social pact proposal into a completed social pact agreement. However, successfully completed social pact agreements are not found to have any consistent effect on the PRRP support of blue-collar workers. While this latter finding is contrary to our expectations, the overall results reported in Tables 4.2 and 4.3 are broadly consistent with our theoretical claims. Namely, when governing parties in Western Europe decide to enact broad-based economic reforms, there is only one way for them to stem the growth of blue-collar support for the

96 Social Identity and Working Class Support for the Populist Radical Right

Table 4.3 Unilateral legislation and working-class support for the populist radical right

	(1)	(2)	(3)	(4)	(5)	(6)
Data	ISSP		EVS		EES	
PRRPs	Basic	All	Basic	All	Basic	All
Unilateral legislation	1.11***	1.25	0.55***	0.30**	0.12***	0.13***
	(0.41)	(0.97)	(0.16)	(0.14)	(0.04)	(0.05)
Female	−0.05	−0.26	−0.31**	−0.49***	−0.28**	−0.35***
	(0.36)	(0.24)	(0.13)	(0.13)	(0.13)	(0.09)
Age	−0.01*	−0.02**	−0.01**	−0.01***	−0.02***	−0.01***
	(0.01)	(0.01)	(0.00)	(0.00)	(0.01)	(0.00)
Education	−0.30**	−0.30***	−0.91***	−0.31	−0.29***	−0.24***
	(0.14)	(0.10)	(0.31)	(0.22)	(0.09)	(0.07)
Political ideology (right)	3.25**	3.11***	0.29***	0.31***	0.26***	0.24***
	(1.66)	(1.17)	(0.05)	(0.04)	(0.04)	(0.03)
Number of political parties	−1.80	4.75**	0.11	0.08	−0.15**	0.02
	(1.18)	(2.29)	(0.19)	(0.16)	(0.08)	(0.07)
Unemployment rate	0.03	−1.08	−0.13	−0.15**	−0.12	−0.05***
	(0.30)	(0.76)	(0.08)	(0.06)	(0.10)	(0.02)
Immigration	−1.44**	0.91***	0.18***	0.08	0.11	0.01
	(0.68)	(0.32)	(0.06)	(0.06)	(0.07)	(0.07)
Social spending	0.47**	0.44	0.15***	0.07	0.02	−0.01
	(0.21)	(0.45)	(0.06)	(0.06)	(0.04)	(0.04)
Corporatism			0.09	0.25	0.23	−0.08
			(0.37)	(0.29)	(0.18)	(0.19)
Constant	−13.88***	−48.69**	−9.05***	−5.84***		
	(5.03)	(24.21)	(1.54)	(1.40)		
−2 x Log likelihood	171.7	238.5	9,185.3	11,994.8	4.332.5	5,550.1
Number of observations	1,405	1,405	33,666	33,666	1,796	2,377

Note: Logistic regression with clustered standard errors (by country/year) is used in Models 1 to 4. Ordered logistic regression with clustered standard errors (by country/year) is used in Models 5 and 6. Clustered standard errors are in parentheses. Results on cut-points are not reported in Models 5 and 6. ***$p < 0.01$, **$p < 0.05$, *$p < 0.1$.

Source: ISSP (2003), EVS (1990, 1999, 2008), and EES (2009).

populist radical right: by proposing and successfully completing a social pact with labour unions. By contrast, either of the other remaining possibilities—to enact economic reform legislation unilaterally or to propose a social pact but fail to convert it into an actual agreement—lead to substantively large increases in blue-collar worker support for the populist radical right.

Mediation Effects of Economic Reforms

To examine whether and to what extent shifts in social identity and/or issue salience can explain the effect of failed social pact proposals and unilaterally enacted economic reform legislation on blue-collar worker support for the populist radical right, we utilize the causal mediation model developed by Imai, Keele, Tingley, and Yamamoto (2011). Causal mediation analysis models are designed to help researchers identify both 'indirect' and 'direct' effects. An indirect effect is when one variable (the 'treatment') affects another (the 'outcome') through its impact on an intermediate variable (the 'mediator'). A direct effect is any remaining effect the treatment has on the outcome after its impact through the mediator has been taken into account. Thus, causal mediation analysis models test whether an independent variable affects a dependent variable through a specific 'causal pathway' and inform us how much of the total effect of that independent variable is explained by that pathway. In our case, we are interested in whether certain policy processes, outputs, and outcomes affect blue-collar workers' support for the populist radical right by altering these workers' social identity and therefore what issues they find most salient; and the extent to which a shift in social identity and issue salience explains the overall effect that these policy processes, outputs, and outcomes have on blue-collar worker support for the populist radical right.

The causal mediation analysis model developed by Imai et al. (2011) has two main advantages over other existing causal mediation analysis models. First, it can be utilized for non-linear models such as logit and probit and thus allows us to employ binary and ordinal dependent variables. Second, it provides a method to conduct sensitivity analyses to determine how much model estimates would change given different degrees of violation of the 'sequential ignorability assumption.'[13]

The Imai, Keele, Tingley, and Yamamoto (2011) model consists of three stages. First, two regression models are produced, one for the mediator and the other for the main outcome of interest.[14] The mediator is modelled as a function of the treatment and a series of control variables. The outcome is modelled as a function of the mediator, the treatment, and a series of

---

[13] The sequential ignorability assumption relates to an assumption regarding exogeneity in each stage of a causal mediation analysis model. First, in the model estimating the mediator, the treatment is assumed to be statistically independent of potential values of the outcome and mediator. Second, in the model estimating the outcome, the mediator is assumed to be statistically independent of potential values of the outcome.

[14] We utilize the 'mediation' Stata package developed by Hicks and Tingley (2011). This package does not allow for the inclusion of multiple mediators in a single model. Thus, we test the effects of different mediators in separate models (Curtis 2016; Nielsen 2018).

control variables, including those incorporated in the model of the mediator.[15] Based on the results of the mediation model, two sets of predictions are produced for the mediator, one under the treatment and the other under the control. For instance, in a model of the effect that social pact agreements (the treatment) have on social identity (the mediator), predicted levels of social identity would be produced given the presence and absence of social pact agreements.

Second, the outcome model is utilized to produce three results for the effect the treatment has on the main outcome of interest: the average causal mediation effect (ACME), the average direct effect (ADE), and the average treatment effect (ATE). The ACME is the effect that the treatment has on the main outcome of interest through the mediator only, the ADE is the effect of the treatment on the main outcome of interest while the effects of all the control variables (including the mediator) are controlled for, and the ATE is the total effect of the treatment, or the sum of the ACME and ADE. These estimates are produced by predicting the outcome of interest under the treatment using the value of the mediator predicted when the treatment is present and predicting the outcome of interest under the treatment but using the value of the mediator under the control condition (i.e., when the treatment is not present). The sum of these two estimates is the ATE, while the ACME is the average difference between the outcome predictions in the two models, and the ADE is the remaining effect of the treatment after accounting for the ACME (i.e., the ATE minus the ACME). For instance, in a causal mediation analysis model of the effect that social pact agreements have on blue-collar worker support for the populist radical right via a change in social identity, the ACME would be the difference between the predicted probability that blue-collar workers will vote for the populist radical right given a change in social identity induced by social pact agreements and given social identity in the absence of social pact agreements (with the actual value of the social pact agreement variable included in these outcome models). The ADE would be the latter estimate only, while the ATE would be the sum of the ACME and ADE. Third, the quasi-Bayesian Monte Carlo approximation of King, Tomz, and Wittenberg (2000) is used to compute confidence intervals for the results.[16]

---

[15] We include control variables used in the model for the outcome variable in the model for the mediator to satisfy, at least partially, the sequential ignorability assumption (Clifford 2017).

[16] In most of our causal mediation analysis models, we have a binary outcome (whether or not a blue-collar worker is supportive of the populist radical right) and ordinal mediators (e.g., the extent to which a blue-collar worker has a class-based or nation-based identity). In such a case, the outcome model used is a probit regression, allowing for the assumption that the error terms are jointly normal with a possibly nonzero correlation ρ. Mathematical details regarding the algorithm and quasi-Bayesian method utilized in this analysis can be found in Imai, Keele, and Tingley (2010).

Using the causal mediation analysis model, we test how significantly the policy effects on blue-collar workers' party support go through their social identity (ISSP), national pride (EVS), and issue salience (EES). In addition, some questions in surveys we employ allow us to test other theories on populist radical right support. We do not claim that social identity and issue salience are the only causal pathways by which these macro-level variables effect blue-collar worker support for the populist radical right. Therefore, in an effort to test alternative causal pathways, we include two additional mediators in several of our models: respondents' opinion on imports and their level of trust in their national parliament.

'Import shocks' (i.e., substantial increases in imports) have been found to be a major factor in blue-collar workers' economic grievances and therefore their support for the populist radical right (Colantone and Stanig 2018b). Since imports increase the economic insecurity of blue-collar workers, we expect policy processes, outputs, and outcomes that are (perceived to be) beneficial to blue-collar workers to improve these workers' perception of international trade and thus decrease their support for the populist radical right. The opinion on imports variable is from the ISSP (2003) and thus only included in models that utilize that survey. The variable is constructed based on blue-collar workers' agreement with the statement, '[MY COUNTRY] should limit the import of foreign products in order to protect its national economy'. Respondents can choose between one of five options: agree strongly; agree; neither agree nor disagree; disagree; or disagree strongly. Higher values of this ordinal variable signify a stronger desire for protectionism and thus a more negative view of imports.

As outlined above, blue-collar workers' distrust of the political establishment and government more generally is a product of their overall political discontent (Jennings et al. 2017). We expect policy processes, outputs, and outcomes that are beneficial to blue-collar workers to improve these workers' perception of the political system and thus to decrease their support for the populist radical right. The trust in the national parliament variable is from the EES (2009, 2014) and thus only included in models that utilize that survey. The variable is constructed based on the extent to which blue-collar workers agree with the statement, 'You trust the national parliament (in your country).' Respondents can choose between one of four options: yes, totally; yes, somewhat; no, not really; or no, not at all. Higher values of this ordinal variable signify that a blue-collar worker has greater trust in the national parliament in their country.[17]

---

[17] Results on the first-stage models are reported in the appendix. Direct effects, ACMEs, and total effects indicate the average marginal effects (not coefficients) of each effect.

100   Social Identity and Working Class Support for the Populist Radical Right

Results of the causal mediation models are reported in Tables 4.4 and 4.5. Model 1 in each table employs the ISSP, Model 2 in each table employs the EVS, and Model 3 in each table employs the EES. The results indicate that at least a portion of the effects that failed social pact proposals and unilaterally enacted economic reform legislation have on blue-collar worker support for the populist radical right can be explained via a shift in these workers social identity, national pride, and the issues they find most salient. Overall, the statistically significantly positive ACMEs of major mediators (national identity, national pride, and issue salience) as well as the statistically significantly positive coefficients of these mediators (i.e., the effects of national identity, national pride, and issue salience on party support) imply that failed social pact proposals strengthen blue-collar workers' PRRP support by reinforcing their national identity, national pride, and salience on immigration-related issues.

The average causal mediation effects (ACME) inform us that national identity (Model 1 in each table) accounts for 16.0 per cent of the total effect of failed social pact proposals and 9.4 per cent of the total effect of unilaterally enacted reform legislation; national pride accounts for 3.2 per cent of the total effect of failed social pact proposals (Model 2 in Table 4.4); and the salience of issues relating to immigration and multiculturalism (Model 3 in each table) accounts for 8.3 per cent of the total effect of failed social pact proposals and 9.8 per cent of the total effect of unilaterally enacted reform legislation.[18] However, the mediated effect of unilateral legislation (through national pride) is not statistically significant (Model 2 in Table 4.5).

Regarding the additional mediators, the results indicate that blue-collar workers' trust in the national parliament significantly mediates the effect that failed social pact proposals and unilaterally enacted reform legislation have on blue-collar workers' support for the populist radical right, but that these workers' opinions of imports have no such mediation effect (Models 1 and 3 in Tables 4.4 and 4.5). In other words, in addition to the mediation effects occurring through national identity, national pride, and issue salience, failed social pact proposals and unilaterally enacted reform legislation strengthen blue-collar workers' support for the populist radical right by reducing their trust in the national parliament. The average causal mediation effects (ACME) inform us that trust in parliament accounts for 20.5 per cent of the total effect of failed social pact proposals and 9.2 per cent of the total effect of unilaterally enacted reform legislation.

---

[18] Although the voting probability variable in the EES is an ordered categorical variable, the mediation package uses the ordinary least squares model because it is currently unable to accommodate such variables (Curtis 2016).

Table 4.4 Failed social pact proposals and working-class support for the populist radical right (Mediation Model)

Data	(1) ISSP	(2) EVS	(3) EES
The treatment (policymaking process)			
Failed social pact proposal	1.38	1.14***	1.12***
	(0.96)	(0.07)	(0.41)
The mediators			
National identity	1.74***		
	(0.60)		
National pride		0.84***	
		(0.07)	
Issue Salience (immigration/multiculturalism)			1.77***
			(0.29)
Opinion on import	0.31		
	(0.37)		
Trust in parliament			−1.30***
			(0.19)
Control variables			
Female	0.10	−0.29***	−0.37**
	(0.59)	(0.06)	(0.18)
Age	−0.00	−0.01***	−0.02***
	(0.02)	(0.00)	(0.01)
Education	−0.25	−0.87***	−0.37***
	(0.26)	(0.10)	(0.13)
Political ideology (right)	2.88***	0.33***	0.32***
	(0.55)	(0.01)	(0.03)
Number of political parties	−0.31	0.03*	−0.39***
	(0.43)	(0.02)	(0.12)
Unemployment rate	−0.23	−0.17***	−0.76***
	(0.21)	(0.01)	(0.10)
Immigration	0.45***	0.18***	0.06
	(0.15)	(0.01)	(0.06)
Social spending	0.25	0.06***	0.15***
	(0.16)	(0.01)	(0.05)
Social pact agreement	0.20	0.08***	0.01
	(0.32)	(0.01)	(0.01)
Corporatism		−0.28***	0.56***

Continued

102 Social Identity and Working Class Support for the Populist Radical Right

Table 4.4 *Continued*

Data	(1) ISSP		(2) EVS	(3) EES	
			(0.06)	(0.20)	
Constant	−26.13***		−6.98***	5.35***	
	(6.79)		(0.28)	(1.04)	
Treatment: Failed social pact proposal					
Mediator	National identity	Opinion on import	National pride	Issue salience	Trust in parliament
Direct effect	0.03	0.024	0.049***	1.09***	1.09***
ACME	0.01***	0.001	0.002***	0.10*	0.28***
Total effect	0.03	0.025	0.051***	1.19***	1.37***
Number of observations	1,140		31,361	1,391	
−2 x Log likelihood	130.0		12,279.1		
R-squared				0.23	

Note: Standard errors are in parentheses. ***p < 0.01, **p < 0.05, *p < 0.1.
Source: ISSP (2003), EVS (1990, 1999, 2008, 2017), and EES (2009, 2014).

Table 4.5 Unilateral legislation and working-class support for the populist radical right (Mediation Model)

Data	(1) ISSP	(2) EVS	(3) EES
Treatment (policymaking process)			
Unilateral legislation	0.93	0.45***	0.18***
	(0.57)	(0.03)	(0.04)
Mediators			
National identity	1.86***		
	(0.66)		
National pride		0.89***	
		(0.07)	
Issue Salience (immigration/multiculturalism)			1.67***
			(0.27)
Opinion on import	0.64		
	(0.45)		
Trust in parliament			−0.79***
			(0.16)

Data	(1) ISSP		(2) EVS		(3) EES
Control variables					
Female	−0.04		−0.31∗∗∗		−0.31*
	(0.69)		(0.07)		(0.16)
Age	−0.00		−0.01***		−0.03***
	(0.02)		(0.00)		(0.01)
Education	−0.08		−0.88***		−0.45***
	(0.28)		(0.11)		(0.11)
Political ideology (right)	3.72***		0.32***		0.37***
	(0.69)		(0.01)		(0.03)
Number of political parties	−1.98		0.10∗∗∗		−0.29***
	(1.22)		(0.02)		(0.07)
Unemployment rate	0.08		−0.14***		−0.20***
	(0.25)		(0.01)		(0.06)
Immigration	−1.03		0.18∗∗∗		0.12**
	(0.76)		(0.01)		(0.05)
Social spending	0.33		0.15***		0.03
	(0.27)		(0.01)		(0.03)
Corporatism			−0.05		0.55***
			(0.07)		(0.13)
Constant	−20.28***		−9.84***		3.76***
	(5.61)		(0.31)		(0.78)
Treatment: Unilateral legislation					
Mediator	National identity	Opinion on import	National pride	Issue salience	Trust in parliament
Direct effect	0.004	0.005	0.014***	0.18***	0.18***
ACME	0.001*	0.000	−0.000	0.02***	0.02***
Total effect	0.005	0.005	0.014***	0.20***	0.20***
Number of observations	1,120		30,755	1,676	
−2 x Log likelihood	101.8		11,704.5		
R-squared				0.21	

Note: Standard errors are in parentheses. ***p < 0.01, **p < 0.05, *p < 0.1.
Source: ISSP (2003), EVS (1990, 1999, 2008, 2017), and EES (2009, 2014).

The Mediation Stata package also allows us to perform a sensitivity analysis to examine how robust the result on the mediation effect is to the sequential ignorability assumption. The sensitivity analysis results show that the ACME remains statistically significant at the 0.95 level as long as the sensitivity parameter *rho* (the correlation of errors from the equation for the mediator and that for the outcome variable) is below 0.3–0.5. Also, an omitted confounder, if there is any, would have to explain at least 10–25 per cent of the remaining variance in each of the mediators and the outcome variable for the ACME to be zero (i.e., statistically insignificant). Although there is no consensus regarding what thresholds are necessary to meet in the sensitivity analysis for the findings to be robust, the figures provided directly above are within an acceptable range according to recent studies that apply similar sensitivity analyses (Curtis 2016; Carreras, Carreras, and Bowler 2019; Hildebrandt, Trüdinger, and Wyss 2019).

Union Membership, Economic Reforms, and the Populist Radical Right

As stated above, we expect the social pact formation process and unilaterally enacted reform legislation to affect the social identity and therefore vote choice of blue-collar workers that belong to a union as well as those that do not. Nonetheless, the direct involvement of labour unions in the social pact formation process suggests that economic reforms will have a larger impact on blue-collar union members than non-union members. This is for three interrelated reasons. First, one of the primary missions of labour unions is to educate their members about electoral politics so that workers can better recognize and act upon what is in their economic self-interest, as well as the interests of their union and the working classes and middle classes more broadly (Ahlquist 2017). Thus, blue-collar union members are likely to be more knowledgeable than blue-collar non-union members about economic reform efforts by the government and whether the policymaking processes and policy outputs pursued are consistent with worker and union interests.

Second, the relatively democratic nature of union organizations means that rank-and-file union members are often actively involved in the social pact formation process, including in decisions regarding whether their union will pursue a social pact agreement with the government, the bargaining positions of their union in any social pact-related negotiations, and whether their union will accept a specific agreement that union leaders have negotiated with the government (Baccaro 2002; Culpepper 2002; Baccaro and Lim 2007; O'Donnell, Adshead, and Thomas 2011; Culpepper and Regan 2014). Thus, a completed social pact agreement is likely to result in a greater sense of political efficacy among blue-collar union workers than blue-collar workers that do not belong to a union.

Third, since labour unions and (less commonly) employers' associations are the only active partners with governing parties in the social pact formation process, social pact agreements generally better reflect the interests of blue-collar union members than blue-collar non-union members (Han and Castater 2023). More specifically, social pact agreements may shelter union 'insiders' from harmful welfare state reforms at the expense of non-union 'outsiders'.[19] For instance, after a centre-right government in Italy collapsed following a failed unilateral effort to reform public pensions in 1994, a centrist government emerged that was willing to engage with the social partners. The result was a social pact that produced one of the most far-reaching pension reforms in Western Europe in the 1990s (Myles and Pierson 2001), but one that protected union interests by distributing the costs of retrenchment over a larger social base and more gradually phasing out seniority pensions[20] than the failed centre-right reform effort (Simoni 2010). Since social pacts may deliver disproportionate benefits to union members, blue-collar workers that belong to a union have more to gain if a social pact agreement is completed and more to lose if a social pact agreement fails to materialize than blue-collar workers that do not belong to a union.

In Table 4.6, we test whether economic reform efforts by the government affect the PRRP support of blue-collar union members more than blue-collar non-union members. We do this by incorporating interaction terms consisting of our policymaking process variables (social pact agreements, failed social pact proposals, and unilaterally enacted reform legislation, respectively) and union membership. Models 1 and 4 employ the ISSP, Models 2 and 5 employ the EVS, and Models 3 and 6 employ the EES.

The results of the models indicate that union membership does not significantly strengthen the effect of economic reform efforts on blue-collar workers' PRRP support. The interaction term containing social pact agreements has a statistically significant coefficient in the expected direction in one out of three models (Model 1). While the interaction terms containing failed social pact proposals have statistically significant coefficients in the expected direction in two out of three models (Models 1 and 3), none of the coefficients of the interaction terms including unilateral legislation is statistically significant.

---

[19] Union weakening and the growing competition among workers' movements in recent years may be forcing organized labour to build coalitions with labour market 'outsiders' and thus also to abandon efforts to shelter union 'insiders' during the social pact formation process (Natili and Puricelli 2023).

[20] Seniority pensions refer to those that allow workers to retire after a certain number of years of service/employment.

106 Social Identity and Working Class Support for the Populist Radical Right

Table 4.6 Union membership, policymaking processes, and support for the populist radical right[a]

Data	(1) ISSP	(2) EVS	(3) EES	(4) ISSP	(5) EVS	(6) EES
Union membership	0.08	−0.58***	−0.03	0.80	0.01	0.02
	(0.68)	(0.19)	(0.22)	(0.56)	(0.33)	(0.33)
Social pact agreement	−1.69	0.10*	−0.06***			
	(1.19)	(0.06)	(0.01)			
Union membership x Social pact agreement	−1.67**	0.04	0.03			
	(0.71)	(0.05)	(0.02)			
Failed social pact proposal	5.76**	0.84**	1.00***			
	(2.24)	(0.41)	(0.12)			
Union membership x Failed social pact proposal	2.90**	0.43	0.37***			
	(1.44)	(0.40)	(0.13)			
Unilateral legislation				1.98***	0.57***	0.19**
				(0.56)	(0.15)	(0.08)
Union membership x Unilateral legislation				0.01	−0.16	0.01
				(0.05)	(0.17)	(0.10)
Female	0.35	−0.35***	−0.21	0.50	−0.36***	−0.17
	(0.42)	(0.12)	(0.17)	(0.72)	(0.14)	(0.16)
Age	0.00	−0.01***	−0.02***	0.01	−0.01**	−0.02***
	(0.01)	(0.00)	(0.00)	(0.01)	(0.01)	(0.01)
Education	−0.66***	−0.92***	−0.49***	−0.64*	−0.88***	−0.35***
	(0.21)	(0.21)	(0.10)	(0.37)	(0.30)	(0.12)
Political ideology (right)	4.48**	0.30***	0.24***	5.64**	0.29***	0.24***
	(1.91)	(0.05)	(0.04)	(2.23)	(0.05)	(0.04)
Effective number of political parties	−0.07	−0.01	0.06***	−3.27**	0.10	−0.08
	(0.60)	(0.10)	(0.02)	(1.29)	(0.17)	(0.06)
Unemployment rate	−0.04	−0.20***	−0.92***	0.35	−0.15*	−0.27*
	(0.38)	(0.07)	(0.10)	(0.43)	(0.08)	(0.14)
Immigration	0.42**	0.16***	−0.25***	−2.58***	0.17***	0.09
	(0.17)	(0.03)	(0.04)	(0.86)	(0.06)	(0.07)
Social spending	0.18	0.07	0.34***	0.43*	0.14**	0.04
	(0.16)	(0.05)	(0.04)	(0.23)	(0.06)	(0.06)
Corporatism		−0.07	−0.75***		0.14	−0.06
		(0.51)	(0.14)		(0.34)	(0.23)

Data	(1) ISSP	(2) EVS	(3) EES	(4) ISSP	(5) EVS	(6) EES
Constant	−28.20** (11.74)	−6.24*** (1.72)		−15.14** (6.84)	−8.84*** (1.43)	
−2 x Log likelihood	116.9	11,056.2	4,264.9	84.0	9,133.6	4,267.7
Number of observations	1,268	33,824	1,353	1,243	33,448	1,353

[a]EES (2014) excludes a union membership variable. Thus, Models 3 and 6 only include survey data from EES (2009).*Note:*Logistic regression with clustered standard errors (by country/year) is used in Models 1, 2, 4, and 5. Ordered logistic regression with clustered standard errors (by country/year) is used in Models 3 and 6. Clustered standard errors are in parentheses. Results on cut-points are not reported in Models 3 and 6. ***p < 0.01, **p < 0.05, *p < 0.1.

Source: ISSP (2003), EVS (1990, 1999, 2008, 2017), and EES (2009).

In Figure 4.2, we present visual representations of the substantive interactive effects of union membership on each policymaking process variable according to the results in Table 4.6. We observe that in all six models (including those containing interaction terms with statistically significant coefficients), the confidence interval of the estimated effect of the economic reform efforts on union members overlaps with that of non-union members. Furthermore, in only one model (Model 6) is a policymaking process variable statistically significant only for union members. In that model, unilaterally enacted reform legislation results in an increased likelihood that union members will support the populist radical right but has no such effect on non-union members. Therefore, despite the statistical significance of some interaction term coefficients in our models, the overall evidence suggests that the policymaking process utilized by governing parties when they (attempt to) enact substantial economic reforms similarly affects the party preferences of union and non-union blue-collar workers.

The results reported in Table 4.6 and visually displayed in Figure 4.2 imply that the steady decline in union membership across Western European countries in recent decades (and discussed in Chapter 2) has, at most, only slightly diminished the effect of the social pact formation process and unilaterally enacted reform legislation on blue-collar support for the populist radical right. This indicates that the high salience level of economic issues among blue-collar workers, substantial news media attention given to economic reform efforts by the government (be they through the social pact formation process or unilaterally enacted legislation), and the credibility bestowed on labour unions by the working class generally translate into union and non-union blue-collar workers being similarly affected by policymaking

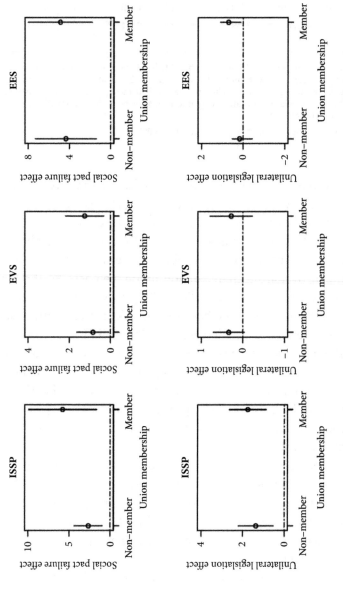

Figure 4.2 Union membership, policymaking processes, and populist radical right-wing party support

Note: Circles indicate the coefficients of the failed social pact proposal and unilateral legislation variables, and lines indicate their confidence intervals.

processes pertaining to organized labour. Thus, even in the context of relatively weak and/or weakening labour unions, governing parties in Western Europe can achieve an electoral benefit (or at least avoid an electoral cost) by actively and successfully engaging with the social partners when attempting to enact far-reaching economic reforms.

Conclusion and Discussion

In recent decades, Western European governments have enacted a series of highly controversial neoliberal welfare state reforms, most of them out of a sense of economic necessity and/or European Union budgetary rules. In this chapter, we considered whether the policymaking processes pursued by governments when they adopted (or attempted to adopt) such reforms affected the PRRP support of blue-collar workers. We argued theoretically and found empirically that if governing parties refuse to engage with the social partners when formulating and implementing reforms or are unable to convert a social pact proposal into a completed social pact agreement, it strengthens the national identity of blue-collar workers and thus also the salience they place on cultural issues, ultimately leading to their increased support for the populist radical right. However, we did not find a strong support-decreasing effect of social pact agreement in this chapter.

Given the active participation of union members in the social pact formation process, their greater knowledge about issues of concern to the working class, and the tendency of social pact agreements to benefit union 'insiders' more than non-union 'outsiders', we also examined whether unionized blue-collar workers are more strongly affected by the policymaking processes utilized by governments when they institute welfare state reforms than non-unionized blue-collar workers. While we did find evidence that union members are likelier than non-union members to support the populist radical right when a social pact agreement fails to materialize and oppose the populist radical right when a social pact agreement is completed, examination of the substantive effects of union membership on each of our policymaking process variables (social pact agreements, failed social pact proposals, and unilaterally enacted reforms) suggested that such effects were modest.

Taken together, the results in this chapter imply that if left-leaning or centre-right governments desire to reduce support for the populist radical right, they should actively attempt to incorporate organized labour in any welfare state reform efforts; and that the general decline in unionization across Western Europe in recent decades has not substantially diminished the effects that policymaking processes related to welfare state reforms have on working-class support for the populist radical right. In the following two chapters, we will respectively consider whether specific policy outputs (government labour market spending and EPL) and policy outcomes (related to inequality in wages and employment) also matter for the PRRP support of the working class.

5

Policy Outputs

Labour Policies and Support for the Populist Radical Right

In this chapter, we examine the effects that policy outputs, or certain national government policies, have on blue-collar worker support for the populist radical right. More specifically, we consider the extent and design of welfare state policies particularly relevant to the working class: EPL and spending on (active and passive) LMPs.

Our central claim is that when governments adopt welfare state policies that improve the relative economic position of the working class (such as strong employment protections and generous labour market spending), it strengthens blue-collar workers' class identity and the salience they place on economic issues, and thus decreases their support for the populist radical right. By contrast, if governments adopt welfare state policies that harm or have little effect on the relative economic position of the working class (such as weak or non-existent employment protections and meagre labour market spending), it strengthens blue-collar workers' national identity and the salience they place on cultural issues, and thus increases their support for the populist radical right.

This chapter is divided into four sections. In the first section, we provide a broad overview of the literature on policy outputs and voting preferences. In the second section, we discuss the recent history of EPL and labour market spending in Western Europe, outline our main theoretical arguments of the chapter, and empirically test our claims. In the third section, we consider whether active or passive labour policies have a greater effect on the social identity and PRRP support of blue-collar workers; if blue-collar workers with secure, long-term employment (i.e., 'labour market insiders') are affected differently by EPL and labour market spending than blue-collar workers without secure, long-term employment (i.e., 'labour market outsiders'); and the implications of any such divergent effects. In the fourth section, we summarize the main arguments and findings in the chapter.

Social Identity and Working Class Support for the Populist Radical Right. Eric G. Castater and Kyung Joon Han, Oxford University Press. © Eric G. Castater and Kyung Joon Han (2025). DOI: 10.1093/9780198953104.003.0005

EPL and LMPs as Policy Outputs in Western Europe

While a plethora of studies have argued and found that policy outcomes—such as the unemployment rate or the levels of economic inequality and immigration—affect voters' party preferences (e.g., see Dassonneville and Lewis-Beck 2013; Hernández and Kriesi 2016; Sørensen 2016), a smaller group of studies have instead focused on the importance of policy outputs. Three broad reasons have been provided by scholars for why policy outputs matter to voters. First, it is difficult for voters to identify the specific causes of socio-economic or socio-cultural outcomes, or to discern between the 'signal' (i.e., an outcome produced by government policy) and the 'noise' (i.e., an outcome produced by factors other than government policy) (Gasper and Reeves 2011). For instance, when voters observe an increase in the unemployment rate, they cannot confidently assess how much of it derives from poor public policy or circumstances beyond government control, such as the condition of the global economy (Sanders 1999; Ebeid and Rodden 2006). Therefore, rather than focus (exclusively) on policy outcomes, voters evaluate governing parties based on the content of their actual policies, as these are relatively easy to assess and attribute to government action (Kriner and Reeves 2012).

Second, voters' evaluation of socio-cultural and socio-economic contexts is the product of both the inherent features of those phenomena as well as the particular government responses to them. For instance, voters are less affected and concerned by poor economic conditions (e.g., a higher unemployment rate) when they are protected by generous welfare state policies (Pacek and Radcliff 1995).[1] Furthermore, while voters may not blame the government for conditions beyond its control (e.g., the destruction caused by a natural disaster), they will punish the government electorally if they perceive that it failed to respond to such conditions with appropriate and necessary policies (e.g., a national disaster declaration) (Healy and Malhotra 2010; Gasper and Reeves 2011).

Third, policy outputs can further or impair the material and/or ideological self-interest of specific voters, regardless of the impact they have on macro-level outcomes (Lewis-Beck and Nadeau 2011). Regarding material self-interest, a voter is likelier to be supportive of (opposed to) a policy and the governing parties that implement it if it produces a clear and direct benefit (cost) to them. For instance, younger voters are more supportive of public education funding than older voters (Brunner and Balsdon 2004), while

---

[1] Relatedly, Vlandas and Halikiopoulou (2019) study how the economic grievance effect of unemployment on populist radical right support is mediated by EPL and unemployment benefits.

older voters punish/reward governing parties more than younger voters in response to changes in public pensions (Chrisp and Pearce 2019). Regarding ideological self-interest, a voter is likelier to be supportive of (opposed to) a policy and the governing parties that implement it if it is consistent with (contradicts) their political values. For instance, voters with left-leaning values respond much more favourably than voters with right-leaning values to governing parties that implement redistributive government policies (Lazarus and Reilly 2010; Armingeon and Weisstanner 2022), while voters with right-leaning values respond much more favourably than voters with left-leaning values to welfare state retrenchment (Schumacher, Vis, and van Kersbergen 2013).

All in all, voters combine multiple information sources when they evaluate socio-cultural and socio-economic conditions. As we argued in Chapter 4, the policymaking process matters, but so too do policy outputs and, as we will discuss further in Chapter 6, policy outcomes. In the following section, we will consider two broad types of policies that we argue are particularly relevant to the quality of life and therefore voting preference of the working class, EPL and (active and passive) LMPs.

EPL, LMPs, and the Working Class

Following much of the labour politics literature, we argue that EPL and LMPs are practically and politically among the most important government policies for blue-collar workers (e.g., see Western 1997; Rueda and Pontusson 2000; Anderson and Pontusson 2007; Rueda 2007; Nelson 2009; Avdagic 2013). EPL refers to those policies that set norms and procedures that govern the hiring and firing of certain workers, such as protection against (arbitrary) dismissals, limitations on the use of temporary contracts, and the regulation of working hours. LMPs broadly refer to those policies that are meant to address unemployment and its effects on the income distribution (Vanhoudt 1997). As we will discuss further below, such policies can be categorized as PLMPs or ALMPs. PLMPs are meant to directly replace income lost due to unemployment, such as unemployment insurance and early retirement schemes. ALMPs, by contrast, are meant to assist the unemployed in finding a new job, such as expanded public sector employment, employment subsidies, the operation of job centres, and job training.[2] We separately discuss EPL and

---

[2] In the political economy literature, PLMPs and ALMPs are sometimes respectively referred to as 'protective policies' and 'productive policies' (Rueda 2007); 'demand-side policies' and 'supply-side policies' (Boix 1998); or 'consumption-oriented policies' and 'investment-oriented policies' (Beramendi et al. 2015).

EPL

It is straightforward that EPL provides the greatest direct benefit to individuals employed in precarious jobs, namely in those private sector occupations requiring relatively little formal education and providing modest compensation, as is the case with many blue-collar jobs. By contrast, job security is a less pressing concern for public-sector workers and individuals in higher earning jobs that require substantial formal education; and policies that make it easier and less expensive to hire and fire workers are generally in the material interests of the self-employed and small business owners (Clark and Postel-Vinay 2009; Voigt and Zohlnhöfer 2020).[3]

A substantial amount of research has examined the micro- and macro-level consequences of EPL. At the micro-level, EPL has been found to strengthen workers' perceived level of job security and their preference for job security over flexible labour markets, as well as their support for government spending on unemployment insurance and industrial subsidies, with this effect particularly large among workers with lower skill levels (Gingrich and Ansell 2012; Balz 2017; Duman and Kemmerling 2020). While the presence of robust EPL appears to increase support for a comprehensive role for government in the economy, it also increases the perceived economic threat posed by immigrants among the unemployed—who may feel locked out of the labour market due to EPL—and decreases the desire to engage in entrepreneurial activities, as EPL improves the desirability of working for an employer (Heizmann 2015).

At the macro-level, there is a scholarly consensus that EPL has at least four broad effects on a country's economy. First, the cost of EPL to employers results in less job turnover, or a lower level of both hiring and firing (Bertola 1990; Heyes and Lewis 2014; Checchi and Leonardi 2016). Second, the cost of EPL for employers results in higher aggregate unemployment (Heimberger

---

[3] There is surprisingly little research examining public opinion and EPL. Nonetheless, the available evidence suggests that those with less formal educated have a stronger preference for EPL than those with more formal education, with the effect magnified in the presence of unemployment (Boeri, Conde-Ruiz, and Galasso 2003).

2021).[4] Third, EPL creates 'labour market dualization' or 'segmentation', or classes of labour market insiders (protected by EPL) and outsiders (not protected by EPL), with the latter being disproportionately populated by migrants and younger workers (more on labour market insiders and outsiders below) (Gangl 2003). Finally, EPL reduces economic inequality by decreasing the risk of job loss and shifting work reallocation costs to employers, with these effects overpowering the higher levels of unemployment generated by EPL (Checchi and García-Peñalos 2008; Barbieri and Cutuli 2016).

In Table 5.1 and Figure 5.1, we utilize an EPL index produced by the OECD.[5] The index hypothetically ranges from 0 to 6, with higher values indicating greater employment protection. In Table 5.1, we provide the average level of EPL between 1990 and 2018 in the 16 Western European countries covered in our analysis. The table informs us that the EPL index has an average score of 2.36 and among the countries covered, with substantial cross-national variation. Two countries, Portugal (4.17) and the Netherlands (3.33), have an EPL index score that is more than one standard deviation (0.78) above the mean, while four countries have an EPL index score that is more than one standard deviation below the mean, Ireland (1.23), the United Kingdom (1.42), Switzerland (1.43), and Denmark (1.5). The remaining 10 countries have EPL index scores ranging between 1.75 (Belgium) and 2.94 (Italy).

Given that EPL was established in Western Europe in the immediate years after World War II and has shown substantial 'path dependence' across countries, cross-national variation in EPL has largely been explained by three broad historical factors (Emmenegger 2014). First, the VOC approach claims that employers in national economies that disproportionately consist of workers with 'specific skills' successfully lobbied governments for EPL to encourage more workers to invest in skills that may not be transferable to other firms, industries, or occupations (Iversen and Soskice 2009). Second, PRT argues that more robust EPL is the result of robust labour movements that through pressure campaigns and the election of centre-left political parties were able to enact policies that strengthened workers vis-à-vis their employers (Korpi 1985; Rueda 2005). Third, the Social Catholicism Thesis

[4] However, in his meta-analysis of articles examining the effect of EPL on unemployment, Heimberger (2021) finds that the existence and size of the effect depends on the journal of publication and the type of ELP measure utilized.

[5] The OECD EPL index includes multiple indicators of employment protection, including employment protection against individual dismissals and collective dismissals.

Table 5.1 EPL index

Country	EPL
Austria	2.45
Belgium	1.75
Denmark	1.50
Finland	2.19
France	2.56
Germany	2.58
Greece	2.93
Ireland	1.23
Italy	2.94
The Netherlands	3.33
Norway	2.33
Portugal	4.17
Spain	2.46
Sweden	2.50
Switzerland	1.43
UK	1.42

Note: The numbers are average employment protection legislation indexes by country from 1990 to 2018.

Source: OECD Indicators of Employment Protection Legislation.

claims that substantial EPL arose in countries with large Catholic populations and in which the Catholic Church played a prominent role. The argument here is that EPL helps preserve the 'male breadwinner model' and therefore traditional forms of family organization (Esping-Andersen 1996; Huo, Nelson, and Stephens 2008).

In Figure 5.1, we provide the average level of the EPL index by year between 1990 and 2018 across the same 16 countries included in Table 5.1. The figure informs us that the average level of EPL in these countries has declined by about 13 per cent over the period, from an average score of 2.53 in 1990 to just over 2.2 in 2018. Furthermore, we observe that the decline in EPL primarily occurred during two relatively brief periods, the early-to-mid 1990s and the early years of the European Debt Crisis (2010–14).

The impetus for labour market reforms in the 1990s and 2010s were persistently high levels of unemployment and weak economic growth, as well as normative concerns about labour market segmentation/dualization in countries with strict EPL, namely in those countries in continental and

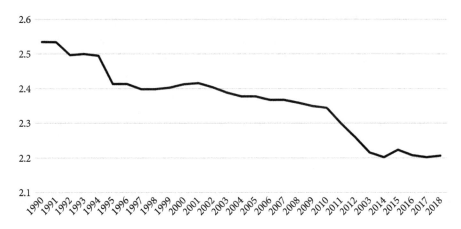

Figure 5.1 EPL index, 1990–2018
Source: OECD Indicators of Employment Protection Legislation.

southern Europe (Emmenegger 2014).[6] In an effort to spur economic growth and increase employment in these countries, many European governments therefore sought to liberalize their labour markets by weakening employment protections for full-time workers with open-ended contracts, while at the same time strengthening such protections for part-time and temporary workers.

Indeed, such an approach became so popular among political elites during these periods that the historical positive association between strong EPL and social democratic governance vanished and may have even reversed, as centre-left parties increasingly sought to woo middle class professionals (Zohlnhöfer and Voigt 2021). Despite such a consensus, however, the relative success of these liberalization efforts has varied substantially across countries and over time as a result of the relative strength and behaviour of labour market insiders (i.e., those with strong employment protections) and the extent of economic turmoil. For instance, liberalization has been on the political agenda in France since at least the early 2000s, with efforts made by the centre-right governments of Presidents Jacques Chirac and Nicolas Sarkozy, the centre-left government of President François Hollande and, more recently, the centrist government of President Emmanuel Macron. However, these efforts have largely failed due to France's relatively modest economic difficulties (compared to countries in the European periphery),

---

[6] For example, Portugal introduced multiple reforms on employment protection between 2011 and 2014 that cut severance pay and add new legitimate reasons for dismissal (OECD 2017). The 2012 reform in Spain also modified policies on employment protection in a similar way (OECD 2013).

mass protests led by France's small but institutionally strong labour movement, and organized labour's tough stance in social pact negotiations. Indeed, France's EPL index score barely budged between 2000 and 2019 (the last year for which data is available), falling only from 2.58 to 2.56. By contrast, Portugal did not engage in liberalization efforts until 2009 but did so in the context of severe economic turmoil, International Monetary Fund and EU conditionality, and a weaker, more fragmented labour movement. The result was that even under successive centre-left governments, the country's EPL index score declined from 4.42 in 2009 to 3.14 in 2014.

LMPs

LMPs provide a disproportionate benefit to those in insecure employment, including many blue-collar workers in the private sector, as such policies are specifically designed to provide income support to those who become unemployed (PLMPs) or resources to assist the unemployed in finding a new job (ALMPs) (Burgoon and Dekker 2010; Rehm 2016; Busemeyer et al. 2023). However, unlike EPL, which is strictly focused on those with employment, LMPs are targeted at the unemployed only. Thus, while EPL helps vulnerable workers maintain employment, LMPs help those who have lost a job to maintain some semblance of the life they knew prior to unemployment and/or provide them with opportunities to find a new (and better) job. By contrast, LMPs are much less in the material interests of the self-employed and small business owners, who experience less job insecurity, may be ineligible to profit from LMPs (because of their status as employers), often must help finance LMPs via taxes, and might need to lift worker pay because of the higher reservation wages that LMPs engender (Browning and Crossley 2001; Rehm 2009).

A substantial amount of research has examined the micro- and macro-level consequences of LMPs, with individual studies often focusing on PLMPs only, ALMPs only, or both independently. At the micro-level, greater spending on LMPs is associated with stronger public support for such policies (Korpi and Palme 1998; De Beer 2007). This association has been explained by the norms of reciprocity promoted by generous welfare state policies, as well as citizens' comfort with policies that have long been established and justified—both in moral and practical terms—in public discourse (Mettler and Soss 2004; Raven et al. 2011). Greater labour market spending has also been found to reduce anti-immigration attitudes and increase support for centre-left parties, as these policies strengthen social cohesion, reduce labour market competition, and act as policy links between workers and social democratic parties. Indeed, the effects of labour market spending on welfare state support, anti-immigration sentiment, and voting for centre-left parties have been found to be greatest among blue-collar workers, the unemployed, and those in precarious employment generally, as it is these individuals who benefit most from such policies (Emmenegger, Marx, and Schraff 2015; Nagayoshi and Hjerm. 2015; Busemeyer and Neimanns 2017; Kweon 2018).

Given the nature of LMPs, it is not surprising that most macro-level studies examining their consequences have focused on the effects they have on (un)employment and economic inequality. The consensus in these studies is that PLMPs decrease employment and ALMPs increase employment, while both types of policies reduce economic inequality. PLMPs decrease aggregate employment because of their 'de-commodifying' character, or by making the individuals less dependent on market income and therefore less motivated to find paid work. By contrast, ALMPs increase aggregate employment because they are geared towards helping individuals find new (and better) jobs, and thus incentivize the unemployed to seek paid work (Blanchard and Wolfers 2000; Murtin and Robin 2018). Once again, these results are particularly strong for the more economically vulnerable, such as those with fewer marketable skills (Escudero 2018). While PLMPs and ALMPs have divergent effects on unemployment, both have been found to reduce economic inequality, either because they replace lost market income (PLMPs) or help workers find new (and better paying) jobs (ALMPs) (Rueda 2015; Pignatti and Van Belle 2018).[7]

In Table 5.2 and Figure 5.2, we utilize a measure for labour market spending as a percentage of GDP provided by the OECD.[8] In Table 5.2, we provide the average level of labour market spending between 1990 and 2018 in the 16 Western European countries covered in our analysis. The table informs us that, on average, Western European countries spent the equivalent of 2.1 per cent of GDP on LMPs annually in the period covered. As with the EPL measure, there is substantial cross-national variation. Three countries, Belgium (3.9 per cent of GDP), Finland (3.41 per cent of GDP), and Spain (3.23 per cent of GDP) spend more than one standard deviation (0.97) above the

---

[7] Despite broad agreement among scholars that ALMPs increase employment, PLMPs decrease employment, and LMPs generally reduce economic inequality, many studies have found these effects to be conditional on the specific LMPs under consideration, the existing policy mix in a country, and the time at which such policies were instituted (Bassanini and Duval 2009; Rueda 2015; Pignatti and Van Belle 2018).

[8] The data is from the OECD Social Expenditure Database. The variable contains spending on both ALMPs and PLMPs, with the latter consisting of spending on unemployment benefits.

120 Social Identity and Working Class Support for the Populist Radical Right

Table 5.2 Government spending on LMPs

Country	Government spending on LMPs
Austria	1.62
Belgium	3.90
Denmark	1.65
Finland	3.41
France	2.59
Germany	2.37
Greece	0.77
Ireland	2.59
Italy	1.10
The Netherlands	2.79
Norway	1.35
Portugal	1.49
Spain	3.23
Sweden	2.68
Switzerland	1.35
UK	0.75

Note: The numbers are average government spending on labour market policies (percentage of GDP) by country from 1990 to 2018.

Source: OECD Social Expenditure Database.

mean, while three other countries spend more than one standard deviation below the mean, the United Kingdom (0.75 per cent of GDP), Greece (0.77 per cent of GDP), and Italy (1.1 per cent of GDP). The remaining 10 countries spend between 1.35 per cent of GDP (Norway and Switzerland) and 2.79 per cent of GDP (the Netherlands) on labour market policies.

As with EPL, PLMPs have been present in Western European countries since at least the immediate post-World War II years and have exhibited substantial path dependence across countries, with cross-national differences typically explained through the lens of the VOC approach or PRT. In the VOC approach, PLMPs are the product of the demands of both workers and employers in Coordinated Market Economies (CMEs), as without adequate unemployment benefits workers may hesitate to invest in the 'specific skills' demanded by employers in such a system (Hall and Soskice 2001; Rhodes 2005). In PRT, PLMPs are explained as resulting from the relative economic and political strength of workers, reflected in broad-based and centralized labour movements and the long-term electoral success of centre-left political parties (Esping-Andersen 1990; Gordon 2015).

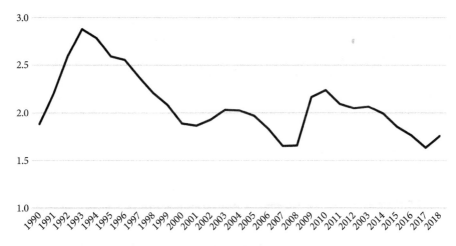

Figure 5.2 Government spending on LMPs, 1990–2018
Source: OECD Social Expenditure Database.

In contrast to EPL and PLMPs, ALMPs are relatively modern inventions, and thus scholarship makes less of a distinction between the cross-national and over-tine determinants of such policies. As we alluded to when covering first- and second-generation social pacts in Chapter 4, the popularity of ALMP grew in the 1980s and 1990s in response to the poor performance of continental and southern European economies relative to those with less comprehensive welfare states, particularly the United States. In brief, generous PLMPs were argued to exacerbate unemployment by disincentivizing job-seeking and raising the reservation wage. By contrast, it was claimed that ALMPs—which are often characterized as 'investments' in workers rather than merely 'insurance' for the unemployed—encourage job-seeking and skill upgrades and therefore also more (and better-paid) employment (Blanchard and Wolfers 2000; Murtin and Robin 2018; Ko and Bae 2020).

In Figure 5.2, we provide the average level labour market spending by year between 1990 and 2018 across the same 16 countries included in Tables 5.1 and 5.2. The figure informs us that the average level of labour market spending peaked in the early to mid-1990s at about 2.9 per cent of GDP and has declined in fits and starts since, with a major fall in the latter half of the mid-1990s followed by much more modest drops (and increases) since. Nonetheless, by 2018, the measure was near its low for the period at about 1.75 per cent of GDP, a decrease of nearly 40 per cent since its high in 1993.

As with EPL, LMPs have been reformed in recent decades ostensibly to address persistently sluggish economic conditions in Western Europe. These changes have affected both spending levels and the LMP policy mix, with the general trend being towards reductions in aggregate LMP spending and a greater share of LMP expenditures dedicated to ALMPs rather than PLMPs. Also relevant for overall labour market spending has been EU budgetary rules, which place strict (but often unenforced) caps on the deficit spending and overall debt levels of member state governments. Scholars have outlined at least four additional factors that affect government spending on PLMPs, ALMPs, or both over time. First, consistent with the VOC approach, the type of market economy present: CMEs reduce labour market spending less than Liberal Market Economies (LMEs), as the historically expansive welfare state and 'specific skills' required in the former generate relatively high levels of public support for labour market policies (Swank 2011). Second, consistent with PRT, the organizational strength of workers: countries with broad-based and centralized labour unions and electorally successful centre-left parties reduce labour market spending less than countries with less worker power, as labour market policies disproportionately benefit the unemployed and those in precarious employment (Noël 2020). Third, economic phenomena and/or aggregate economic conditions: those economic factors that generate greater worker insecurity, such as increased exposure to international trade and deindustrialization, increase spending on LMPs through their effect on popular demand for such policies. In the short term, higher unemployment can also be expected to increase overall spending on LMPs, as a growing number of individuals qualify to benefit from such policies. By contrast, a larger share of workers in precarious employment and long-lasting elevated levels of unemployment reduce LMP spending, as the former results in fewer workers qualifying for LMPs and the latter puts pressure on the government budget and/or on political leaders to engage in LMP reforms (Pontusson and Weisstanner 2018). Finally, the type of political system and government matter for LMP spending: countries with fewer partisan and institutional veto points have seen more LMP reform—including cuts in LMP spending—than countries with more veto points, as the popularity of such programmes makes them difficult to dismantle or substantially alter if numerous actors must sign-off on the policy change (Swank 2011).[9]

---

[9] In a somewhat contrary fashion, Marinova (2020) claims that social democratic parties become more likely to support cuts to LMPs when many partisan and institutional veto points are present, as such an environment reduces clarity of responsibility and thus allows centre-left parties to adopt policies that may improve aggregate economic conditions but also turn off many of the party's core supporters.

EPL, LMPs, and Working-Class Support for the Populist Radical Right

Since stronger EPL and more generous LMPs improve the relative economic standing of the working class, we expect such policies to weaken blue-collar workers' national identity and the salience they place on cultural issues, and therefore also their support for the populist radical right. We test these relationships in this sub-section with three sets of survey data: the ISSP (2003), the EVS (1990, 1999, 2008, 2017), and the EES (2009, 2014).

First, we test the direct effects of EPL and LMPs on PRRP support by utilizing logistic and ordered logistic regression models. Results on the effects of EPL are reported in Table 5.3. Models 1 and 2 employ the ISSP, Models 3 and 4 employ the EVS, and Models 5 and 6 employ the EES. Models 1, 3, and 5 include the basic list of PRRPs and Models 2, 4, and 6 add 'borderline' PRRPs outlined in Chapter 2.

The results inform us that strong EPL weakens blue-collar workers' support for the populist radical right. The coefficient of the EPL variable has a negative sign and is statistically significant in all six models. Furthermore, the substantive size of the effect is found to be large across all the models, although its magnitude does differ based on the type of survey data used. The largest effect is found in the model that utilizes the ISSP (Model 1), which informs us that as the EPL measure moves from its 10th percentile to its 90th percentile value, blue-collar workers' probability of supporting the populist radical right declines by about 90 per cent, from 0.11 to 0.01. The smallest effect of EPL is found in the model that utilizes the EVS (Model 3), which suggests that the probability of blue-collar workers supporting the populist radical right 'only' decreases from 0.06 to 0.02 when the EPL measure moves from its 10th to 90th percentile value, a decline of about two-thirds. Finally, in the model that utilizes the EES (Model 5), we observe that increasing the EPL measure from its 10th to 90th percentile value increases the probability that blue-collar workers are 'not at all' likely to vote for the populist radical right (i.e., the dependent variable = 0) by over 80 per cent, from 0.35 to 0.64. By contrast, the same change in the EPL measure decreases the probability that blue-collar workers are 'very probable to vote' for the populist radical right (i.e., the dependent variable = 10) by over 70 per cent, from 0.11 to 0.03.[10]

In Table 5.4, we report the results of the models examining the effects of LMPs on working class support for the populist radical right. The models presented are identical to those included Table 5.3, but with the LMP variable

---

[10] All the other variables are fixed at their mean values when a predicted probability is calculated.

124 Social Identity and Working Class Support for the Populist Radical Right

Table 5.3 EPL and working-class support for the populist radical right

	(1)	(2)	(3)	(4)	(5)	(6)
Data	ISSP		EVS		EES	
PRRPs	Basic	All	Basic	All	Basic	All
EPL	−1.17***	−1.38**	−0.53***	−0.31*	−0.36***	−0.34***
	(0.43)	(0.61)	(0.15)	(0.17)	(0.09)	(0.08)
Female	−0.27	−0.18	−0.29**	−0.47***	−0.39***	−0.37***
	(0.24)	(0.24)	(0.13)	(0.13)	(0.08)	(0.08)
Age	−0.01	−0.02*	−0.01***	−0.01***	−0.02***	−0.02***
	(0.01)	(0.01)	(0.00)	(0.00)	(0.00)	(0.00)
Education	−0.36***	−0.51**	−1.02***	−0.39*	−0.34***	−0.32***
	(0.13)	(0.21)	(0.27)	(0.24)	(0.10)	(0.10)
Political ideology (right)	3.49**	3.03***	0.30***	0.32***	0.25***	0.25***
	(1.38)	(1.13)	(0.05)	(0.04)	(0.03)	(0.03)
Number of political parties	3.10***	2.24**	0.19**	0.18***	0.10**	0.06
	(0.86)	(0.95)	(0.07)	(0.06)	(0.05)	(0.05)
Unemployment rate	−2.16***	−1.18	−0.12	−0.18***	−0.07***	−0.07***
	(0.72)	(0.98)	(0.07)	(0.06)	(0.02)	(0.03)
Immigration	0.59***	0.27	0.11***	0.06**	−0.08**	−0.09**
	(0.20)	(0.29)	(0.03)	(0.03)	(0.04)	(0.04)
Social spending	1.37***	0.71	0.14***	0.08**	−0.01	−0.01
	(0.45)	(0.61)	(0.05)	(0.04)	(0.02)	(0.03)
Constant	−53.60***	−32.56	−7.48***	−5.24***		
	(17.03)	(20.15)	(1.89)	(1.34)		
−2 x Log likelihood	217.1	254.9	10,945.1	14,083.8	8,426.8	8,616.0
Number of observations	1,430	1,430	34,054	34,054	2,324	2,377

Note: Logistic regression with clustered standard errors (by country/year) is used in Models 1 to 4. Ordered logistic regression with clustered standard errors (by country/year) is used in Models 5 and 6. Clustered standard errors are in parentheses. Results on cut-points are not reported in Models 5 and 6. ***$p < 0.01$, **$p < 0.05$, *$p < 0.1$.

Source: ISSP (2003), EVS (1990, 1999, 2008, 2017), and EES (2009, 2014).

replacing the measure for EPL. The results imply that generous LMPs weaken blue-collar workers' support for the populist radical right. In all six models, the coefficient for the LMP variable is negative, with it reaching statistical significance in five of the models, including all three of the 'basic' versions. The calculation of predicted probabilities suggests that the substantive sizes of the effects are comparable to those found for EPL. In Models 1 and 3 (which

Policy Outputs   125

Table 5.4 LMP and working-class support for the populist radical right

	(1)	(2)	(3)	(4)	(5)	(6)
Data	ISSP		EVS		EES	
PRRPs	Basic	All	Basic	All	Basic	All
LMP	-1.92^{***}	-1.61^{**}	-0.64^{***}	-0.40	-0.26^{***}	-0.23^{**}
	(0.52)	(0.64)	(0.22)	(0.27)	(0.09)	(0.09)
Female	-0.26	-0.18	-0.21^{*}	-0.42^{***}	-0.38^{***}	-0.35^{***}
	(0.25)	(0.24)	(0.13)	(0.13)	(0.08)	(0.08)
Age	-0.01	-0.02^{**}	-0.01^{**}	-0.01^{***}	-0.02^{***}	-0.02^{***}
	(0.01)	(0.01)	(0.00)	(0.00)	(0.00)	(0.00)
Education	-0.41^{***}	-0.52^{***}	-1.01^{***}	-0.37	-0.29^{***}	-0.28^{***}
	(0.14)	(0.18)	(0.29)	(0.23)	(0.09)	(0.09)
Political ideology (right)	3.45^{**}	2.98^{***}	0.30^{***}	0.32^{***}	0.25^{***}	0.25^{***}
	(1.39)	(1.12)	(0.05)	(0.04)	(0.03)	(0.03)
Number of political parties	3.03^{***}	1.95^{**}	0.18^{*}	0.17^{*}	0.27^{***}	0.21^{**}
	(0.82)	(0.94)	(0.10)	(0.09)	(0.09)	(0.09)
Unemployment rate	-1.91^{***}	-0.87	-0.07	-0.14^{**}	-0.10^{***}	-0.10^{***}
	(0.67)	(1.00)	(0.07)	(0.06)	(0.02)	(0.03)
Immigration	0.67^{***}	0.29	0.13^{***}	0.07^{***}	-0.06	-0.07
	(0.21)	(0.28)	(0.02)	(0.03)	(0.05)	(0.06)
Social spending	1.43^{***}	0.61	0.18^{***}	0.11^{**}	0.03	0.03
	(0.44)	(0.61)	(0.06)	(0.05)	(0.02)	(0.02)
Constant	-57.17^{***}	-31.85	-8.43^{***}	-6.06^{***}		
	(17.43)	(19.82)	(1.79)	(1.30)		
−2 x Log likelihood	213.5	254.3	11,021.9	14,125.4	8,479.4	8,671.2
Number of observations	1,430	1,430	34,054	34,054	2,324	2,377

Note: Logistic regression with clustered standard errors (by country/year) is used in Models 1 to 4. Ordered logistic regression with clustered standard errors (by country/year) is used in Models 5 and 6. Clustered standard errors are in parentheses. Results on cut-points are not reported in Models 5 and 6. ***p < 0.01, **p < 0.05, *p < 0.1.

Source: ISSP (2003), EVS (1990, 1999, 2008, 2017), and EES (2009, 2014).

utilize the ISSP and EVS, respectively), a change in the LMP measure from its 10th percentile value (0.5 per cent of GDP) to its 90th percentile value (3 per cent of GDP) decreases blue-collar workers' probability of supporting the populist radical right from 0.11 to 0.01 (Model 1) and 0.06 to 0.02 (Model 3), both identical to the effects found for EPL in their corresponding models in Table 5.3. In Model 5 (which utilizes the EES), the same change in the LMP measure increases the probability that blue-collar workers are 'not at all' likely to vote for the populist radical right from 0.5 to 0.7 (a rise of 40 per cent) and decreases the probability that blue-collar workers are 'very probable to vote' for the populist radical right from 0.06 to 0.03 (a decline of 50 per cent).

Mediation Effects of Labour Policies

Taken together, the above models provide strong evidence that EPL with strong worker protections and generous LMPs weaken working-class support for the populist radical right. To determine whether at least some of these effects go through blue-collar workers' national identity and the issues they find most salient, we once again employ the casual mediation analysis model developed by Imai, Keele, Tingley, and Yamamoto (2011). As we discussed in Chapter 4, we test the mediation effect of national identity with the ISSP, the mediation effect of issue salience with the EES, and the mediation effect of national pride with the EVS. In addition, we examine how the effects of ELP and LMPs are mediated through blue-collar workers' economic grievances (their opinion of imports) with the ISSP and through their political discontent (their trust in the national parliament) with the EES.[11] Table 5.5 reports the results for the models with the EPL measure and Table 5.6 reports the results for the models with the LMP variable.

The results reported in Table 5.5 inform us that the EPL effect on working class support for the populist radical right is substantially mediated by blue-collar workers' national identity, national pride, and the issues they find most salient, with the ACMEs of our main mediators statistically significant in all three models. In general, the statistically significantly negative ACMEs of the mediators in our theory (national identity, national pride, and issue salience) and the statistically significantly positive coefficients of the mediators (i.e., the effects of national identity, national pride, and issue salience on party support) mean that strong EPL weakens blue-collar workers' PRRP support by reducing their national identity, national pride, and salience on immigration-related issues.

In Model 1 (which utilizes the ISSP), a change in national identity explains 11.5 per cent of the EPL effect; in Model 2 (which utilizes the EVS), a change in national pride explains 5.7 per cent of the EPL effect; and in the table's most substantive result, Model 3 (which utilizes the EES) finds that a change

---

[11] Results on the first-stage models are reported in the appendix.

Table 5.5 EPL and working-class support for the populist radical right (Mediation Model)

Data	(1) ISSP	(2) EVS	(3) EES
The treatment (policy output)			
EPL	−0.56	−0.52***	−0.28**
	(0.57)	(0.03)	(0.13)
The mediators			
National identity	1.50***		
	(0.47)		
National pride		0.75***	
		(0.07)	
Issue Salience (immigration/multiculturalism)			1.68***
			(0.24)
Opinion on import	−0.18		
	(0.21)		
Trust in parliament			−1.43***
			(0.14)
Control variables			
Female	−0.52	−0.28***	−0.70***
	(0.43)	(0.06)	(0.15)
Age	−0.02	−0.01***	−0.03***
	(0.01)	(0.00)	(0.00)
Education	−0.29	−0.99***	−0.41***
	(0.18)	(0.10)	(0.10)
Political ideology (right)	3.39***	0.32***	0.40***
	(0.41)	(0.01)	(0.03)
Number of political parties	3.17***	0.21***	0.25***
	(0.46)	(0.02)	(0.05)
Unemployment rate	−2.21***	−0.08***	−0.12***
	(0.34)	(0.01)	(0.02)
Immigration	0.66***	0.12***	−0.17***
	(0.13)	(0.01)	(0.02)
Social spending	1.38***	0.14***	−0.01
	(0.26)	(0.01)	(0.02)
Constant	−57.65***	−8.64***	6.47***
	(8.74)	(0.28)	(0.87)

Continued

128 Social Identity and Working Class Support for the Populist Radical Right

Table 5.5 *Continued*

Data	(1) ISSP		(2) EVS		(3) EES
Treatment: EPL					
Mediator	National identity	Opinion on import	National pride	Issue salience	Trust in parliament
Direct effect	−0.018	−0.017	−0.036***	−0.29***	−0.29***
ACME	−0.003***	−0.001	−0.002***	−0.15***	−0.16***
Total effect	−0.020*	−0.017	−0.038***	−0.44***	−0.44***
Number of observations	1,305		31,361	2,185	
−2 x Log likelihood	188.3		12,279.1		
R-squared				0.21	

Note: Standard errors are in parentheses. ***$p < 0.01$, **$p < 0.05$, *$p < 0.1$.

Source: ISSP (2003), EVS (1990, 1999, 2008, 2017), and EES (2009, 2014).

in what issues blue-collar workers' find most salient explains nearly half (34.4 per cent) of the total EPL effect. Regarding the other mediators included in the table, trust in the national parliament is also found to have a significant role in mediating the EPL effect (Model 3), while no such effect is found for opinion of imports (Model 1).

The results reported in Table 5.6 inform us that the LMP effect on working-class support for the populist radical right is also mediated by blue-collar workers' identity, national pride, and the issues they find most salient. Once again, the ACMEs of our main mediators are statistically significant across all the models. In Model 1 (the ISSP), a change in national identity explains 9.2 per cent of the LMP effect; in Model 2 (the EVS), a change in national pride explains 4.8 per cent of the LMP effect; and in Model 3 (the EES), a change in what issues blue-collar workers find most salient explains 31.0 per cent of the total LMP effect. Similar to the results in Table 5.5 and results on economic reforms in Chapter 4, Table 5.6 informs us that the LMP effect is also mediated by blue-collar workers' trust in the national government, but not their opinion of imports.[12]

In summary, we find that strong EPL and generous LMP spending—two broad types of labour policies that provide a disproportionate benefit

---

[12] In the analyses in Tables 5.5 and 5.6, the ACMEs remain statistically significant at the 0.95 level as long as the sensitivity parameter *rho* is below 0.2–0.4. Also, an omitted confounder, if there is any, would have to explain at least 20–40 per cent of the remaining variance in each mediator and outcome variable for the ACME to be zero.

Policy Outputs 129

Table 5.6 LMP and working-class support for the populist radical right (Mediation Model)

Data	(1) ISSP		(2) EVS	(3) EES	
The treatment (policy output)					
LMP	−1.29		−0.60***	−0.25***	
	(0.88)		(0.05)	(0.09)	
The mediators					
National identity	1.42***				
	(0.45)				
National pride			1.12***		
			(0.07)		
Issue Salience (immigration/ multiculturalism)				1.62***	
				(0.25)	
Opinion on import	−0.16				
	(0.20)				
Trust in parliament				−1.46***	
				(0.15)	
Control variables					
Female	−0.52		−0.15**	−0.68***	
	(0.43)		(0.07)	(0.15)	
Age	−0.02		−0.01***	−0.03***	
	(0.01)		(0.00)	(0.00)	
Education	−0.34*		−0.84***	−0.41***	
	(0.19)		(0.10)	(0.11)	
Political ideology (right)	3.37***		0.29***	0.41***	
	(0.41)		(0.01)	(0.03)	
Number of political parties	3.15***		0.19***	0.44***	
	(0.56)		(0.02)	(0.07)	
Unemployment rate	−2.05***		−0.06***	−0.17***	
	(0.36)		(0.01)	(0.03)	
Immigration	0.71***		0.15***	−0.16***	
	(0.19)		(0.01)	(0.03)	
Social spending	1.44***		0.17***	0.05*	
	(0.36)		(0.01)	(0.03)	
Constant	−60.15***		−9.09***	3.58***	
	(11.79)		(0.28)	(0.74)	
Treatment: LMP					
Mediator	National identity	Opinion on import	National pride	Issue salience	Trust in parliament
Direct effect	−0.034*	−0.033*	−0.048***	−0.26***	−0.26***
ACME	−0.004***	−0.001	−0.002***	−0.11***	−0.12***

Continued

Table 5.6 *Continued*

Data	(1) ISSP		(2) EVS	(3) EES	
Total effect	−0.038*	−0.033*	−0.051***	−0.37***	−0.37***
Number of observations	1,305		30,935	2,139	
−2 x Log likelihood	186.0		8,900.2		
R-squared				0.20	

Note: Standard errors are in parentheses. ***p < 0.01, **p < 0.05, *p < 0.1.

Source: ISSP (2003), EVS (1990, 1999, 2008, 2017), and EES (2009, 2014).

to the working class—weaken blue-collar workers' support for the populist radical right. Consistent with our social identity theory, the results of our causal mediation analysis models informed us that a substantial share of the EPL and LMP effect is driven by how these policies alter blue-collar workers' social identity and the issues they find most salient.[13] More specifically, strong EPL and generous LMP spending decrease blue-collar workers' support for the populist radical right by reducing nationalism and the salience of immigration-related issues among the working class. We also found that some of the EPL and LMP effects come through political trust: as EPL and LMP become more favourable to workers, blue-collar workers trust the country's national parliament more and thus support the populist radical right less.

PLMPs, ALMPs, and the Insider–Outsider Divide

Thus far, we have argued that stronger EPL and greater aggregate LMP spending reduce working-class support for the populist radical right through their effects on the social identity of blue-collar workers and the issues they find most salient. In this section, we consider whether the type of LMP spending (PLMP or ALMP) matters for working class support for the populist radical right, and if the EPL and LMP effects differ between 'labour market insiders' and 'labour market outsiders'.

---

[13] Similarly, Halikiopoulou and Vlandas (2016) argue and find that strong EPL and generous LMPs reduce the support of PRRPs, particularly when there is a high level of aggregate unemployment. However, their analysis focuses on the relative costs and benefits of such policies to all workers, and thus does not concentrate exclusively on the working class or consider the effect of such policies on individuals' social identity.

ALMPs and PLMPs

As noted above, ALMPs have been adopted by Western European governments in recent decades at least partly out of the belief that the decommodifying nature of PLMPs discourages job-seeking and increases the reservation wage; and that a substantial amount of research in comparative political economy has confirmed that ALMPs produce better employment outcomes than PLMPs. Nonetheless, the different types of benefits provided by these LMPs and the diverging positions of PRRPs on them suggest that blue-collar workers' support for such parties is influenced more by PLMPs than ALMPs.

First, PLMPs provide direct financial support to workers that allows them to maintain their quality of life when unemployed (e.g., through unemployment checks), while ALMPs deliver indirect benefits in the form of *potential* future employment (Bronchetti 2012; Rueda 2015). This reality leads the working class—which is more vulnerable to unemployment and pessimistic about upward mobility than the middle class—to have a stronger preference for PLMPs than ALMPs (Kweon 2018; Pontusson and Weisstanner 2018; Häuusermann et al. 2022). Consequently, generous PLMPs are expected to improve blue-collar workers' perception of their economic and political status more than generous ALMPs, and thus also to have a greater effect on diminishing working-class support for the populist radical right.

Second, PRRPs have the toughest stance against ALMPs of any party family, but are overtly supportive of more traditional welfare state policies like PLMPs and public pensions (Enggist and Pinggera 2022). Such an observation has been explained by the desire of PRRPs to restore and protect traditional socio-economic identities and hierarchies rather than facilitate a transition to new types of employment and more flexible labour markets (Fenger 2018). Therefore, generous PLMPs are expected to undermine working-class support for the populist radical right more than generous ALMPs by reducing the distinctiveness—and consequently the political potency—of that party family's preferred welfare state policies.

To test our claims, we utilize the same models as those included in Table 5.4, but with the LMP variable being replaced by a measure for ALMPs and PLMPs, respectively. The results reported in Table 5.7 confirm, though not very strongly, our expectations. ALMPs are found to significantly reduce working-class support for the populist radical right in only one of three models the measure is contained within (Model 3), but only at the 0.10 significant level. Indeed, the ALMP coefficient even comes up positive (and statistically insignificant) in another model (Model 1). By contrast, PLMPs are found to

132 Social Identity and Working Class Support for the Populist Radical Right

Table 5.7 Effects of ALMPs and PLMPs

Data	(1) ISSP	(2)	(3) EVS	(4)	(5) EES	(6)
ALMP	0.28		−1.21*		−0.59	
	(5.73)		(0.67)		(1.56)	
PLMP		−0.09		−0.57**		−0.40**
		(0.26)		(0.29)		(0.16)
Female	−0.12	−0.01	−0.27**	−0.21*	−0.27*	−0.30**
	(0.24)	(0.01)	(0.12)	(0.12)	(0.14)	(0.14)
Age	−0.01	−0.36**	−0.01**	−0.01**	−0.01***	−0.01***
	(0.01)	(0.15)	(0.01)	(0.00)	(0.00)	(0.00)
Education	−0.11	2.86**	−0.82***	−1.11***	−0.29***	−0.36***
	(0.18)	(1.31)	(0.23)	(0.28)	(0.10)	(0.10)
Political ideology (right)	2.79**	0.01	0.30***	0.30***	0.27***	0.27***
	(1.18)	(0.22)	(0.05)	(0.05)	(0.04)	(0.04)
Number of political parties	0.02	0.18	0.08	0.17	0.10	0.20**
	(0.19)	(0.18)	(0.11)	(0.11)	(0.08)	(0.09)
Unemployment rate	−0.11	0.29***	−0.11	−0.08	−0.15**	−0.09
	(0.17)	(0.10)	(0.07)	(0.08)	(0.08)	(0.06)
Immigration	0.26**	0.21	0.14***	0.13***	−0.12**	−0.08*
	(0.13)	(0.17)	(0.03)	(0.03)	(0.05)	(0.04)
Social spending	0.18	−1.70***	0.17***	0.14**	0.05*	0.04
	(0.15)	(0.60)	(0.06)	(0.06)	(0.03)	(0.03)
Constant	−18.96***	−20.12***	−8.23***	−8.04***		
	(5.96)	(5.73)	(1.90)	(1.83)		
−2 x Log likelihood	206.5	195.3	11,034.7	11,169.2	5,269.6	5,250.2
Number of observations	1,430	1,430	34,054	34,054	1,676	1,676

Note: Logistic regression with clustered standard errors (by country/year) is used in Models 1 to 4. Ordered logistic regression with clustered standard errors (by country/year) is used in Models 5 and 6. Clustered standard errors are in parentheses. Results on cut-points are not reported in Models 5 and 6. ***p < 0.01, **p < 0.05, *p < 0.1.

Source: ISSP (2003), EVS (1990, 1999, 2008, 2017), and EES (2009, 2014).

significantly reduce working-class support for the populist radical right in two out of three models the measure is contained within (Models 4 and 6).[14]

---

[14] Both the ALMP and PLMP variables have significant and negative coefficients in the models that include data from the EES (Models 3 and 4). Although the absolute value of the ALMP coefficient is larger than that for PLMP in these models, higher levels of PLMP spending relative to ALMP spending across countries means that the substantive effects are comparable. As the values of the ALMP and PLMP

Policy Outputs

These findings ironically imply that a policy that scholarship has found harms aggregate employment (PLMPs) reduces working class support for the populist radical right more than a policy that research has found increases aggregate employment (ALMPs). As stated above, we believe this counterintuitive finding can be explained by the divergent nature of these policies and PRRPs' stances on them: PLMPs provide a direct and decommodifying benefit, and thus improve the perceived status of blue-collar workers more than ALMPs, which provide an indirect and potential future benefit; and there is less reason for blue-collar workers to support the populist radical right if one of their major welfare state policy prescriptions—namely, more PLMP spending—is already reflected in public policy.

Insiders and Outsiders

Since Rueda (2005, 2007) established his Insider–Outsider Model, a substantial body of research has emerged in comparative political economy dedicated to examining the divergent political preferences and behaviours of labour market insiders and outsiders, as well as under what conditions public policy will reflect the interests of each (Häusermann, Kemmerling, and Rueda 2020). Labour market insiders refer to those in 'secure employment', including individuals with full-time, regular, and open-ended (paid) jobs. By contrast, labour market outsiders refer to those who are unemployed or in 'insecure employment', including individuals with part-time, temporary, and/or fixed term (paid) jobs. In general, this literature claims that labour market insiders favour welfare state policies aimed at helping people in secure employment and oppose welfare state policies meant to assist those in insecure employment, while the opposite is the case for labour market outsiders. In each case, it is argued that policies that benefit those in secure jobs inhibit the ability of labour market outsiders to find similar work, while policies that benefit the unemployed or those in insecure work harm the economic position of labour market insiders. Thus, the policy preferences of labour market insiders and outsiders are self-interested and inherently in conflict with each other.

One of the most common arguments in the insider–outsider literature is that labour market insiders favour strong EPL and oppose generous LMPs,

---

variables increase from their minimum values (0.2 per cent for each) to their maximum values (2.1 per cent for ALMPs and 4.3 per cent for PLMPs) in our data, blue-collar workers' probability of voting for a PRRP decreases to the same degree, from 0.05 to 0.01.

while labour market outsiders oppose strong EPL and favour generous LMPs (Rueda 2007; Lindvall and Rueda 2014; Schwander 2019).[15] The explanations provided for these expectations are straightforward: EPL helps those in secure work maintain their employment status, but in the process reduces job turnover and employment opportunities for the unemployed and those in insecure work; while LMPs help the unemployed and those in insecure work find (better) jobs, but result in higher taxes on labour market insiders and thus also redistribution from the latter to the former.

Given that EPL provides a greater relative benefit to those in secure employment and LMPs provide a greater relative benefit to the unemployed and those in insecure employment, we expect strong EPL to weaken the national identity and thus also the PRRP support of labour market insiders more than outsiders; and generous LMPs to weaken the national identity and thus also the PRRP support of labour market outsiders more than insiders. Unfortunately, the ISSP, EVS, and EES do not have questions pertaining to respondents' type of labour contract, precluding our ability to identify the full range of labour market insiders and outsiders. However, the ESS does include such questions, including whether a respondents' contract provides them with a full-time or part-time job and whether that work is of limited or unlimited duration. Therefore, to test our claims by utilizing a logistic regression model and nine waves of the ESS (2002, 2004, 2006, 2008, 2010, 2012, 2014, 2016, 2018). We label 'labour market insiders' as those with a contract providing them with a full-time job of unlimited duration and 'labour market outsiders' as those with a contract providing them with a part-time job and/or work of a limited duration. Based on these two types of workers, we construct a binary variable of *insider*, which takes a value of one when a blue-collar worker is a labour market insider and zero if a blue-collar worker is a labour market outsider. We then include interaction terms in our models consisting of the *insider* variable and EPL and LMP, respectively. If our expectations are confirmed, the interaction term with EPL will have a statistically significant negative sign (indicating that EPL reduces PRRP support of labour market insiders more than outsiders) and the interaction term with LMP will have a statistically significant positive sign (indicating that LMPs reduce PRRP support of labour market outsiders more than insiders).

---

[15] Despite the consensus in the literature that labour market insiders and outsiders are affected differently by EPL and LMPs and thus have dissimilar preferences regarding welfare state policies, micro-level studies have found that such differences are more modest and conditional than much of this research suggests (Guillaud and Marx 2014; Biegert 2019).

Table 5.8 EPL, LMPs, and working-class support for the populist radical right (ESS)

	(1)	(2)
PRRPs	Basic	All
Insider	−0.02	0.26
	(0.29)	(0.35)
EPL	−0.14	−0.07
	(0.16)	(0.21)
Insider x EPL	−0.25**	−0.42***
	(0.11)	(0.16)
LMP	−0.45**	−0.31*
	(0.19)	(0.18)
Insider x LMP	0.28**	0.32**
	(0.13)	(0.14)
Female	−0.23***	−0.20**
	(0.06)	(0.08)
Age	−0.01***	−0.01***
	(0.00)	(0.00)
Education	−0.61***	−0.98***
	(0.12)	(0.21)
Political ideology (right)	0.34***	0.33***
	(0.02)	(0.02)
Effective number of political parties	0.20***	0.05
	(0.06)	(0.09)
Unemployment rate	−0.22***	−0.16***
	(0.04)	(0.05)
Immigration	0.10***	0.15***
	(0.02)	(0.04)
Social spending	0.13***	0.12**
	(0.03)	(0.05)
Constant	−5.54***	−6.47***
	(0.83)	(1.41)
−2 x Log likelihood	9,080.3	6,449.9
Number of observations	18,340	18,340

Note: Logistic regression with clustered standard errors (by country/year) is used. Clustered standard errors are in parentheses. ***$p < 0.01$, **$p < 0.05$, *$p < 0.1$.

Source: ESS (2002, 2004, 2006, 2008, 2010, 2012, 2014, 2016, 2018).

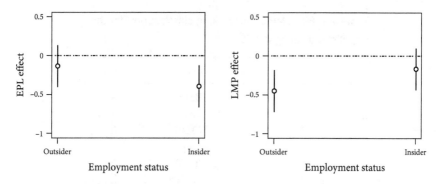

Figure 5.3 Labour policies and working-class support for the populist radical right

Note: Circles indicate the coefficients of employment protection legislation (EPL) or labour market policy (LMP), and lines indicate their confidence intervals.

The results reported in Table 5.8 confirm our expectations. In both our models (one including the basic list of PRRPs and the other adding the borderline cases), the coefficients on the interaction terms are in the expected direction and statistically significant. The different effects of EPL and LMP are graphically presented in Figure 5.3. The vertical axes of the graphs indicate potential conditional coefficients of EPL and LMPs, respectively, for blue-collar labour market insiders and outsiders. The small circles indicate the conditional coefficients when all the variables in the model are held at their mean level, with the lines extending from the circles representing the confidence intervals. The graph on the left informs us that strong EPL only reduces PRRP support of labour market insiders. By contrast, the graph on the right informs us that generous LMPs only reduce the PRRP for labour market outsiders.

Although the overlapping confidence intervals in each graph suggest that these results should be viewed with caution, the reported findings combined with the trends on LMP and EPL reported above imply that the weakening of EPL and reductions in the generosity of LMPs in recent decades have led to increased working-class support for the populist radical right among both labour market insiders and outsiders. Such an expectation is supported by the ESS. Figure 5.4 visually displays the share of blue-collar labour market insiders and outsiders, respectively, that support the populist radical right by year in the 16 countries covered in our analysis. The figure informs us that in 2002, less than 3 per cent of each group supported the populist radical right. However, by 2018, that number had grown to 12 per cent of labour market insiders and over 6 per cent of labour market outsiders.[16] A further discussion of these findings will be provided in the final chapter of this book, including

---

[16] Consequently, between 2002 and 2018, the share of working-class supporters of the populist radical right that were labour market insiders increased from 25.4 per cent to 41.8 per cent.

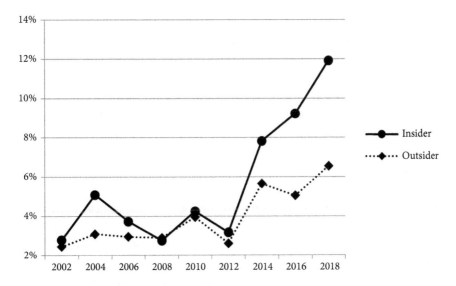

Figure 5.4 Working-class support for the populist radical right, 2002–18

Note: The percentage is the percentage of insider (or outsider) manual workers who support a populist radical right party.

Source: ESS (2002, 2004, 2006, 2008, 2010, 2012, 2014, 2016, 2018)

a tentative explanation for why support has grown more among labour market insiders and what implications this has for the policies promoted by PRRPs.

Conclusion and Discussion

In recent decades, Western European governments have reduced employment protections for those in secure employment and decreased spending on the unemployed and those in insecure employment, ostensibly to improve macro-economic conditions in their countries and, in some cases, meet EU budgetary rules. After examining the processes by which such reforms were enacted and their consequences in Chapter 4, here we considered whether the actual policy outputs produced by national governments affected the PRRP support of blue-collar workers. We argued theoretically and found empirically that weaker EPL and less generous LMPs increase working-class support for the populist radical right at least partially by strengthening these workers' national identity and thus also the salience they place on cultural issues relative to economic issues.

After our initial analysis, we also assessed which of the two main types of LMPs—PLMPs or ALMPs—have a greater influence on working class support for the populist radical right and whether EPL and LMPs generally have divergent effects on labour market insiders and outsiders. Given that PLMPs are decommodifying, provide a direct benefit to recipients, and are much more strongly supported by PRRPs than ALMPs, we argued that the former matter more for blue-collar worker support for these parties than the latter. Furthermore, since employment protections primarily benefit those in secure employment and welfare state spending most assists the unemployed and those in insecure employment, we anticipated that stronger EPL will have a greater effect on the PRRP support of labour market insiders, while LMPs will have a greater effect on labour market outsiders. The results of our empirical analysis largely confirmed our expectations: generous PLMPs were found to reduce working class support for the populist radical right more consistently than generous ALMPs; EPL only affects the PRRP support of labour market insiders; and LMPs only affect the PRRP support of labour market outsiders.

Taken together, the results in this chapter imply that working-class support for the populist radical right has grown in recent years due to welfare state policy reforms that disproportionately harmed (the perceived status of) members of the working class, regardless of their employment conditions. Combined with the analysis in the previous chapter, this suggests that if left-leaning or centre-right governments desire to reduce support for the populist radical right, they should not only attempt to incorporate organized labour in any welfare state reform efforts, but also enact those welfare state policies that both subjectively and objectively improve the economic and political standing of blue-collar workers (irrespective of the macro-economic effects of such policies). In Chapter 6, we turn our attention to examining whether macro-economic conditions—including those affected by welfare state policies—also matter for the PRRP support of the working class.

6
Policy Outcomes

Economic Inequality and Support for the Populist Radical Right

In this chapter, we examine the effects that policy outcomes, or macro-economic conditions shaped by policy outputs, have on blue-collar worker support for the populist radical right. More specifically, we consider two types of economic inequality particularly relevant to the working class: wage inequality (between blue- and white-collar workers) and unemployment inequality (between those without and with a college degree). Our central claim is that if macro-economic conditions are relatively unfavourable to the working class (i.e., wage inequality and unemployment inequality are comparatively high), it strengthens blue-collar workers' national identity and the salience they place on cultural issues, and thus increases their support for the populist radical right.

This chapter is divided into four sections. In the first section, we provide a broad overview of the literature on policy outcomes and voting preferences, with a particular focus on economic voting. In the second section, we discuss cross-national and over-time trends in wage inequality and unemployment inequality in Western Europe, outline our main theoretical arguments of the chapter, and empirically test our claims. In the third section, we consider whether the effects of wage inequality and unemployment inequality on PRRP support differ among less and more highly skilled blue-collar workers and the implications of any such divergent effects. In the fourth section, we summarize the main arguments and findings in the chapter.

Policy Outcomes in Western Europe: Economic Voting

A plethora of studies have argued and empirically found that policy outcomes affect Europeans' vote choice and national electoral results more generally. By far the most common types of policy outcomes examined in this literature

Social Identity and Working Class Support for the Populist Radical Right. Eric G. Castater and Kyung Joon Han, Oxford University Press. © Eric G. Castater and Kyung Joon Han (2025). DOI: 10.1093/9780198953104.003.0006

relate to the state of the (national) economy.[1] While there are points of contention within this research on 'economic voting',[2] there are at least three broad areas of scholarly consensus (Lewis-Beck and Stegmaier 2018).

First, voters in the aggregate hold incumbent governing parties accountable for the state of the (national) economy. More specifically, incumbent parties/politicians are rewarded with more votes when economic conditions in the recent past were strong and are punished with fewer votes when economic conditions in the recent past were weak (Lewis-Beck and Stegmaier 2013). Therefore, vote choice is based on 'retrospective' rather than 'prospective' views of the economy, with such perceptions being mostly consistent with objective economic performance (Nadeau and Lewis-Black 2001; Lewis-Beck, Martini, and Kiewiet 2013).

Second, voters base their economic vote choice much more on the state of the national economy (i.e., 'sociotropic voting') than their own personal finances ('egotropic voting') (Duch and Stevenson 2008; Nadeau, Lewis-Beck, and Bélanger 2013). Such sociotropic voting has been explained as resulting from numerous factors, including altruistic concerns and self-interested future expectations (Wang 2017).

Third, the main indicators that matter for the economic vote are economic (or real income) growth and the unemployment rate (Powell and Whitten 1993; Dassonneville and Lewis-Beck 2013), phenomena that are relatively easy for voters to accurately ascertain and that have obvious relevance for the employment and money-making prospects of working-age citizens.

Wage Inequality, Unemployment Inequality, and the Working Class

Following much of the economic voting literature, we examine the economic vote of the working class by considering macro-level indicators regarding income and unemployment. However, since our social identity theory is concerned with the relative status of blue-collar workers (rather than aggregate macro-economic conditions), we utilize measures that attempt to capture how the working class is performing compared to upper classes in terms of

---

[1] Other prominent issues examined in the policy outcome literature include corruption (Ecker, Glinitzer, and Meyer 2016), crime (Cummins 2009), and war casualties (Karol and Miguel 2007).

[2] Areas of disagreement in the economic voting research include the exact time horizon voters use when assessing incumbent parties/politicians, the types of countries or political systems likely to have (more) economic voting, and the types of voters most likely to engage in economic voting (e.g., see Healy and Lenz 2014; Achen and Bartels 2016; Wimpy and Whitten 2017; Stiers, Dassonneville, and Lewis-Beck 2020).

Policy Outcomes **141**

earned income and unemployment. Thus, our analysis in this chapter focuses on wage inequality between blue-collar and white-collar workers and unemployment inequality between those without and with a college degree. In the sub-sections below, we separately discuss wage inequality and unemployment inequality, including how we measure these factors, why they matter for blue-collar workers, and how and why their levels differ over time.

Wage Inequality

While wage inequality—or the extent of earnings differentials in a country—can be a matter of concern for all economic classes, there is good reason to expect it to be particularly important to the working class. First, blue-collar workers derive nearly all their income from wages, unlike those in the upper classes, who generate a substantial and growing share of their income from investments. Second, blue-collar workers are disproportionately represented near the middle of the wage distribution, with their presence more common below than above the median wage. For instance, utilizing European Union Statistics on Income and Living Conditions (EU-SILC), Goedemé, Nolan, Paskov, and Weissstanner (2021) categorize workers in 30 European countries into nine occupational groupings, two of which ('routine occupations' and 'skilled manual workers') are dominated by blue-collar workers.[3] The authors find that those in routine occupations (low- and medium-skilled manual labour and service jobs) made below the median wage in all 16 of the Western European countries analysed here, while skilled manual workers made below the median wage in all but three of those countries (the lone exceptions being Denmark, Sweden, and the United Kingdom). Furthermore, in all 16 countries there was at least one occupational grouping that earned less than those in routine occupations, with half of the countries having at least two such occupations.[4] Given that blue-collar workers are generally neither at the top or very bottom of the wage distribution, a change in wage inequality is likely to be a direct consequence of the relative standing of these workers, as well as an indication of their future employment and wage-earning prospects. Third, and as covered in detail in Chapters 2 and 4, blue-collar workers have particularly struggled in recent decades

---

[3] A third occupational grouping, 'higher grade blue-collar workers', was found to earn above the median wage in over half of the 16 Western European countries. However, this category consists only of those who supervise manual work.

[4] Other than routine occupations, the occupational groupings most commonly found near the bottom of the wage distribution were 'small farmers' and 'lower white collar' workers. In all countries, the occupational grouping with the highest median wage was the 'high salariat', or well-educated professionals.

due to deindustrialization, labour union decline, and welfare state retrenchment, which taken together have led to fewer employment opportunities, lower wages, and less job security for the working class. Thus, rising inequality is substantially a result of worsening economic conditions for blue-collar workers (although as we outlined in previous chapters and discuss further below, not all blue-collar workers have experienced similarly deteriorating conditions).

A substantial amount of research has examined the micro- and macro-level consequences of economic inequality, with most of this research focused on income inequality rather than wage inequality alone.[5] At the micro-level, higher levels of economic inequality have been found to alter preferences regarding redistribution and redistributive government policies (Finseraas 2010; Alt and Iversen 2017);[6] depress political interest and participation (Solt 2008); reduce trust in government (Anderson and Singer 2008); weaken support for incumbent governments, particularly when perceptions of the aggregate economy are poor (Goubin, Hooghe, Okolikj, and Stiers 2020); and increase support for populist, radical political parties of the left and right (March 2012; Han 2016; Engler and Weisstanner 2021). Furthermore, these effects are generally concentrated among those with lower and moderate incomes, individuals who experience the largest relative losses because of rising inequality (Alt and Iversen 2017). Thus, higher economic inequality leads to greater pessimism among large segments of the voting public, and thus also greater demands for changes to the political status quo (De Grauwe 2017).

At the macro-level, there is a scholarly consensus that high levels of economic inequality generate a host of negative socio-economic and political outcomes. These include, but are not limited to, the erosion of democratic institutions and civil liberties (Reenock, Bernhard, and Sobek 2007; Landman and Larizza 2009); lower voter turnout (Anderson and Baramendi 2012); less trust in individuals and private institutions (i.e., social trust)

---

[5] 'Income inequality' encompasses not only wages, but also other market generated revenue (e.g., capital gains) and, at times, government taxes and transfers. Furthermore, income inequality is often measured at the household rather than the individual level.

[6] While many theoretical models predict that rising economic inequality increases support for redistribution, particularly among those near the middle of the wage/income distribution, numerous scholars have identified what is referred to as the 'Robin Hood Paradox', or that more unequal countries redistribute less than more equal countries (e.g., see Huber and Stephens 2001; Rueda 2008). To explain this apparent paradox, an expansive literature has emerged. While a full accounting of this research is beyond the scope of this chapter, it has generally argued that inequality only translates into greater support for redistribution in certain macro contexts, such as when labour market segmentation or party polarization are low, or ethnic minority populations are modest (Finseraas 2010; Alt and Iversen 2017).

(Rothstein and Uslaner 2005); and greater political polarization (Pontusson and Rueda 2008).

In brief, these findings are explained as resulting from large and growing gaps between the lifestyles of the very rich/wealthy and everyone else, diverging redistributive demands among lower and higher economic classes, and a general sense that the political system is corruptly working on behalf of the well-connected few rather than the citizenry more broadly.

In Table 6.1 and Figure 6.1, we utilize a measure of wage inequality produced by Eurostat. The variable is a ratio that expresses the average earnings of white-collar workers relative to blue-collar workers, with higher values indicating higher levels of inequality between these two occupational groupings. In Table 6.1, we provide the average wage inequality between 2006 and 2018 in the 16 Western European countries covered in our analysis. The table informs us that the wage inequality has an average score of 1.72 and among the countries covered, with substantial cross-national variation. Three countries, Ireland (1.35), Norway (1.35), and Denmark (1.41), have a wage inequality that is more than one standard deviation (0.1) below the mean (signifying relatively low levels of inequality), while two countries have a wage inequality that is more than one standard deviation above the mean (signifying relatively high levels of inequality), Portugal (2.65) and Italy (2.29). The remaining 11 countries have wage inequality scores ranging between 1.49 (Sweden) and 1.96 (Germany).

While most research on the determinants of wage inequality focuses on explaining changes within countries since the 1970s or 1980s (more on that below), persistent differences in economic inequality across countries over many decades has led some scholars to extend their analysis further back in time to understand such long-lasting disparities. This scholarship has primarily focused on a broad set of interrelated political, economic, institutional, and cultural factors that have existed in countries since at least the early decades of the twentieth century.

First, PRT argues that countries with more enduring working-class power—expressed through consistent leftwing and/or Christian Democratic party success and strong labour movements—have persistently lower levels of wage inequality, as the working class is more supportive of wage compression and robust welfare states than those in the middle or upper classes (Esping-Andersen 1990; Korpi 2006).

Second, the VOC approach claims that while leftwing and centrist party success and the power of organized labour matter for long-term cross-national differences in wage inequality, these features are not the result of

Table 6.1 Wage inequality between blue-collar and white-collar workers

Country	Wage inequality
Austria	1.94
Belgium	1.68
Denmark	1.41
Finland	1.60
France	1.76
Germany	1.96
Greece	1.57
Ireland	1.35
Italy	2.29
The Netherlands	1.61
Norway	1.35
Portugal	2.65
Spain	1.79
Sweden	1.49
Switzerland	1.59
UK	1.56

Note: The numbers indicate the ratios of average earnings of white-collar workers to those of blue-collar workers.

Source: Eurostat, Structure of Earnings Survey: Annual Earnings.

the long-lasting strength of the working class. Instead, they are a product of pre-industrial forms of economic cooperation (e.g., through guilds and rural cooperatives), which eventually evolved into centralized wage bargaining institutions in which unions and employers' associations bargain over compensation, as well as proportional representation electoral systems, the latter of which encourages the creation of centre-left coalitions and thus more generous welfare states (Iversen and Soskice 2009).

Third, some countries' populations consistently have a greater 'taste for equality' than others and thus are more or less likely to adopt institutions and policies that promote greater egalitarianism. Such cross-national variation in cultural norms have themselves been explained by numerous factors, including a country's geographic size, degree of urbanization, religious traditions, and historic level of ethnic homogeneity, all of which determine the extent of pscyho-emotional bonds between workers and citizens more broadly (Esping-Andersen 1990; Alesina and Glaeser 2004; Scheve and Stasavage 2009).

Policy Outcomes 145

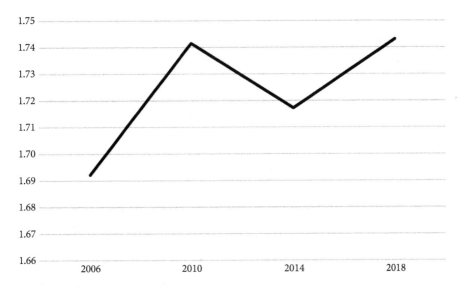

Figure 6.1 Wage inequality between white-collar and blue-collar workers, 2006–18
Note: The numbers indicate the ratios of average earnings of white-collar workers to those of blue-collar workers.
Source: Eurostat, Structure of Earnings Survey: Annual Earnings.

In Figure 6.1, we provide the average level of the wage inequality by year between 2006 and 2018 across the same 16 countries included in Table 6.1. The figure informs us that the average wage inequality in these countries increased from an average score of 1.70 in 2006 to 1.74 in 2018.[7] Furthermore, we observe that the rise in inequality occurred primarily in the run up to, and the early years of, the European Debt Crisis (2010–14).

A plethora of research has emerged to explain over-time variation in wage inequality in the wealthy democracies since the 1970s or 1980s, with this literature focusing on changes in labour market institutions, welfare state policies, globalization-related phenomena, industrial or manufacturing employment, and technology utilized by workers. Although the arguments and findings in this literature are far from uniform, researchers have generally determined

---

[7] Other measures of wage inequality have also captured a general rise in inequality in Western European countries in recent decades, although they differ regarding the extent of the rise and the exact years in which it occurred. For instance, perhaps the most popular measure for wage inequality in the existing literature is an earnings ratio from the Organization of the Economic Cooperation and Development (OECD) that compares wages at the 90th percentile to those at the 10th percentile. Although there are a substantial number of missing observations in the dataset, it suggests a similar average rise in wage inequality of about 4 per cent between the latter decades of the twentieth century and 2020, the last year for which comprehensive data was available (Pontusson, Rueda, and Way 2002; OECD Economic Outlook 2023).

that those conditions that improve the relative market position and bargaining power of (lower-paid) workers reduce inequality, while those that improve the relative market position and bargaining power of employers and/or higher-paid workers increase inequality.[8] Given the general upward trend in wage inequality in recent decades, most of these factors are aimed at explaining increases in inequality, or at least why some countries appear to have experienced a (large) rise in inequality while others have not.

First, declining unionization and the breakdown of centralized wage bargaining institutions has contributed to an increase in wage inequality, as such institutions compress wages by 'predistributing' earnings from owners/top managers to workers and higher-paid workers to lower-paid workers (Korpi 1985; Iversen and Soskice 2010).[9] Furthermore, fewer less skilled and lower paid workers among union members, growing imports from the Global South, and more feasible 'exit options' for international investors may have reduced unions' ability to reduce wage inequality in recent decades (Golden and Wallerstein 2011; Pontusson 2013; Castater and Han 2016). Second, neo-liberal welfare state reforms have led to greater wage inequality by reducing the job security (e.g., through the weakening or elimination of EPL) and the 'reservation wage'[10] (e.g., via less generous unemployment benefits) of workers (Golden and Wallerstein 2011; Mooi-Reci 2012). Third, globalization-related factors that increase labour market competition between workers in the Global North and Global South lead to a rise in wage inequality in the wealthy democracies, as cheaper imports and immigration from less developed countries, as well as offshoring, lead to less available employment and/or lower wages for native born workers (Wood 1995; Card 2001; Criscuolo and Garicano 2010; Hummels, Munch, and Xiang 2018). Fourth, a substantial decline in employment in the manufacturing and industrial sectors has reduced the number of good-paying middle-income jobs, and thus led to greater wage inequality (Alderson and Nielsen 2002). Finally, technological advancements have led to diminished demand for less skilled/educated workers and greater demand for more highly skilled/educated workers, as the latter are able to effectively operate and manage the newer computer software and hardware, equipment, and machinery. Since more highly skilled/educated workers generally receive

---

[8] Rochat (2023) provides a comprehensive recent review of the literature on the determinants of economic inequality in the wealthy democracies.

[9] Unions may do this directly through the collective bargaining process or indirectly through non-union employers offering higher wages in response to union bargained contracts (Rueda and Pontusson 2000; Rosenfeld and Western 2012).

[10] A 'reservation wage' is the lowest wage at which a worker is willing to accept paid employment (Kesternich, Schumacher, Siflinger, and Valder 2022).

greater pay than less skilled/educated workers even before any such technological progress, these advancements have led to a rise in wage inequality (more on such 'skill-biased technological change' below) (Berman and Machin 2000; Haskel and Slaughter 2002).

Unemployment Inequality

There are at least two reasons why unemployment—or being without paid work but actively seeking it—is a particular matter of concern for the working class. First, and as stated above, the working class is more dependent on wages than those in higher economic classes (who receive considerable income from investments) (Schlenker and Schmid 2015). Thus, a loss of employment will matter more for the economic security of blue-collar workers than white-collar workers. Second, the risk and incidence of unemployment is greater among blue-collar workers than other economic classes, including those in low end service occupations. For instance, a recent analysis for the European Commission utilized 2021 Eurostat data to examine unemployment by economic class in 10 EU countries (Requena 2023). The investigation found that blue-collar workers made up slightly above 20 per cent of all employed people in the countries examined, but over 40 per cent of the unemployed. Furthermore, manual workers of all skill levels represented above average shares of the long-term unemployed, with about one-third of unemployed blue-collar workers being without work for at least one year. Such a high occurrence of unemployment among the working class has been explained by the relatively 'substitutable' skills of manual workers and the fact that blue-collar workers are more often employed on (limited duration) contracts than those in service sector jobs (Hall and Franzese 1998; Korpi 2002; Requena 2023).

As with economic inequality, a substantial amount of political science research has examined the micro- and macro-level consequences of contextual level unemployment.[11] Most of this literature focuses on the effect such unemployment has on two interrelated phenomena: (support for) the welfare state and partisan preferences.[12] At the micro level, higher unemployment has

---

[11] 'Contextual level unemployment' refers to the unemployment rate at the national or regional level rather than the employment status of a specific individual (Johnston et al. 2005; Sipma and Lubbers 2020).

[12] There is also a large body of research that examines the effect of unemployment on political participation, especially voter turnout. However, there is little consensus in this literature, with some findings supportive of the 'mobilization' thesis (or that unemployment increases political participation in response to dissatisfaction with government policy) and others the 'withdrawal' thesis (or that unemployment decreases political participation, as it leads to less 'internal efficacy' for the unemployed and more focus on personal struggles than macro-level issues associated with politics) (Rosenstone 1982; Smets and van Ham 2013; Azzollini 2021).

been found to increase support for redistribution and the desire for social insurance, including generous benefits for the unemployed, sick, and elderly (Blekesaune and Quadagno 2003; Wehl 2019; Ahrens 2022); weaken support for incumbent and rightwing parties, the latter of which has less 'ownership' of unemployment-related issues than leftwing parties (Helgason and Mérola 2017); and strengthen support for populist radical parties, particularly of the left, which emphasize class-based divisions and promote a pro-redistribution policy agenda (Gomez and Ramiro 2019; Sipma and Lubbers 2020). Unsurprisingly, these findings are generally stronger for those most (likely to be) affected by higher unemployment, including the (long-term) unemployed, individuals in occupations at greater risk of unemployment, and those in lower economic classes generally. Thus, higher unemployment is associated with more favourable views of the welfare state and greater support for opposition, left leaning, and 'anti-system' political parties, especially among the most economically vulnerable.

Similarly, macro-level studies on the effects of unemployment have focused substantially on its consequences for the welfare state and especially partisan preferences, with the findings largely consistent with those found at the micro-level. First, higher unemployment generally leads to more welfare state spending and greater government redistribution, at least in the short-term (Bradley et al. 2003; Rueda 2015; Hooghe, Dassonneville, and Oser 2019). This is primarily the result of the unemployed being disproportionately from the lower economic classes and the existence of 'automatic economic stabilizers' (e.g., unemployment benefits) and other government LMPs (e.g., ALMP) targeted at the unemployed.[13] Second, higher unemployment leads to vote loss for incumbent and centre-right political parties, but vote gain for opposition and populist radical parties, particularly of the left (Dassonneville and Lewis-Beck 2013; Helgason and Mérola 2017; Gomez and Ramiro 2019; Sipma and Lubbers 2020).[14] Taken together, substantial evidence exists at the micro- and macro-levels that contextual unemployment matters for the policy and partisan preferences of voters, particularly blue-collar workers, and that higher unemployment rates translate into more welfare state spending, greater government redistribution, and altered electoral outcomes, with mainstream parties and incumbent governments suffering and radical and opposition parties benefiting.

---

[13] Although there is a scholarly consensus that unemployment leads to greater government redistribution, this effect has been found to differ based on welfare state design and the time period analysed (e.g., see Rueda 2015).

[14] The impact of unemployment on partisanship has also been found to be conditioned by contextual factors, including welfare state design (Vlandas and Halikiopoulou 2019; Zohlnhöfer and Voigt 2021).

In Table 6.2 and Figure 6.2, we present an unemployment rate ratio constructed by the authors with data from the OECD. The ratio measures the unemployment rate of people without a college degree to that of people with a college degree, with greater values indicating higher levels of inequality between these two educational groupings. Since blue-collar workers are much less likely to have a college degree than members of the middle and upper classes, we assume that this ratio is reflective of the relative economic standing of the working class.[15] In Table 6.2, we provide the average level of the unemployment ratio between 1989 and 2019 in the 16 Western European countries covered in our analysis. The table informs us that the unemployment ratio has an average score of 2 among the countries covered, with substantial cross-national variation. Three countries, Belgium (2.8), Germany (2.8), and Ireland (2.6) have an unemployment ratio that is more than one standard deviation (0.44) above the mean (indicating higher levels of unemployment inequality), while three countries have an unemployment ratio that is more than one standard deviation below the mean (indicating lower levels of unemployment inequality), Greece (1.3), Italy (1.4), and Portugal (1.5). The remaining 10 countries have an unemployment ratio ranging between 1.6 (Spain) and 2.3 (Norway).

Given persistent differences in unemployment rates across Western European countries (and, for a time, between Western European countries and the United States), a substantial scholarly literature has arisen to explain what types of partisan governments, welfare state policies, and labour market institutions are associated with higher or lower levels of unemployment in the wealthy democracies. However, very little consensus has emerged in this research. First, scholars in the PRT tradition argue that countries with a long history of left-leaning governments have relative low levels of unemployment, while those promoting the Insider–Outsider Model suggest that such governments more often adopt policies that keep unemployment elevated.[16] Fundamentally, the disagreement stems from different assumptions regarding the main electoral constituency of leftwing parties, and therefore these parties' priorities and the types of policies they adopt. Those in the PRT tradition claim that leftwing parties' main constituency is the working

---

[15] For instance, according to the OECD, the average share of 25- to 64-year-olds with at least a college degree in 2017 for the 16 countries analysed here was 30.4 per cent, ranging from a low of 17 per cent in Austria to a high of 43 per cent in Switzerland. By contrast, only 9 per cent of blue-collar workers held *any* degree beyond secondary education in the 2008 and 2017 EVS.

[16] Numerous scholars have found that the partisan effect on unemployment has diminished in recent decades, as leftwing governments have been less able to adopt pro-employment welfare state and trade policies in the context of European integration (including EU budgetary rules) and globalization generally (Bandau and Ahrens 2020; Jensen and Wenzelburger 2021).

Table 6.2 Unemployment inequality between education groups

Country	Unemployment rate ratio
Austria	2.1
Belgium	2.8
Denmark	1.7
Finland	2.2
France	2.0
Germany	2.8
Greece	1.3
Ireland	2.6
Italy	1.4
The Netherlands	1.8
Norway	2.3
Portugal	1.5
Spain	1.6
Sweden	2.0
Switzerland	1.8
UK	2.1

Note: The numbers indicate the ratios of the unemployment rate of people without tertiary education to that of people with tertiary education.

Source: OECD, Unemployment Rate Indicator.

class (and lower economic classes generally), a group particularly vulnerable to unemployment. Thus, leftwing governments adopt wage and welfare state policies that attempt to maximize job creation (Korpi 1991; Veiga and Chappell Jr. 2002). By contrast, those promoting the Insider–Outsider Model claim that leftwing parties' main constituency is (blue-collar) workers in full-time employment, and therefore leftwing governments adopt wage and welfare state policies that primarily benefit 'labour market insiders' (i.e., those in secure employment), with these policies often coming at the expense of employment opportunities for 'labour market outsiders' (e.g., the unemployed and those in part-time work) (Rueda 2007, 2014).[17]

Second, scholarly disagreement exists over whether generous welfare state policies aimed at the unemployed (e.g., unemployment benefits or ALMPs) and ostensibly pro-worker regulations (e.g., EPL) decrease, increase, or have no effect on national unemployment rates. On the one hand, those adhering

[17] For instance, ALMPs and PLMPs targeted at part-time workers or the unemployed are primarily financed by (well-paid) full-time workers (Lindvall and Rueda 2014).

to the 'disincentive perspective' argue that welfare state policies that 'decommodify' labour (e.g., via higher unemployment insurance replacement rates or longer durations to receive unemployment benefits) elevate the reservation wage and thus increase unemployment (Layard, Nickell, and Jackman 2005; Schmieder and von Waechter 2016). On the other hand, the 'job search subsidy perspective'—often promoted by those in the VOC tradition—claim that generous social insurance policies for the unemployed lead to a workforce with more specialized skills and better job matches, and thus lower unemployment in the long run (Estevez-Abe, Iversen, and Soskice 2001; Biegert 2017). Similarly, disagreement exists on the unemployment effect of EPL, which some assert increases unemployment by elevating the cost of hiring and firing workers, and others claim decreases unemployment by reducing layoffs (e.g., due to procedural costs of dismissal) (Avdagic 2015; Heimberger 2021).

Third, supporters of the 'institutional' or 'pro-regularly' approach claim that strong union organizations and/or centralized collective bargaining institutions reduce unemployment, while promoters of the 'deregulatory' approach take the opposite perspective and argue they increase unemployment (Baccaro and Rei 2007; Avdagic and Salardi 2013).[18] In the former case, the encompassing nature of union organizations and employers' associations (often with the participation of the government) facilitate the ability of workers, employers, and government leaders to 'internalize externalities' and thus adopt compensation, employment, and welfare state policies that benefit the aggregate economy, not only those economic actors involved in the collective bargaining process (Garret and Way 1999; Kenworthy 2002; Bassanini and Duval 2009). In the latter case, strong unions artificially elevate the cost of labour for employers and thus result in higher overall unemployment (Siebert 1997). Furthermore, a substantial amount of research—including in the VOC literature—has indicated that the effect of collective bargaining on unemployment is determined by numerous contextual factors, including type of welfare state policies, the extent of globalization, the establishment of the Eurozone, and the size of the public sector fiscal burden, as well as

---

[18] Calmfors and Driffill (1988) propose that highly centralized and decentralized collective bargaining systems perform best regarding unemployment, while moderately centralized systems perform the worst. In short, the argument is that highly centralized systems allow labour unions and employer associations to 'internalize externalities' and thus adopt policies that benefit the aggregate economy, while decentralized systems have relatively fragmented and weak labour unions that have little effect on national level unemployment. By contrast, moderately centralized systems have strong enough labour unions to elevate the cost of doing business, but not enough coordination to ensure that policies adopted will provide benefits to those excluded from the collective bargaining process.

country-specific wage bargaining rules and the economic sectors dominant in the collective bargaining process (Hall and Franzese 1998; Garrett and Way 1999; Traxler and Kittel 2000; Mares 2006; Bassanini and Duval 2009; Biegert 2017).

In Figure 6.2, we provide the average level of the unemployment ratio by year between 1989 and 2019 across the same 16 countries included in Table 6.1. The figure informs us that the average unemployment ratio in these countries followed a U-shaped pattern during the years covered, with relatively high levels of the measure from 1989 to 1992 and between 2008 to 2019, but relatively low levels in the late 1990s and mid-2000s. Overall, the unemployment ratio declines from a high of about 2.1 in 1989 to a low of about 1.7 in 2003 (a decrease of ~19 per cent), before rising to over 2 in 2010 (an increase of ~18 per cent) and then stabilizing at about 1.9 from 2013 to 2019. Taken together, this suggests that unemployment inequality between those without and with a college degree declined throughout much of the 1990s and mid-2000s but has since risen to levels comparable to the late 1980s and early 1990s.

Despite relatively persistent differences in unemployment across Western European countries, there have been several distinct periods of high, rising, or declining unemployment across the continent in recent decades, each

Figure 6.2 Unemployment inequality between people with tertiary education and those without it, 1989–2019

Note: The numbers indicate the ratios of the unemployment rate of people without tertiary education to that of people with tertiary education.

Source: OECD, Unemployment Rate Indicator.

explained by different phenomena. In the 1970s and 1980s, elevated levels of unemployment—even during times of economic growth—led to the coining of the term 'Eurosclerosis', a description meant to convey not only the poor employment performance in Europe compared to the United States and Japan, but also the excessive labour market regulations and welfare state policies that were claimed to have been at the root of the divergence (Giersch 1985).

From the mid-1990s until the late 2000s, Western European countries experienced a consistent decline in unemployment, resulting in a more than 25 per cent reduction in the unemployment rate of the original 12 EU countries during this period (with no such decline observed in the United States or Japan) (Boeri and Garibaldi 2009). The most prominent explanations for this decline have been the 'disincentive' and 'deregulatory' theories outlined above, or that welfare state retrenchment, fewer workers covered by collective bargaining contracts, and the decentralization of collective bargaining during this period reduced the reservation wage for workers and the cost to employers of hiring and firing workers (Regini 2003; Layard, Nickell, and Jackman 2005; Boeri and Garibaldi 2009). However, as the debate between these approaches and those of the 'job search subsidy' and 'institutional' perspectives indicate, this explanation is far from universally accepted, with others emphasizing different factors, such as increasing European integration; European countries catching up to the United States in terms of service-sector job creation (as well as agricultural and industrial job loss); 'flexicurity' arrangements, whereby government reforms improve labour market 'flexibility' but also maintain somewhat generous social insurance policies to provide 'security' against those experiencing (increased) labour market risk (Viebrock and Clasen 2009); or, similarly, 'workfare' arrangements, whereby greater labour market flexibility is accompanied by more generous ALMPs, which are meant to improve (potential) workers' ability to acquire a (good paying) job (Rueda 2015).

During the European Debt Crisis (2009 to the mid-2010s), European countries again experienced a substantial rise in unemployment, with the largest increases in European periphery countries at the centre of the crisis, such as Greece, Italy, and Spain. Broadly, the crisis was brought about by a 'sudden stop' of international investments to Eurozone countries, triggered by the financial fallout from the subprime mortgage crisis in the United States and the public admission by Greece that they had been concealing the extent of their sovereign debt (Copelovitch, Frieden, and Walter 2016). The crisis finally started to ebb largely due to the historic efforts of the European Central Bank, which reduced interest rates close to zero and purchased trillions of euros worth of government bonds through 'quantitative easing' (Gabor 2014; Mody and Nedeljkovic 2024).[19]

Finally, since the mid-2010s, unemployment has declined to various degrees across Western Europe, with this trend largely continuing even during the depths of the COVID-19 pandemic (Béland, Cantillon, Hick, and Moreira 2021).[20]

Economic Inequality and Working-Class Support for the Populist Radical Right

Since higher levels of wage and unemployment inequality imply that the working class is in a relatively weak economic position, we expect higher levels of wage and unemployment inequality to strengthen blue-collar workers' national identity and the salience they place on cultural issues, and therefore also their support for the populist radical right. We test these relationships in this sub-section with three sets of survey data: the ISSP (2003), the EVS (2008, 2017), and the EES (2009, 2014).

First, we test the direct effects of wage inequality and unemployment inequality on PRRP support by utilizing logistic and ordered logistic regression models. Results on the effects of wage inequality are reported in Table 6.3. Models 1 and 2 employ the ISSP, Models 3 and 4 employ the EVS, and Models 5 and 6 employ the EES.[21] Models 1, 3, and 5 include the basic list of populist radical right-wing parties and Models 2, 4, and 6 add 'borderline' populist radical right-wing parties listed in Chapter 2.

The results suggest that greater wage inequality between blue- and white-collar workers strengthens working-class support for the populist radical right. The coefficient of the wage inequality variable has a positive sign and is statistically significant in five of the six models. Furthermore, the substantive size of the effect is large across all the basic models, although the magnitude differs based on the type of survey data used. The largest effect is found in the model that utilizes the ISSP (Model 1), which finds that as the wage

---

[19] Evidence is mixed regarding whether EU and International Monetary Fund bailouts helped resolve the crisis, as they provided hundreds of billions of Euros in emergency funds to Eurozone governments, but also conditioned their dispersion on 'austerity' policies that likely exacerbated and prolonged the crisis (Dosi, Pereira, Roventini, and Virgillito 2019).

[20] During the pandemic, most European countries adopted or substantially increased subsidies to businesses to allow them to maintain their existing workforce. This is in contrast to the United States, which, instead of supporting businesses directly, substantially increased the generosity and duration of unemployment benefits (in addition to providing regular 'stimulus' checks to individuals and households) (Béland, Cantillon, Hick, and Moreira 2021).

[21] Since the wage data is available only from 2006, the 1990 and 1999 EVS waves are excluded from Models 3 and 4.

Policy Outcomes   155

Table 6.3 Wage inequality and manual workers' support for the populist radical right

Data	(1) ISSP	(2)	(3) EVS	(4)	(5) EES	(6)
Populist radical right parties	Basic	All	Basic	All	Basic	All
Wage inequality	2.47**	1.81**	3.58*	1.16	1.74**	1.82**
	(1.11)	(0.85)	(1.87)	(1.51)	(0.77)	(0.79)
Female	−0.39	−0.31	−0.34**	−0.49***	−0.35***	−0.34***
	(0.28)	(0.23)	(0.14)	(0.12)	(0.10)	(0.09)
Age	−0.01	−0.02**	−0.00	−0.01**	−0.01***	−0.01***
	(0.01)	(0.01)	(0.00)	(0.00)	(0.00)	(0.00)
Education	−0.26**	−0.34**	−0.14	−0.07	−0.25***	−0.24***
	(0.13)	(0.14)	(0.21)	(0.17)	(0.09)	(0.09)
Political ideology (right)	3.73**	3.29**	0.43***	0.42***	0.24***	0.24***
	(1.65)	(1.30)	(0.04)	(0.04)	(0.03)	(0.03)
Number of political parties	3.49***	2.61***	0.15	0.23**	0.11*	0.08
	(0.88)	(0.82)	(0.12)	(0.10)	(0.06)	(0.06)
Unemployment rate	−0.97***	−0.44	−0.13	−0.19**	−0.07***	−0.07***
	(0.30)	(0.45)	(0.12)	(0.10)	(0.02)	(0.02)
Immigration	2.54***	1.78**	0.15***	0.08***	−0.14***	−0.14***
	(0.88)	(0.78)	(0.04)	(0.03)	(0.02)	(0.02)
Social spending	0.88***	0.37	0.15**	0.07	−0.01	−0.01
	(0.32)	(0.37)	(0.07)	(0.04)	(0.03)	(0.03)
Constant	−81.48***	−55.44**	−13.08***	−7.52***		
	(28.72)	(23.87)	(2.80)	(2.21)		
−2 x Log likelihood	178.3	218.2	3,725.4	4,634.2	8,110.4	8,293.4
Number of observations	1,405	1,405	7,498	7,498	2,254	2,307

Note: Logistic regression with clustered standard errors (by country/year) is used in Models 1 to 4. Ordered logistic regression with clustered standard errors (by country/year) is used in Models 5 and 6. Clustered standard errors are in parentheses. Results on cut-points are not reported in Models 5 and 6.
***$p < 0.01$, **$p < 0.05$, *$p < 0.1$.
Source: ISSP (2003), EVS (2008, 2017), and EES (2009, 2014).

inequality variable changes from its 10th percentile value to its 90th percentile value, blue collar workers' probability of voting for a PRRP increases from 0.01 to 0.05. Smaller but similar effects are found in the models utilizing the EVS (Model 3) and the EES (Model 5). In the former, a change in the wage inequality from its 10th to 90th percentile value raises the probability that a blue-collar worker will support a PRRP from 0.04 to 0.12, while in the latter it increases the probability that a blue-collar worker is 'very probable to vote' for a PRRP (i.e., the dependent variable = 10) from 0.04 to 0.08 and decreases the probability they are 'not at all' likely to vote for a PRRP (i.e., the dependent variable = 0) from 0.56 to 0.39.[22]

In Table 6.4, we report the results of the models examining the effects of unemployment inequality between those without and with a college degree on working-class support for the populist radical right. The models included are identical to those in Table 6.3, but with the unemployment inequality variable replacing the wage inequality variable. The results imply that unemployment inequality between those without and with a college degree strengthens blue-collar workers' support for the populist radical right, although the results are not as robust as those for wage inequality. As anticipated by our theory, the coefficient for the unemployment inequality is positive in five of the six models (the lone exception being Model 3), with it reaching statistical significance in three of the models, including two of the 'basic' versions (Models 1 and 5). The calculation of predicted probabilities suggests that the substantive size of the effects is smaller in Model 1 (which utilizes the ISSP) and larger in Model 5 (which utilizes the EES) than the comparable models with the wage inequality reported in Table 6.3. In Model 1, a change in the unemployment inequality measure from its 10th percentile value (1.4) to its 90th percentile value (2.8) increases blue-collar workers' probability of supporting the populist radical right from 0.01 to 0.02 (a rise of 100 per cent). In Model 5, the same change in the unemployment inequality measure decreases the probability that blue-collar workers are 'not at all' likely to vote for the populist radical right from 0.6 to 0.36 (a decline of 40 per cent) and increases the probability that blue-collar workers are 'very probable to vote' for the populist radical right from 0.04 to 0.1 (a rise of 150 per cent).[23]

Mediation Effects of Economic Inequality

Taken together, the above models provide strong evidence that wage inequality between blue- and white-collar workers increases working-class support for the populist radical right, and more modest evidence that unemployment inequality between those without and with a college degree does the same. To determine whether at least some of these effects go through blue-collar workers' national identity and the issues they find most salient, we again apply

---

[22] All the other variables are fixed at their mean values when a predicted probability is calculated.
[23] All the other variables are fixed at their mean values when a predicted probability is calculated.

Policy Outcomes 157

Table 6.4 Unemployment inequality and manual workers' support for the populist radical right

	(1)	(2)	(3)	(4)	(5)	(6)
Data	ISSP		EVS		EES	
Populist radical right parties	Basic	All	Basic	All	Basic	All
Unemployment inequality	2.96***	4.06***	−0.56	0.05	0.64**	0.34
	(0.72)	(1.18)	(0.68)	(0.46)	(0.31)	(0.57)
Female	−0.28	−0.29**	−0.53***	−0.68***	−0.34***	−0.30**
	(0.20)	(0.15)	(0.13)	(0.12)	(0.09)	(0.12)
Age	−0.01	−0.02**	−0.00	−0.01	−0.01***	−0.02***
	(0.01)	(0.01)	(0.01)	(0.01)	(0.00)	(0.01)
Education	−0.23	−0.28	−0.63***	−0.10	−0.29***	−0.39***
	(0.17)	(0.18)	(0.23)	(0.16)	(0.09)	(0.11)
Political ideology (right)	3.28***	3.21***	0.39***	0.39***	0.24***	0.26***
	(1.27)	(1.19)	(0.04)	(0.04)	(0.03)	(0.04)
Number of political parties	1.13**	0.26	0.19**	0.16*	−0.02	0.01
	(0.56)	(0.32)	(0.08)	(0.09)	(0.07)	(0.08)
Unemployment rate	−0.93**	−0.11	−0.06	−0.15**	−0.06	−0.22**
	(0.41)	(0.36)	(0.09)	(0.07)	(0.04)	(0.09)
Immigration	0.36***	0.13	0.23***	0.08*	−0.16***	−0.09
	(0.14)	(0.11)	(0.04)	(0.05)	(0.06)	(0.09)
Social spending	0.64**	0.12	0.19***	0.06	−0.02	0.06
	(0.27)	(0.23)	(0.07)	(0.05)	(0.03)	(0.04)
Constant	−38.19***	−25.24***	−11.45***	−6.33***		
	(12.45)	(7.87)	(2.13)	(1.76)		
−2 x Log likelihood	213.2	234.3	6,815.5	10,283.9	8,095.6	8,282.4
Number of observations	1,543	1,543	27,976	27,976	1,724	2,310

Note: Logistic regression with clustered standard errors (by country/year) is used in Models 1 to 4. Ordered logistic regression with clustered standard errors (by country/year) is used in Models 5 and 6. Clustered standard errors are in parentheses. Results on cut-points are not reported in Models 5 and 6. ***p < 0.01 **p < 0.05 *p < 0.1.

Source: ISSP (2003), EVS (1990, 1999, 2008, 2017), and EES (2009, 2014).

the causal mediation analysis model developed by Imai, Keele, Tingley, and Yamamato (2011). As we discussed in Chapter 1 and noted in the previous two chapters, we test the mediation effect of national identity with the ISSP, the mediation effect of national pride with the EVS, and the mediation effect of issue salience with the EES. We also examine how the effects of wage and

158 Social Identity and Working Class Support for the Populist Radical Right

unemployment inequality are mediated through blue-collar workers' economic grievances (opinion of imports) with the ISSP and political discontent (trust in the national parliament) with the EES.[24] Table 6.5 reports the results for the models with the wage inequality and Table 6.6 reports the results for the models with the unemployment inequality.

The results reported in Table 6.5 inform us that the effect of wage inequality on working-class support for the populist radical right is substantially mediated by blue-collar workers' national identity, national pride, and the issues they find most salient, with the ACMEs of our main mediators statistically significant in all three models. In Model 1 (which utilizes the ISSP), a change in national identity explains 9.2 per cent of the wage inequality effect; in Model 2 (which utilizes the EVS), a change in national pride explains 5.2 per cent of the wage inequality effect; and in Model 3 (which utilizes the EES), a change in what issues blue-collar workers' find most salient explains 15.8 per cent of the total wage inequality effect. Regarding the other mediators included in the table, consistent with results in previous chapters, while opinion regarding imports is not found to have a significant role in mediating the wage inequality effect, trust in the national parliament is (in Models 1 and 3, respectively).

The results reported in Table 6.6 inform us that the unemployment inequality effect on working-class support for the populist radical right is also mediated by blue-collar workers' identity and the issues they find most salient, but not by their national pride. In Model 1 (which utilizes the ISSP), a change in national identity explains 9.2 per cent of the unemployment inequality effect; and in Model 3 (which utilizes the EES), a change in what issues blue-collar workers find most salient explains 5.2 per cent of the total unemployment inequality effect. Consistent with previous results, the mediation effect of blue-collar workers' opinion regarding imports is not significant. However, unlike previous results, the mediation effect of blue-collar workers' trust in the national parliament turned out to be statistically insignificant as well.[25]

In summary, we find that wage inequality and unemployment inequality—measured in such a way to ascertain differences between blue- and white-collar workers—strengthen working-class support for the populist radical right. Consistent with our social identity theory, the results of our causal

---

[24] Results on the first-stage models are reported in the appendix.

[25] Consistent with previous chapters, the ACME remains statistically significant at the 0.95 level as long as the sensitivity parameter *rho* is below 0.2–0.4 in the analyses in Tables 6.5 and 6.6. Also, an omitted confounder, if there is any, would have to explain at least 20 per cent (EES)–40 per cent (ISSP) of the remaining variance in each mediator and outcome variable for the ACME to be zero.

Policy Outcomes 159

Table 6.5 Wage inequality and manual workers' support for the populist radical right (Mediation Model)

Data	(1) ISSP	(2) EVS	(3) EES
The treatment (policy outcomes)			
Wage inequality	1.84**	2.49***	1.70*
	(0.90)	(0.65)	(0.99)
Mediators			
National identity	1.91***		
	(0.54)		
National pride		0.90***	
		(0.13)	
Issue Salience (immigration/multiculturalism)			1.58***
			(0.21)
Opinion on import	−0.04		
	(0.23)		
Trust in parliament			−0.71***
			(0.15)
Control variables			
Female	−0.69	−0.41***	−0.59***
	(0.50)	(0.12)	(0.15)
Age	−0.03*	−0.01*	−0.02***
	(0.02)	(0.00)	(0.00)
Education	−0.16	−0.20	−0.31***
	(0.21)	(0.13)	(0.11)
Political ideology (right)	3.68***	0.39***	0.39***
	(0.47)	(0.02)	(0.03)
Number of political parties	4.06***	0.13***	0.22***
	(0.63)	(0.03)	(0.05)
Unemployment rate	−1.01***	−0.14***	−0.12***
	(0.34)	(0.02)	(0.02)
Immigration	2.67***	0.09***	−0.24***
	(0.63)	(0.02)	(0.03)
Social spending	0.78**	0.21***	−0.01
	(0.34)	(0.02)	(0.02)
Constant	−81.32***	−12.74***	5.00***
	(17.95)	(0.79)	(0.98)

Continued

160 Social Identity and Working Class Support for the Populist Radical Right

Table 6.5 *Continued*

Data	(1) ISSP		(2) EVS	(3) EES	
Treatment: Wage inequality					
Mediator	National identity	Opinion on import	National pride	Issue salience	Trust in parlia-ment
Direct effect	0.20***	0.21***	0.07***	1.68	1.68
ACME	0.02***	0.00	0.00***	0.33***	−0.23***
Total effect	0.22***	0.21	0.08***	2.01***	1.45
Number of observations	1,280		6,804	2,119	
−2 x Log likelihood	146.6		3,106.6		
R-squared				0.18	

Note: The mediation Stata package is used. Standard errors are in parentheses.***$p < 0.01$, **$p < 0.05$, *$p < 0.1$.

Source: ISSP (2003), EVS (2008 and 2017), and EES (2009 and 2014)

mediation analysis models informed us that a substantial share of the wage and unemployment inequality effects is driven by how these policy outcomes alter blue-collar workers' social identity and the issues they find most salient. More specifically, greater wage inequality and unemployment inequality between white- and blue-collar workers increases working-class support for the populist radical right by strengthening nationalism and the salience of immigration-related issues among the working class.

Economic Inequality and the Skill Divide between Blue-Collar Workers

Although most formulations of PRT assume that blue-collar workers are relatively monolithic in terms of their labour market experience and therefore also their policy and partisan preferences (Korpi 1985; Rueda and Pontusson 2000; Ahlquist 2017), scholars in other theoretical traditions have long recognized that such a categorization of the working class is overly simplistic (e.g., see Rueda 2005; Cusack, Iversen, and Rehm 2006; Thelen and Martin 2007; and O'Donnell, Adshead, and Thomas 2011). As we discussed in Chapters 4 and 5, there are strong theoretical and empirical reasons to suspect divergent interests and preferences among union and non-union blue-collar workers

Policy Outcomes 161

Table 6.6 Unemployment inequality and manual workers' support for the populist radical right (Mediation Model)

Data	(1) ISSP	(2) EVS	(3) EES
The treatment (policy outcomes)			
Unemployment inequality	5.40***	0.03	0.79***
	(1.80)	(0.06)	(0.24)
Mediators			
National identity	1.69***		
	(0.47)		
National pride		0.88***	
		(0.07)	
Issue Salience (immigration/multiculturalism)			1.10***
			(0.21)
Opinion on import	−0.20		
	(0.19)		
Trust in parliament			−0.79***
			(0.14)
Control variables			
Female	−0.22	−0.67***	−0.54***
	(0.43)	(0.07)	(0.15)
Age	−0.01	−0.01***	−0.03***
	(0.01)	(0.00)	(0.00)
Education	−0.35*	0.01	−0.39***
	(0.19)	(0.07)	(0.10)
Political ideology (right)	2.96***	0.37***	0.38***
	(0.36)	(0.01)	(0.03)
Number of political parties	−0.25	0.15***	−0.00
	(1.07)	(0.02)	(0.05)
Unemployment rate	−1.21**	−0.15***	−0.12***
	(0.57)	(0.01)	(0.03)
Immigration	0.59**	0.09***	−0.26***
	(0.25)	(0.01)	(0.03)
Social spending	0.98**	0.06***	−0.02
	(0.47)	(0.01)	(0.02)
Constant	−45.31***	−6.24***	6.52***
	(10.71)	(0.27)	(0.81)

Continued

162 Social Identity and Working Class Support for the Populist Radical Right

Table 6.6 *Continued*

Data	(1) ISSP		(2) EVS	(3) EES	
Treatment: Unemployment inequality					
Mediator	National identity	Opinion on import	National pride	Issue salience	Trust in parliament
Direct effect	0.0038***	0.0038***	0.0010	0.78***	0.78***
ACME	0.0002**	−0.0001	−0.0001	0.04**	−0.05
Total effect	0.0040***	0.0037***	0.0009	0.83***	0.73***
Number of observations	1,321		27,482	2,255	
−2 x Log likelihood	166.5		6,477.0		
R-squared				0.19	

Note: The mediation Stata package is used. Standard errors are in parentheses. ***p < 0.01, **p < 0.05, *p < 0.1.

Source: ISSP (2003), EVS (1990, 1999, 2008, and 2017), and EES (2009 and 2014)

(regarding the social pact formation process) and working-class economic 'insiders' and 'outsiders' (regarding LMPs and EPL). Here, we argue that the skill profile of blue-collar workers affects how these actors respond to changes in wage and unemployment inequality, with our focus on such inequalities within the working class rather than between economic classes.

A substantial amount of micro-level research has demonstrated that 'highly skilled' and 'less skilled' blue-collar workers have divergent policy and partisan preferences, with these largely explained by the greater compensation and job security of the former compared to the latter.[26] As we noted above, less skilled blue-collar workers are generally near the bottom of the wage and income distributions, while their more highly skilled counterparts are typically closer to the middle (Goedemé, Paskov, Weissstanner, and Nolan 2021); and unemployment incidence falls as skill or education level rises. For instance, in the analysis by Requena (2023) of 2021 Eurostat survey

---

[26] The existing literature on the causes and consequences of workers' skill levels generally defines 'skills' in terms of the actual qualifications or applied knowledge of workers gained through education/training; the ability required to complete a specific type of job; or, more ambiguously, how a particular socio-cultural context can lead some workers or jobs to be labelled more or less 'skilled', regardless of the objective abilities of these workers or the actual characteristics of the work performed (Warhurst, Tilly, and Gatta 2017). Here, we are utilizing the first and second definition of 'skill', as we are concerned about both the current job status and earnings profile of blue-collar workers (encapsulated in the first definition) and the economic opportunities available to blue-collar workers (captured by the second definition).

data for 10 EU countries, the author found that the unemployment rate for 'semi-/non-skilled' manual workers was nearly twice as high as that for 'skilled' manual workers (10.4 per cent compared to 5.5 per cent).

Given the different labour market experiences of more and less skilled members of the working class, it is unsurprising that existing research has largely shown that those with lower skill levels favour greater wage compression, more generous social insurance policies, and stronger redistributive efforts by the government than their more highly skilled counterparts (Hall and Thelen 2007; Nijhuis 2009; Iversen and Soskice 2010; Han and Castater 2016). Broadly, such findings are explained as resulting from the narrow self-interest of these workers. Since less skilled blue-collar workers earn less compensation and are at greater risk of unemployment than more skilled blue-collar workers (due to the highly 'substitutable' nature of their labour), the former are also likelier to support those conditions, policies, and government actions that imply a net benefit for those in more vulnerable labour market conditions.

In addition to the inherently more insecure labour market position of less skilled workers, socio-economic phenomena associated with technological change, globalization, and organized labour have further eroded the relative market power of these workers in recent decades. First, technological innovations have led to the introduction of new computers and automated equipment into manufacturing processes and thus increased the relative demand for workers who possess the skills to operate and manage these computers and equipment (Berman, Bound, and Machin 1998).[27]

Second, greater international trade and, relatedly, offshoring have reduced the demand for less skilled members of the working class. Theories of international economics, such as Ricardo's theory of comparative advantage and the Heckscher-Ohlin theory, explain why less skilled blue-collar jobs in wealthy countries are replaced by imports from industrializing (or newly industrialized) countries, most of which have a comparative advantage in less skilled labour. By contrast, highly skilled workers in wealthy democracies can take advantage of technological change, as such countries invest heavily in research and development and have social policies that enlarge educational opportunities (Bartel and

---

[27] Some scholars have argued against the claim that technological change has a 'bias' against the less skilled (e.g., see Flynn 1988; Bogliacino and Lucchese 2016). Nonetheless, many empirical studies, including those that employ a natural experiment approach (e.g., Fernandez 2001), a cross-country comparative approach (e.g., Berman and Machin 2000), and a cross-sector approach (e.g., Haskel and Slaughter 2002) confirm the skill-biased technological change hypothesis: technological advancements in the workplace have worsened the economic status of less skilled workers relative to more skilled workers.

Lichtenberg 1987; Sachs and Shatz 1996).[28] Offshoring—or multinational corporations moving production of goods or services to the same enterprise or a non-affiliated enterprise in a foreign country—also diminishes the relative demand of less skilled blue-collar workers, as companies can more easily offshore those processes that can be performed by those with modest skill levels (Geishecker and Görg 2005; Keuschnigg and Ribi 2009).

Third, de-unionization and the decline of centralized collective bargaining institutions have particularly harmed less skilled blue-collar workers (Card and DiNardo 2002). Technological change, greater import competition from international trade, and offshoring have led to greater loss of union jobs among those with fewer skills and lower incomes, leading to national labour movements with more highly skilled and well-paid members than in the past (Pontusson 2013; Han and Castater 2016). Thus, benefits and labour protections provided by unions are increasingly reserved for the highly skilled and those in more sheltered sectors of the economy (Garrett and Way 1999; Mosimann and Pontusson 2022).

The relatively vulnerable labour market position of less skilled blue-collar workers compared to more skilled blue-collar workers and the concurrent trends of technological change, globalization, and union decline suggest rising inequality not only between blue- and white-collar workers, but also between blue-collar workers of different skill levels. To examine whether this intuition has empirical support, we present data on the earnings of blue-collar workers by skill level and unemployment by level of formal education. First, in Figure 6.3, we utilize Eurostat data to present the average ratio of earnings between more and less skilled blue-collar workers from 2006 to 2018 in the 16 countries analysed here. The data inform us that wage inequality between these workers has risen during the period analysed, with highly skilled blue-collar workers' earning the equivalent of about 126 per cent of that of less skilled blue-collar workers in 2018, an increase of about 6 percentage points since 2006.

To the best of our knowledge, there is no consistent cross-national and over-time data on the unemployment rates between blue-collar workers with different skill levels. However, the OECD provides data that allows us to construct an unemployment rate ratio between those with upper secondary (but not tertiary) education and no upper-secondary education. Given the positive correlation between formal education and skill level,[29] we assume that

---

[28] Nonetheless, there is disagreement regarding whether international trade has widened the income gap between those workers with more and less skills (e.g., Krugman and Lawrence 1993; Wood 1995).

[29] For instance, in the ISSP (2003), 76 per cent of less skilled blue-collar workers did not finish upper-secondary education compared to 63 per cent of more highly skilled blue-collar workers. Furthermore,

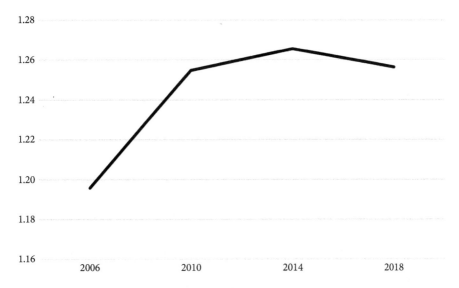

Figure 6.3 Wage inequality between more skilled and less skilled blue-collar workers, 2006–18
Note: The numbers indicate the ratios of average earnings of highly skilled blue-collar workers to those of less skilled blue-collar workers by country from 2006 to 2018.
Source: Eurostat, Structure of Earnings Survey: Annual Earnings.

this ratio is reflective of the relative market position of less and more skilled blue-collar workers. Figure 6.4 presents the average of this unemployment rate ratio from 1989 to 2019 for the 16 countries in our analysis. The figure demonstrates that unemployment inequality between those with some and no upper secondary education has generally risen since the 1990s, so that in 2019 it was near its highest for the period. In 1994 and 1999, the unemployment rate ratio fell to its lowest point, just below 1.4. By 2018 and 2019 (the last two years presented in the graph), the ratio stood at about 1.7, an increase of nearly 25 per cent.

Thus far, we have considered how our social identity theory applies to inequality between blue- and white-collar workers. However, persistent and rising inequality within the working class suggests that intra-class inequality may matter as well. If it does, then our social identity theory would anticipate rising inequality within the working class to lead to divergent partisan preferences among less and more skilled workers, with the former becoming even more likely to support PRRPs than previously.

---

the Pearson's chi-squared test informs us that blue-collar workers' skill level (whether they are more or less skilled) and educational attainment (whether they completed upper-secondary education) are statistically correlated at the 0.01 level (p = 0.0000).

Figure 6.4 Unemployment inequality between people with upper-secondary education (without tertiary education) and those without upper-secondary education, 1989–2019

Note: The numbers indicate the ratios of the unemployment rate of people without upper-secondary education to that of those with upper-secondary (but no tertiary) education.
Source: OECD, Unemployment Rate Indicator.

To test whether this intuition has empirical validity, we utilize logistic and ordered regression models identical to those presented in Tables 6.3 and 6.4, but that include two interaction terms, each consisting of a dummy variable for less skilled blue-collar workers.[30] One interaction term includes the wage inequality between less and more skilled blue-collar workers, while the other the unemployment rate inequality between those with some and no upper secondary education. As with the models above, Models 1 and 2 employ the ISSP, Models 3 and 4 employ the EVS, and Models 5 and 6 employ the EES. Models 1, 3, and 5 include the interaction term of skill level and wage inequality and Models 2, 4, and 6 employ the interaction term of skill level and unemployment inequality. The results of the models are reported in Table 6.7 and comport, though not very strongly, with our expectations. The coefficients of the interaction terms have an expected, positive, sign in all the models, but they are statistically significant in four out of six models. The results imply that rising wage inequality among blue-collar workers and

---

[30] In the EVS and EES, 'unskilled manual workers' are categorized as less skilled workers, and 'plant and machine operators and assemblers' are categorized as less skilled workers in the ISSP.

rising unemployment inequality between those with some and no upper secondary increase the likelihood of supporting a PRRP particularly among less skilled blue-collar workers.

The divergent effects of wage inequality and unemployment inequality on more and less skilled blue-collar workers are graphically presented in Figure 6.5. The vertical axes of the graphs indicate the conditional coefficients and their confidence intervals, with findings for wage inequality presented in the top three graphs and that for the unemployment inequality presented in the bottom three graphs. The small circles indicate the conditional coefficients when all the variables in the model are held at their mean level, with the confidence intervals represented by the lines extending from the circles. Though the interaction terms of inequality and less skilled worker are statistically significant in four out of six models in Table 6.7, the substantive meaning of the interactive effect seems to be not very large in many models. The top three graphs demonstrate that the working-class wage inequality effect is statistically significant (ISSP) or insignificant (EVS) among both highly skilled and less skilled workers.[31] Wage inequality shows different effects between highly skilled and less skilled workers only in the last model (EES): working-class wage inequality increases less skilled blue-collar workers' support for PRRPs, but does not modify party support of highly skilled blue-collar workers. Two of the three bottom graphs (those employing the EVS and the EES) inform us that while unemployment inequality increases less skilled blue-collar workers' support for PRRPs, it does not change highly skilled blue-collar workers' support for these parties. However, such an interactive effect is not clearly observed in the first model (that uses the ISSP).

Our results, combined with rising inequality within the working class in recent decades, suggest that PRRPs have attracted greater electoral support among less skilled blue-collar workers than more skilled blue-collar workers. This implication is borne out by the survey data utilized in this analysis, with EVS informing us that less skilled blue-collar workers' share of PRRP support grew from 19.5 per cent to 23.8 per cent between 1990 and 2017, while that of highly skilled blue-collar workers declined from 13.4 per cent to 3.4 per cent during that period. Thus, while less skilled blue-collar workers were 1.4 times more likely to be a supporter of a PRRP in 1990, they were about seven times more likely in 2017. A further discussion of these findings will be

---

[31] Though the wage inequality effects are statistically insignificant among both highly skilled and less skilled workers in the EVS models at the 0.05 level, both of them are statistically significant at the 0.10 level in the models.

168 Social Identity and Working Class Support for the Populist Radical Right

Table 6.7 Skill level and inequality effects on party support

Data	(1) ISSP	(2)	(3) EVS	(4)	(5) EES	(6)
Less skilled worker	0.93***	0.11	0.19	0.11	0.59*	−0.45
	(0.23)	(0.09)	(0.19)	(0.19)	(0.34)	(0.29)
Wage inequality	2.36**		3.18*		1.09	
	(1.11)		(1.79)		(0.83)	
Less skilled worker x Wage inequality	0.29***		0.49		1.46**	
	(0.07)		(1.59)		(0.73)	
Unemployment inequality		3.12***		0.42		0.35*
		(0.78)		(0.40)		(0.18)
Less skilled worker x Unemployment inequality		0.14		0.67**		0.23*
		(0.14)		(0.32)		(0.14)
Female	−0.38	−0.31	−0.27***	−0.44***	−0.35***	−0.37***
	(0.29)	(0.22)	(0.10)	(0.11)	(0.09)	(0.08)
Age	−0.02*	−0.01*	−0.01**	−0.01	−0.01***	−0.01***
	(0.01)	(0.01)	(0.00)	(0.00)	(0.00)	(0.00)
Education	−0.26**	−0.23	−0.20	−0.71***	−0.28***	−0.29***
	(0.13)	(0.15)	(0.15)	(0.16)	(0.09)	(0.09)
Political ideology (right)	3.71**	3.27***	0.41***	0.40***	0.25***	0.25***
	(1.64)	(1.25)	(0.04)	(0.04)	(0.03)	(0.03)
Number of political parties	3.51***	1.12**	0.16	0.33***	0.10	0.08
	(0.88)	(0.57)	(0.13)	(0.07)	(0.06)	(0.05)
Unemployment rate	−0.97***	−0.91**	−0.13	−0.07	−0.07***	−0.05***
	(0.30)	(0.43)	(0.11)	(0.07)	(0.02)	(0.02)
Immigration	2.53***	0.36***	0.14***	0.20***	−0.14***	−0.14***
	(0.88)	(0.14)	(0.04)	(0.03)	(0.03)	(0.03)
Social spending	0.88***	0.64**	0.13*	0.17***	−0.01	−0.01
	(0.32)	(0.27)	(0.07)	(0.05)	(0.03)	(0.02)
Constant	−56.96***	−38.34***	−8.78***	−11.65***		
	(17.69)	(12.43)	(2.00)	(1.64)		
−2 x Log likelihood	177.9	212.7	3,714.1	6,755.1	7,818.4	7,804.9
Number of observations	1,405	1,430	9,545	29,849	2,192	2,192

Note: Logistic regression with clustered standard errors (by country/year) is used in Models 1 to 4. Ordered logistic regression with clustered standard errors (by country/year) is used in Models 5 and 6. Clustered standard errors are in parentheses. Results on cut-points are not reported in Models 5 and 6. ***$p < 0.01$, **$p < 0.05$, *$p < 0.1$.

Source: ISSP (2003), EVS (1990, 1999, 2008, 2017 in Model 3; 2008 and 2017 in Model 4), and EES (2009, 2014)

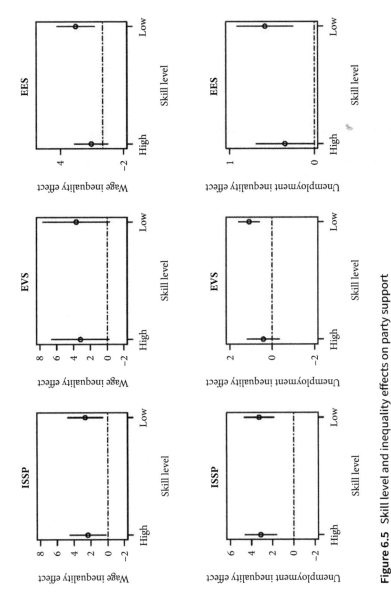

Figure 6.5 Skill level and inequality effects on party support

Note: Circles indicate the coefficients of the wage inequality variable or the unemployment inequality variable, and lines indicate their confidence intervals.

provided in the following chapter, including what implications greater relative support for PRRPs among less educated blue-collar workers has for the policies promoted by PRRPs.

Conclusion and Discussion

Since the mid-2000s, Western European countries have experienced a rise in both wage inequality and unemployment inequality among blue- and white-collar workers, likely resulting from the effects of the European Debt Crisis and the (neo-liberal) policy reforms adopted in response to it. After examining the processes by which such reforms were enacted in Chapter 4 and actual government policy outputs in Chapter 5, here we examined whether policy outcomes relating to wage and unemployment inequality between blue- and white-collar workers matter for working-class support for PRRPs. We argued theoretically and found empirically that greater wage inequality and unemployment inequality between blue- and white-collar workers increase working-class support for the populist radical right at least partially by strengthening these workers' national identity and thus also the salience they place on cultural issues relative to economic issues.

After our initial analysis, we also assessed whether wage inequality and unemployment inequality have divergent effects on working-class support for PRRPs based on the skill level of blue-collar workers. Given the divergent preferences regarding wages and welfare state policies among blue-collar workers with different skill levels and that technological changes and economic globalization have harmed the economic standing of less skilled blue-collar workers more than highly skilled blue-collar workers, we argued that wage and unemployment inequality matter more for the PRRP support of the former than the latter. The results of our empirical analysis confirmed our expectations: higher wage inequality and unemployment inequality have a greater effect on the PRRP support of less-skilled blue-collar workers than more highly skilled blue-collar workers. In other words, wage inequality and unemployment inequality among blue- and white-collar workers primarily affect the PRRP support of manual workers via less-skilled members of the working class.

Our results appear in conflict with the analysis by Burgoon, van Noort, Rooduijn, and Underhill (2019), which finds that rising inequality leads to greater support for radical political parties of the left and right, with a voter becoming more likely to support the radical left when the gap between them and the rich grows and more likely to support the radical right when the gap between them and the poor shrinks. The authors' argument is that greater gains for the rich increase the appeal of the radical left's 'soak the rich' message and policy platform, while greater gains for the poor increase the appeal of the radical right's scapegoating of immigrants and other ethnic minorities. However, there are at least two reasons why these authors' arguments and findings do not necessarily contradict our claims here.

First, Burgoon, van Noort, Rooduijn, and Underhill (2019) focus on all potential voters, not just the working class. As discussed above, blue-collar workers are disproportionately represented in the lower half of the wage and income distributions, with less skilled manual workers generally situated near the bottom. Thus, there is little reason to expect relative wage and income gains of bottom-income earners to lead to greater grievances on the part of the working class.[32] Second, when the authors utilize a general measure of income inequality—mean decile growth minus a respondent's decile's growth—they find that rising inequality increases support for both the radical left and right, even controlling for the effect of rising differentials between them and the rich and shrinking differentials between them and the poor. The empirical results in this chapter similarly suggest that the least paid blue-collar workers (those with fewer skills) become more likely to support PRRPs when they lose ground to the highest paid blue-collar workers (those with more skills), individuals situated near the middle of the wage and income distribution.

Taken together, the results in this chapter imply that working-class support for the populist radical right has grown in recent years due to rising wage and unemployment inequality between the working and middle classes, as well as among blue-collar workers. Combined with the analyses in the previous chapters, this suggests that working-class support for PRRPs is weakest when (left-leaning or centre-right) governments incorporate organized labour in welfare state reform efforts, enact welfare state policies that improve the economic and political standing of blue-collar workers, and macro-economic conditions (policy outcomes) are relatively favourable to the working class, particularly regarding wages and employment outcomes. In Chapter 7, we consider the implications of our analysis for the broader PRRP literature, the 'crisis of democracy' in Western Europe and the United States, and the self-reinforcing nature of inequality in these regions.

---

[32] For instance, in the Comparative Study of Electoral Systems (Module 5, 2016–21), 32.8 per cent of people who belong to the bottom income quintile were blue-collar workers.

7
Concluding Remarks

Despite their decreasing share of the workforce, blue-collar workers still make up a sizable minority of voters in Western European democracies. Indeed, the considerable rise in PRRP popularity in these countries in recent decades has been disproportionately driven by the working class, who have shifted their support to PRRPs from mainstream political parties, particularly of the left. We have argued here that the three main scholarly explanations for why blue-collar workers are increasingly backing PRRPs (the economic grievance, cultural grievance, and political discontent theories) are unable to explain two interrelated stylized facts about working-class support for PRRPs: that blue-collar workers are increasingly concerned about 'cultural issues' rather than 'economic issues' (even in the context of rising economic insecurity among the working class) and are shifting their support from a party family they are largely aligned with on economic issues (i.e., the social democrats or centre-left) to one they are more aligned with on cultural issues (i.e., PRRPs).

Our analysis has sought to explain this puzzle by outlining how political and economic adversity increases blue-collar workers' PRRP support by strengthening their national identity relative to their class identity and thus also the salience they place on cultural issues such as immigration and multiculturalism, issues that are widely recognized to be under the 'ownership' of PRRPs. To test our theoretical claims, we utilized a causal mediation analysis model developed by Imai et al. (2011), which allowed us to determine whether certain macro-level factors (or 'treatments') affect PRRP support through the specific 'causal pathways' (or 'mediators') proposed by our theory, and how much of the macro-level factors' total effects can be explained by those causal pathways.

This final chapter will consist of four sections. The first section summarizes our theoretical argument and the main findings of the empirical chapters (4, 5, and 6) and discusses what implications our analysis has for the (future) disposition, policies, and electoral prospects of PRRPs. The second and third sections consider what these implications suggest for economic

---

Social Identity and Working Class Support for the Populist Radical Right. Eric G. Castater and Kyung Joon Han, Oxford University Press. © Eric G. Castater and Kyung Joon Han (2025). DOI: 10.1093/9780198953104.003.0007

inequality and the crisis of democracy in Western Europe, respectively. The final section concludes with some closing remarks about recent PRRP electoral successes.

Policymaking Processes, Policy Outputs, and Policy Outcomes: Social Identity and Working-Class Support for the Populist Radical Right

Why, despite generally deteriorating economic conditions, do working-class voters increasingly support PRRPs, a party family primarily focused on socio-cultural issues? To explain this puzzle, we utilized the literature on social identity to develop a three-stage theory that describes how relatively poor economic and political circumstances for the working-class lead blue-collar workers to focus more on socio-cultural issues than economic issues and thus also to support the populist radical right. In particular, our analysis focused on the consequences that policymaking processes (i.e., how the national government produces wage and welfare state policies), policy outputs (i.e., the type of welfare state policies adopted by the national government), and policy outcomes (i.e., national economic conditions) have for working-class PRRP support.

The social identity literature suggests that the meaning of various social identities is malleable, individuals have numerous social identities that they can embrace or downgrade, and people derive self-esteem from the social groups that they identify with. Thus, we argue in the first stage of our social identity theory that policymaking processes, policy outputs, and policy outcomes relatively unfavourable to the working class lead them to abandon their economic (or class-based) identity and instead embrace their national identity, the other major social identity with political implications in Western Europe. Since our most strongly held social identities lead us to care more about issues that align with the perceived interests of those identities, the second stage of our social identity theory expects blue-collar workers with a stronger nationalist identity to have a greater focus on socio-cultural issues (such as those related to immigration or multiculturalism) than economic issues (such as those related to the welfare state). Finally, in the third stage of our theory, the 'ownership' that PRRPs have over socio-cultural issues such as immigration and the generally right-leaning positions of working-class voters on these issues mean that blue-collar workers who care more about socio-cultural issues are likelier to support the populist radical right.

In Chapters 4 through 6, we separately explored whether certain policymaking processes, policy outputs, and policy outcomes affect working-class support for PRRPs in the way anticipated by our theory. In Chapter 4, we considered policymaking processes by examining the consequences of how governing parties adopt (neoliberal) welfare state reforms, with the focus on whether governing parties completed social pact agreements with labour unions (and employers' associations), proposed a social pact to labour unions but could not complete it, or acted unilaterally without consulting organized labour; in Chapter 5, we considered policy outputs by examining the consequences of welfare state policies, with the focus on policies with particular relevance to the working class, EPL, and (different types of) LMPs; and in Chapter 6, we considered policy outcomes by examining the consequences of wage and unemployment inequality between blue-collar and white-collar workers and blue-collar workers of different skill and education levels.

Our empirical analyses largely confirmed our theoretical claims, although there were a small number of findings that ran counter to what we anticipated. Broadly, we found that PRRPs perform best when governing parties (of the left, centre, or centre-right) adopt welfare state policies unilaterally or are unable to convert social pact proposals into completed social pact agreements; EPL is weak and LMP spending—especially of the PLMP variety—is low; and wage and unemployment inequality between blue-collar and white-collar workers and more and less educated blue-collar workers is high. Furthermore, the evidence we provided suggests that blue-collar workers respond differently to policy outputs and outcomes depending on their labour market status, and thus that the working class should not be viewed by governing leaders or scholars as a monolithic group with similar interests or preferences. For instance, we found that weaker EPL has led to greater support for PRRPs only among working-class voters in secure employment (economic insiders), reductions in the generosity of LMPs has only reduced PRRP support among working-class voters in insecure employment (economic outsiders), and rising inequality within the working class has led to greater support for PRRPs among less skilled (and thus less paid) blue-collar workers, but not those with higher skill (and thus pay) levels. Contrary to our expectations, we found only weak evidence that social pact agreements reduce working-class support for PRRPs, or that blue-collar union members are more responsive than blue-collar non-union members to policymaking processes associated with the welfare state.

Taken together, our findings suggest, and survey data confirms, that working-class economic insiders and blue-collar workers with relatively low skill levels have become growing constituencies for PRRPs. We believe that this reality has at least two major and interrelated implications for PRRPs, the first regarding the changing constituency of these parties and the second pertaining to policy. First, greater support among economic insiders and less skilled blue-collar workers implies that PRRP voters have moved further to the right on socio-cultural issues and further to the left on economic issues in recent years. This is due to less skilled (and educated) blue-workers having a stronger nationalist disposition than more highly skilled (and educated) blue-collar workers, and both economic insiders and less skilled blue-collar workers being strong supporters of different aspects of the welfare state (e.g., EPL in the case of the former and greater welfare state spending in the case of the latter). Second, PRRPs—recognizing the change in their voting base as well as the general popularity of right-leaning socio-cultural positions and left-leaning economic positions among large segments of the public—have taken and will continue to take increasingly strident positions on socio-cultural issues (where these parties have 'ownership'), but more 'moderate' positions on economic issues (Rovny and Polk 2019). This reality can have the effect of 'blurring' distinctions on economic issues between traditionally left leaning and centrist parties on the one hand and PRRPs on the other, potentially leading to greater emphasis on the socio-cultural issues that PRRPs thrive on politically (Han 2020b). Furthermore, this tendency can be exacerbated by more mainstream parties, which are increasingly adopting right-leaning positions on socio-cultural issues to undermine PRRP support, but that may have the unintended effect of increasing voters' concerns about these issues and thus lead to greater support for PRRPs (Down and Han 2020).

In terms of the substantive effects of our main macro-level indicators (or treatments), our empirical results suggest that policymaking processes have the largest effect on working-class support for PRRPs, while policy outcomes have the smallest effect. Although the different nature of the treatment variables makes them difficult to directly compare, our logistic regression models inform us that just one failed social pact proposal in the previous five years or twice enacting welfare state reforms unilaterally during the same time period (both a common occurrence among the countries we examined) increases the probability that a blue-collar worker will support a PRRP by a factor of 5 to 10, with failed social pact proposals having a larger impact than unilaterally enacted legislation. By contrast, a similarly large effect is only found for policy outputs (EPL and LMPs) and outcomes (wage inequality between blue-collar and white-collar workers) when moving from their 90th to 10th percentile value as reflected in our entire dataset, a magnitude of shift that none of the 16 countries considered here experienced during the period examined. Furthermore, the policy output of unemployment inequality between those without and with a college degree had only modest effects on working-class support for PRRPs, increasing support by a factor of just 2 or 3.

Taken together, the above findings provide promising news for governing parties of the left, centre, and centre-right, as they suggest that those features of public policy that they have the most control over—the policymaking process and, to a lesser extent, policy outputs—matter more for blue-collar PRRP support than that feature governing parties are least able to impact, policy outcomes. As we discussed at length in Chapter 3, this is particularly true in an age of globalization and Europeanization, phenomena that reduce the policymaking autonomy of national governments and increase the vulnerability of national economies to international events or other features of the global economy.

Given these findings and the implications regarding PRRP voters and public policies discussed above, we offer the following advice to left-leaning and mainstream governments that wish to reduce working-class support for PRRPs. First, and most broadly, these governments should primarily focus on (bread and butter) economic issues, such as those pertaining to the welfare state and wages, while 'blurring' their position on socio-cultural and related foreign policy issues, including on multiculturalism, immigration, and EU membership. Not only will this reduce the overall salience of the issues PRRPs thrive on, it will also re-emphasize blue-collar workers' economic identity and address a main underlying cause of PRRP support, economic grievances among the working class.

Second, left-leaning and mainstream governments should redouble their efforts to incorporate interest groups that represent the working class—namely, organized labour—into the policymaking process, particularly regarding economic policies of direct and immediate concern to blue-collar workers. However, every effort should be made by governing leaders to ensure that any such consultation or negotiation with working-class organizations be more than mere public relations efforts; and that they conclude with an agreement that governing parties will adopt policies supported and promoted by organized labour.

Third, and relatedly, welfare state and wage policies endorsed and enacted by left-leaning and centre-right governments need to focus on helping those voters who are most attracted to the nativist, populist, and authoritarian appeals of the PRRP—blue-collar workers. Our analysis suggests that two types of policies that would be particularly beneficial to working-class voters are stronger EPL (to improve the job security of economic insiders) and more generous PLMPs (to reduce economic outsiders' dependence on market income). Furthermore, when tripartite bargaining occurs between employers' associations, labour unions, and elected leaders (which it has to at least some degree in all the countries examined in this analysis), governing parties should push for agreements that reduce employment and wage disparities between less and more highly skilled/formally educated workers, as this will help produce those policy outcomes associated with less aggregate working-class support for PRRPs (lower levels of wage and unemployment inequality among blue-collar workers).

Two recent examples, one in Western Europe and the other in the United States, demonstrate the alternative strategies governing leaders can adopt when developing policies related to the welfare state and wages. In April 2023, French President Emanuel Macron unilaterally adopted—without parliamentary approval or a formal agreement with organized labour—pension reform that rose the retirement age in France to 64 from 62. In response to this action, labour unions in the country organized protests that brought millions of people into the streets over the course of weeks. The leader of the populist radical right National Rally, Marine Le Pen, appeared to engage in position blurring on the issue by officially coming out against the pension reforms but keeping her distance from the protests, which substantially consisted of labour activists and far-left voters and broke out in sporadic violence. Despite the apparent unpopularity of the reforms, Macron refused to back down, and the pension law remains in effect at the time of writing. While this might be considered a policy win for Macron who made pension reform a centrepiece of his second term agenda, it has had clear negative effects on his party's electoral fortunes and helped boost the far-right National Rally. A March 2024 survey of French voters by Ipsos-Sopra Steria for that year's European Parliament elections found the National Rally leading the field with 31 per cent support, well ahead of the 18 per cent support held by Macron's Renaissance party. The centre-left socialists, who received only 2 per cent of the vote two years earlier in the first round of the presidential vote, now stood in third place at 11 per cent, within striking distance of the president's party.

By contrast, US President Joe Biden became the first president in his country's history to join a picket line in support of striking auto workers in September of 2023. The president joined the United Auto Workers and their leader Shawn Fain in the perennial swing state of Michigan to help the union in their ultimately successful efforts to secure record wage increases from automakers. This followed other pro-organized labour policies and announcements by Biden and his administration, including support for the

Protect the Right to Organize (PRO) Act, which has yet to pass in a divided Congress but would be the most pro-labour legislation in the United States since Franklin Roosevelt's New Deal in the 1930s; and vocal support for unionization efforts at Amazon facilities in the Deep South.[1] By contrast, former president Donald Trump did not join the UAW picket line. Instead, he held a rally with 400 to 500 people at a non-unionized automotive plant in Clinton Township in Michigan, where he showed only tepid support for union demands, criticized UAW leadership, played down the importance of the labour negotiations that spurred the strike, and claimed that the real conflict was not between UAW management and employees, but 'American labour' and 'environmental lunatics' who support the auto industry's transition to electric vehicles.[2] Less than three months later, the UAW endorsed Biden over Trump. In response, the president invited the union's leader Fain to his State of the Union address in March 2024, the last prior to the 2024 general election. In the address, Biden not only recognized the UAW leader from the podium, but emphasized bread and butter 'economic issues' throughout his speech, including positive trends in unemployment and inflation; historic state investments in infrastructure and manufacturing; government subsidies towards health care coverage; efforts to bring down the cost of prescription drugs and housing; and public–private partnerships for job training. Biden also explicitly emphasized his historically strong support for organized labour when he stated, 'Wall Street didn't build America... The middle class built the country, and unions built the middle class. . .[3]

In terms of the substantive effects of our theorized causal pathways (or mediators), the results of our causal mediation analyses suggest that our social identity theory is better able to explain how policy outputs and outcomes affect PRRP support than policymaking processes. In other words, while policymaking processes appear to have a larger aggregate substantive effect on working-class support for PRRPs than policy outputs or outcomes, changes in social identity driven by the macro-level factors considered here matter more for explaining working-class support for PRRPs through policy outputs and outcomes. This finding has at least two major implications for researchers seeking to explain (working-class) support for PRRPs. First, the effects of policy outputs and outcomes—which have heretofore been the main focus of the research on PRRP support—are substantially explained by

---

[1] Katie Rogers and Karen Weise, 'Biden Appears to Show Support for Amazon Workers Who Voted to Unionize', *New York Times*, 6 April 2022.

[2] Tom Perkins, 'Voter Drive: Biden and Trump Battle for Blue-Collar Votes in Auto Heartland', *The Guardian*, 30 September 2023.

[3] The White House website (https://www.whitehouse.gov/briefing-room/speeches-remarks/2024/03/08/remarks-by-president-biden-in-state-of-the-union-address-3/).

our social identity theory. Thus, future research on the determinants of PRRP support should move beyond existing theories pertaining to political discontent, economic grievances, and cultural grievances, and more consistently consider social identity and the macro-level factors that help shape and produce it. Second, the influence of policymaking processes—which have been examined by scholars far less than policy outputs and outcomes in the research on PRRP support—need to be considered more frequently and seriously in the literature, with a particular focus on the exact causal pathway(s) by which such effects occur. Given the modest explanatory power of our social identity theory regarding the effect of policymaking processes, we believe that the likeliest drivers of such effects are political discontent and, to a lesser extent, economic grievances (rather than cultural grievances), as unilateral legislation and failed social pact proposals matter more for PRRP support than social pact agreements and there is no obvious, consistent connection between the social pact formation process and socio-cultural issues. Therefore, not incorporating organized labour when making major decisions regarding the welfare state, wages, and other matters of concern to the working class, likely leads to more 'protest voting' and greater demand for an 'anti-system', populist party among blue-collar workers.

PRRPs and Economic Inequality

As we discussed throughout this book, economic inequality has been increasing across much of Western Europe in recent decades. One of the major insights from the scholarly research examining the causes of this rise is that economic inequality is often self-reinforcing, or that higher levels of inequality produce social and political conditions that are likely to exacerbate inequality further. In most cases, explanations for the self-reinforcing nature of inequality focus on how it changes the cost-benefit analysis of numerous political actors, including union members, voters, and elected leaders. For instance, greater earnings differentials between workers could erode support for organized labour, as workers increasingly believe that unions are unable or unwilling to compress wages; reduce the popularity of welfare state policies, as workers desire to maintain their income rather than pay more for benefits that they are unlikely to receive; and more right-leaning economic policies from the government, as political parties shift their positions on economic issues to accommodate changes in public opinion and the growing influence of the wealthy as inequality rises and unions weaken.

By contrast, our analysis suggests that inequality is self-reinforcing because it alters the social identity of blue-collar workers, leading them to care more about cultural issues relative to economic issues. We believe this process not only leads to less support for left-leaning political parties and their policy agenda (which are generally associated with less inequality), but also erodes solidarity among the working class—a sentiment necessary to build and maintain labour organizations (which reduce inequality further). Indeed, greater cultural and political divisions within the working class and growing support among blue-collar workers for the populist radical right has increasingly led to efforts by PRRPs to weaken or dismantle unions and corporatist institutions. Ideologically, PRRPs oppose institutionalized collaboration between unions and governing parties because they divide society based on class (rather than nation) and the supposed corruption such coordination implies. Practically, PRRPs oppose organized labour and corporatist institutions because they have traditionally led to strong bonds between the working class and left-leaning political parties, and the outsider status of PRRPs has precluded the party family's ability to participate in corporatist policy concertation (Rathgeb and Klitgaard 2022).

There are at least two ways by which PRRPs have attempted to weaken organized labour, by attempting to create their own independent labour unions and diminishing the institutional power of unions in corporatist decision-making. For example, the National Rally in France has attempted to create labour unions of public servants, including police officers, prison officers, and public transportation employees, by emphasizing such workers' supposed alienation from political elites and threats to public safety posed by immigrants (Kim forthcoming); and the Sweden Democrats have proposed to replace Ghent-organized unemployment funds (funded and controlled by organized labour) with a public system financed by general taxes and managed by the state (Rathgeb and Klitgaard 2022). While such efforts have thus far been largely unsuccessful, PRRPs' growing electoral success and participation in government suggest looming threats to organized labour and its efforts to instill solidarity and facilitate collective action among the working class.

PRRPs and the Crisis of Democracy

As we discussed in Chapter 1, scholars are increasingly concerned about a 'crisis of democracy' in Western Europe and other wealthy democracies, especially the United States. This crisis is reflected in numerous indicators, including declining public support for democratic institutions, growing tolerance for political violence, and opposition to ethnic diversity. Given that PRRPs have an 'authoritarian' and 'populist' disposition and have gained considerable electoral support by (implicitly and explicitly) criticizing ethnic minorities and emphasizing opposition to multiculturalism and immigration, we believe that their rise poses obvious threats to liberal democracy as well. We have argued and demonstrated here that rising inequality between classes and within the working class has led to greater support for PRRPs among (different types of) blue-collar workers; and that this effect occurs through a specific causal pathway: a change in social identity and, by consequence, issue salience. Taken together, our analysis has at least two broad implications for the crisis of democracy. First, higher inequality threatens democracy by leading the working class to focus more on cultural issues and the social changes bringing them about, domains in which their lower levels of education make them relatively susceptible to prejudice and authoritarian inclinations (Strabac, Listhaug, and Jakobsen 2012; Hagendoorn and Nekuee 2018).[4] Authoritarian attitudes are incompatible with liberal democracy because they disapprove of individual or group differences and strive for the unity and homogeneity of the society by submitting any differences to an authority (Sibley, Robertson, and Wilson 2006). Consequently, these attitudes frequently conflict with the core principles of liberal democracy that endorse the equal treatment of people in the society and the protection of their rights and freedom; checks and balances; and the rule of law. Furthermore, while stronger authoritarian attitudes among the working class make blue-collar workers likelier to support PRRPs, any ensuing PRRP electoral success can further enforce such authoritarian inclinations as PRRP views become more accepted and 'normalized' in the broader society (van Spanje 2010; Han 2015a; Abou-Chadi 2016; Schumacher and van Kersbergen 2016).

Second, the greater focus on cultural issues brought about by higher inequality and ensuing PRRP support elevates the level of affective polarization in the society (Gidron, Adams, and Horne 2020; Harteveld, Mendoza, and Roodujin 2021). Affective polarization indicates that voters increasingly hold contrasting emotional attitudes towards political parties, party

---

[4] Although there is no consistent over-time survey data on authoritarian attitudes, existing evidence suggests authoritarian perspectives are on the rise in Western Europe. For instance, between 1999 and 2017, the share of Europeans who thought it was 'very good' or 'fairly good' to have 'a strong leader who does not have to bother with parliament and elections' grew from 30 per cent to 38 per cent (the European Values Study); and the percentage of Western European respondents who agree that 'ordinary people should make political decisions' declined from 48 per cent to 32 per cent between the first (1996–2001) and fifth (2016–21) waves of the Comparative Study of Electoral Systems.

leaders, and party supporters. More specifically, voters demonstrate stronger favouritism towards those associated with the party they support and stronger animosity towards the party (or parties) they oppose. While voters take a relatively pragmatic approach to economic issues, they take a more principled approach to cultural issues (Tavits 2007). Voters apply morality to cultural issues more strongly than to economic issues because of the former's principle-, value-, and belief-oriented characteristics (Han forthcoming). Moralization justifies and strengthens preferential treatment of 'us', who share the same moral beliefs, and intensifies antipathy toward 'them', who hold conflicting moral views (Garrett and Bankert 2018).

In recent decades, affective polarization has grown in both the United States and Western Europe, particularly the negative feelings voters feel towards their political opposition (Iyengar et al. 2019; Gidron, Adams, and Horne 2019; Reiljan 2020; Han forthcoming). While Broockman, Kalla, and Westwood (2023) argue that the relationship between people's affective polarization and their perception of democratic norms is correlational, not causal, Kingzette et al. (2021) find that partisans who are affectively polarized demonstrate different views on democratic norms (such as equal treatment under the law), depending on whether their political party controls the government. Furthermore, the populist approach to politics promoted by PRRPs exacerbates affective polarization further, as domestic political opponents are 'otherized' and, in the process, dehumanized.

Closing Remarks

When we began writing this book, PRRPs had participated in governing coalitions in only a couple of Western European countries and had not held a national chief executive position in the region since the end of World War II. Nonetheless, the rising popularity of PRRPs and their nativist, populist, and authoritarian persuasion made them a particular matter of concern and their growing support among blue-collar workers posed a unique puzzle in a time of rising inequality. Why would the working class provide greater and greater support to a party family primarily focused on 'cultural issues' linked to ethnic minorities when there were other party options—most obviously on the centre- and far-left—that were proposing and sometimes adopting policies that were objectively—and to even many of these voters, subjectively—better for blue-collar workers? In addition to academic curiosity, we were also motivated to examine this research question to provide advice to mainstream and leftwing governments (who we believe are currently far more supportive of democratic norms and institutions than representatives of PRRPs) on how to reduce support for the populist radical right and preempt their takeover of Western European governments.

However, since that time, populist radical right support has grown even further, with recent elections resulting in PRRPs winning the most votes in the Netherlands and Switzerland; becoming the main opposition party in Belgium, the Netherlands, and Sweden; joining governing coalitions in Finland, Switzerland, and Italy; and, according to some observers, winning a chief executive position in Italy.[5] Furthermore, recent national surveys suggest that PRRPs are surging in France (where the National Rally is currently expected to win the most votes in the 2024 European elections) and Germany (where Alternative for Germany is now the second most popular party, behind only the centre-right Christian Democratic Union/Christian Social Union). Meanwhile, PRRPs remain a minority but perennial force in countries such as Austria and Norway and are now an increasing electoral threat in Portugal and Spain. Thus, it now seems appropriate to not only consider how to explain (and halt) the rise of the populist radical right, but also how PRRPs serving in government—and holding the chief executive position—may impact future PRRP support and, most importantly, democracy and civil peace.

---

[5] While the international news media often refers to Italian Prime Minister Giorgia Meloni's Brothers of Italy party as 'rightwing' and 'far-right', there is scholarly disagreement about whether it represents a PRRP. While the party has organizational and historic links with the National Alliance, the rightwing heir to the fascist Italian Social Movement, and conservative positions on immigration-related issues, it has also focused substantially on matters not obviously related to ethnic diversity, including the protection of small- and medium-sized enterprises and the 'traditional' family (Zulianello 2020; Pirro forthcoming).

APPENDIX A

A Multinomial Logistic Analysis of Social Identity

Table A.1 The macro context and social identity

	(1)	(2)	(3)	(4)	(5)	(6)
1. National identity						
Policymaking process						
Social pact agreement	−0.20					
	(0.77)					
Social pact failure	0.73*					
	(0.37)					
Unilateral legislation		0.68*				
		(0.36)				
Policy output						
EPL			−0.39**			
			(0.16)			
LMP				−0.85***		
				(0.31)		
Policy outcome						
Wage inequality					3.93***	
					(1.00)	
Unemployment inequality						0.95**
						(0.42)
Control variables						
Female	0.29	0.29	0.24	0.27	0.30	0.26
	(0.21)	(0.21)	(0.21)	(0.20)	(0.21)	(0.20)
Age	−0.00	−0.00	−0.00	−0.01*	−0.01*	−0.01
	(0.00)	(0.00)	(0.00)	(0.00)	(0.00)	(0.00)
Education	0.10	0.10	0.05	0.09	−0.04	0.05
	(0.13)	(0.13)	(0.12)	(0.10)	(0.09)	(0.12)
Immigration	−0.13**	−0.14***	0.01	−0.04	−0.04	−0.01
	(0.05)	(0.05)	(0.05)	(0.05)	(0.08)	(0.04)
Constant	3.30***	3.55***	1.83***	2.72**	−0.27	−0.36
	(1.11)	(1.07)	(0.61)	(1.08)	(1.86)	(1.21)

Appendix A **185**

	(1)	(2)	(3)	(4)	(5)	(6)
2. Gender identity						
Policymaking process						
Social pact agreement	1.58***					
	(0.40)					
Social pact failure	−0.34					
	(0.37)					
Unilateral legislation		0.70**				
		(0.35)				
Policy output						
EPL			−0.58***			
			(0.08)			
LMP				0.51		
				(0.46)		
Policy outcome						
Wage inequality					2.92**	
					(1.26)	
Unemployment inequality						0.19
						(0.63)
Control variables						
Female	−0.26	−0.27	−0.35*	−0.26	−0.25	−0.28
	(0.19)	(0.18)	(0.19)	(0.18)	(0.18)	(0.18)
Age	0.00	0.00	0.00	0.00	0.00	0.00
	(0.00)	(0.00)	(0.00)	(0.00)	(0.00)	(0.00)
Education	0.02	−0.00	−0.10	0.07	−0.10*	0.04
	(0.08)	(0.09)	(0.06)	(0.12)	(0.06)	(0.09)
Immigration	−0.12*	−0.07	0.07**	−0.01	0.03	0.01
	(0.07)	(0.09)	(0.03)	(0.05)	(0.09)	(0.06)
Constant	2.53*	1.56	0.85*	−0.17	−1.58	−0.05
	(1.38)	(1.81)	(0.48)	(0.82)	(2.19)	(1.59)
3. Age identity						
Policymaking process						
Social pact agreement	0.38					
	(0.47)					
Social pact failure	−0.08					
	(0.23)					
Unilateral legislation		0.16				
		(0.34)				
Policy output						
EPL			−0.30**			
			(0.13)			
LMP				0.36		
				(0.31)		

Continued

Appendix A

Table A.1 *Continued*

	(1)	(2)	(3)	(4)	(5)	(6)
Policy outcome						
Wage inequality					2.58***	
					(0.89)	
Unemployment inequality						0.46
						(0.40)
Control variables						
Female	−0.57***	−0.57***	−0.65***	−0.58***	−0.59***	−0.62***
	(0.13)	(0.13)	(0.14)	(0.15)	(0.14)	(0.13)
Age	0.03***	0.03***	0.03***	0.03***	0.03***	0.03***
	(0.01)	(0.01)	(0.01)	(0.01)	(0.01)	(0.01)
Education	−0.02	−0.03	−0.10*	−0.01	−0.15***	−0.06*
	(0.05)	(0.05)	(0.06)	(0.06)	(0.04)	(0.03)
Immigration	−0.09	−0.08	−0.03	−0.08**	−0.03	−0.06
	(0.07)	(0.08)	(0.04)	(0.03)	(0.07)	(0.04)
Constant	0.78	0.63	0.92*	0.33	−1.54	−0.26
	(1.54)	(1.67)	(0.54)	(0.94)	(1.74)	(1.16)
Constant						

4. Partisan identity

Policymaking process						
Social pact agreement	1.74***					
	(0.58)					
Social pact failure	−0.27					
	(0.62)					
Unilateral legislation		0.94**				
		(0.43)				
Policy output						
EPL			−0.34			
			(0.24)			
LMP				0.82		
				(0.54)		
Policy outcome						
Wage inequality					1.33	
					(1.82)	
Unemployment inequality						−1.31*
						(0.78)
Control variables						
Female	−0.33*	−0.35**	−0.34**	−0.25	−0.29	−0.32*
	(0.18)	(0.17)	(0.17)	(0.17)	(0.18)	(0.19)
Age	0.01	0.01	0.01	0.01	0.01	0.01
	(0.02)	(0.02)	(0.02)	(0.02)	(0.02)	(0.02)

	(1)	(2)	(3)	(4)	(5)	(6)
Education	−0.19 (0.18)	−0.23 (0.22)	−0.26 (0.22)	−0.15 (0.15)	−0.21 (0.24)	−0.07 (0.15)
Immigration	−0.07 (0.05)	−0.01 (0.07)	0.00 (0.08)	−0.06 (0.06)	0.08 (0.07)	−0.10** (0.04)
Constant	−0.07 (1.69)	−1.20 (1.42)	0.18 (1.49)	−0.89 (1.21)	−3.39** (1.70)	2.83 (2.13)

5. Family identity
Policymaking process

Social pact agreement	0.08 (0.65)					
Social pact failure	0.11 (0.37)					
Unilateral legislation		0.17 (0.39)				

Policy output

EPL			−0.37** (0.17)			
LMP				0.17 (0.36)		

Policy outcome

Wage inequality					3.67*** (1.09)	
Unemployment inequality						0.85 (0.54)

Control variables

Female	−0.31 (0.24)	−0.31 (0.24)	−0.49* (0.26)	−0.44 (0.27)	−0.34 (0.23)	−0.47* (0.26)
Age	0.04*** (0.01)	0.04*** (0.01)	0.04*** (0.01)	0.04*** (0.01)	0.04*** (0.01)	0.04*** (0.01)
Education	0.01 (0.12)	0.01 (0.11)	−0.07 (0.10)	0.04 (0.13)	−0.15 (0.10)	−0.06 (0.10)
Immigration	−0.18** (0.08)	−0.18** (0.09)	−0.01 (0.06)	−0.06 (0.06)	−0.11 (0.07)	−0.02 (0.06)
Constant	0.41 (1.56)	0.39 (1.66)	−1.88** (0.93)	−2.33* (1.28)	−2.79* (1.68)	−3.91** (1.78)

6. Religious identity
Policymaking process

Social pact agreement	15.70*** (1.86)					
Social pact failure	−14.10*** (1.07)					

Continued

188 Appendix A

Table A.1 *Continued*

	(1)	(2)	(3)	(4)	(5)	(6)
Unilateral legislation		0.72				
		(0.78)				
Policy output						
EPL			−0.93**			
			(0.43)			
LMP				2.04		
				(1.31)		
Policy outcome						
Wage inequality					6.09**	
					(2.94)	
Unemployment						1.04
inequality						(1.22)
Control variables						
Female	−1.00	−0.99	−1.12	−0.86	−0.99	−1.05
	(0.77)	(0.76)	(0.77)	(0.73)	(0.77)	(0.77)
Age	0.03	0.03	0.03	0.02	0.02	0.02
	(0.02)	(0.02)	(0.02)	(0.02)	(0.02)	(0.02)
Education	−0.91**	−0.95***	−1.08***	−0.93**	−1.10***	−1.00***
	(0.38)	(0.33)	(0.32)	(0.38)	(0.26)	(0.33)
Immigration	−0.26	−0.16	0.10	−0.08	0.02	0.02
	(0.25)	(0.22)	(0.09)	(0.10)	(0.15)	(0.13)
Constant	2.84	0.93	−1.38	−3.65	−5.77	−3.99
	(5.10)	(4.52)	(2.25)	(2.66)	(4.30)	(3.87)
7. Regional identity						
Policymaking process						
Social pact agreement	−0.27					
	(0.60)					
Social pact failure	0.46					
	(0.33)					
Unilateral legislation		0.34				
		(0.40)				
Policy output						
EPL			−0.23			
			(0.17)			
LMP				−0.01		
				(0.37)		
Policy outcome						
Wage inequality					2.88***	
					(1.02)	
Unemployment						0.60*
inequality						(0.34)

	(1)	(2)	(3)	(4)	(5)	(6)
Control variables						
Female	−0.68*	−0.68*	−0.76**	−0.73*	−0.69*	−0.74**
	(0.38)	(0.38)	(0.37)	(0.38)	(0.38)	(0.37)
Age	0.01***	0.01***	0.01***	0.01***	0.01**	0.01**
	(0.00)	(0.00)	(0.00)	(0.00)	(0.00)	(0.00)
Education	−0.03	−0.03	−0.06	0.01	−0.15	−0.06
	(0.17)	(0.17)	(0.17)	(0.15)	(0.16)	(0.14)
Immigration	−0.10*	−0.11*	−0.02	−0.06	−0.04	−0.03
	(0.06)	(0.06)	(0.04)	(0.04)	(0.04)	(0.03)
Constant	0.76	0.91	−0.10	−0.24	−1.76*	−1.51
	(1.35)	(1.35)	(0.57)	(0.85)	(0.97)	(1.02)
−2 x Log likelihood	6,201.6	6,264.1	6,573.3	6,451.3	6,240.5	6,564.2
Number of observations	1,959	1,959	2,049	2,049	1,959	2,049

Data: ISSP (2003).

Note: Multinomial logistic regression with clustered standard errors (by country) is used. The reference outcome is class identity. Clustered standard errors are in parentheses. ***$p < 0.01$, **$p < 0.05$, *$p < 0.1$.

APPENDIX B

Robustness Checks with the International Social Survey Programme (2013)

Table B.1 The macro context and social identity

	(1)	(2)	(3)	(4)	(5)	(6)
Policymaking process						
Social pact agreement	0.04					
	(0.03)					
Social pact failure	0.42***					
	(0.14)					
Unilateral legislation		−0.02				
		(0.04)				
Policy output						
EPL			−0.33**			
			(0.16)			
LMP				−0.41**		
				(0.19)		
Policy outcome						
Wage inequality					2.01**	
					(0.87)	
Unemployment inequality						0.63
						(0.70)
Control variables						
Female	−0.05	−0.01	−0.04	−0.04	−0.02	−0.06
	(0.08)	(0.09)	(0.10)	(0.09)	(0.09)	(0.09)
Age	0.00	0.00	0.00	0.00	0.00	0.00
	(0.00)	(0.00)	(0.00)	(0.00)	(0.00)	(0.00)
Education	−0.12***	−0.11*	−0.12**	−0.11*	−0.11**	−0.09**
	(0.04)	(0.06)	(0.05)	(0.06)	(0.04)	(0.04)
Immigration	0.02	−0.05	−0.03**	−0.02	−0.03**	−0.01
	(0.01)	(0.03)	(0.01)	(0.02)	(0.01)	(0.01)
−2 x Log likelihood	7,759.7	7,325.9	7,784.7	7,794.3	7,777.4	7,802.5
Number of observations	2,977	2,791	2,977	2,977	2,977	2,977

Data: ISSP (2013).

Note: Ordered logistic regression with clustered standard errors (by country) is used. Clustered standard errors are in parentheses. Results on cut-points are not reported. ***$p < 0.01$, **$p < 0.05$, *$p < 0.1$.

Table B.2 National identity and national pride

	(1)	(2)
Social identity (National identity)	0.35***	0.32***
	(0.04)	(0.04)
Female		0.14*
		(0.08)
Age		0.01***
		(0.00)
Education		−0.07**
		(0.03)
Cut point 1	−3.26***	−2.97***
	(0.11)	(0.19)
Cut point 2	−1.57***	−1.28***
	(0.06)	(0.17)
Cut point 3	0.60***	0.91***
	(0.05)	(0.16)
−2 x Log likelihood	6,323.0	6,207.2
Number of observations	2,993	2,949

Data: ISSP (2013).

Note: Ordered logistic regression is used. Standard errors are in parentheses.
***$p < 0.01$, **$p < 0.05$, *$p < 0.1$.

APPENDIX C

Results of First-Stage Models in Causal Mediation Analyses

Table C.1 Effects of failed social pact proposals on mediators

	(1)	(2)	(3)	(4)	(5)
Data	ISSP		EVS	EES	
Dependent variable	National identity	Opinion on import	National pride	Issue salience	Trust in parliament
Failed social pact proposal	0.16***	0.15***	0.19***	−0.03	−1.11***
	(0.04)	(0.05)	(0.03)	(0.21)	(0.21)
National identity		0.05			
		(0.04)			
Opinion on import	0.02				
	(0.02)				
Issue salience					−0.59**
					(0.28)
Trust in parliament				−0.61**	
				(0.27)	
Female	0.00	−0.12***	0.02	−0.17	−0.17
	(0.03)	(0.05)	(0.02)	(0.20)	(0.14)
Age	0.00***	−0.00	0.00***	0.01	0.00
	(0.00)	(0.00)	(0.00)	(0.01)	(0.00)
Education	−0.05***	−0.03	0.11***	−0.17	0.61***
	(0.01)	(0.02)	(0.03)	(0.14)	(0.10)
Political ideology (right)	0.03**	0.02	−0.05***	0.03	−0.17***
	(0.02)	(0.02)	(0.01)	(0.04)	(0.02)
Number of political parties	−0.00	0.10***	−0.07***	0.17**	0.08
	(0.02)	(0.02)	(0.01)	(0.08)	(0.07)
Unemployment rate	−0.03***	−0.01	−0.06***	−0.03	0.07
	(0.01)	(0.01)	(0.00)	(0.14)	(0.07)
Immigration	−0.00	−0.02**	0.00	0.04	−0.01
	(0.01)	(0.01)	(0.00)	(0.07)	(0.05)
Social spending	0.00	−0.00	0.05***	0.04	0.03
	(0.01)	(0.01)	(0.00)	(0.07)	(0.03)
Social pact agreement	0.03***	−0.01	−0.03***	−0.04*	0.01
	(0.01)	(0.02)	(0.00)	(0.02)	(0.01)

Appendix C   **193**

	(1)	(2)	(3)	(4)	(5)
Data		ISSP	EVS		EES
Dependent variable	National identity	Opinion on import	National pride	Issue salience	Trust in parliament
Corporatism			0.03	−0.49**	0.36**
			(0.02)	(0.21)	(0.15)
Constant	1.93***	1.79***	−0.13	−2.77***	−3.40***
	(0.17)	(0.24)	(0.09)	(1.01)	(0.68)
Number of observations	1,140	1,140	31,361	1,500	1,500
R-squared	0.06	0.04			
−2 x Log likelihood			42,366.5	841.6	1,507.0

Note: Standard errors are in parentheses. ***$p < 0.01$, **$p < 0.05$, *$p < 0.1$.
Source: ISSP (2003), EVS (1990, 1999, 2008, 2017), and EES (2009, 2014).

Table C.2 Effects of unilateral legislation on mediators

	(1)	(2)	(3)	(4)	(5)
Data		ISSP	EVS		EES
Dependent variable	National identity	Opinion on import	National pride	Issue salience	Trust in parliament
Unilateral legislation	0.04*	0.06*	0.02	0.09**	−0.03
	(0.02)	(0.03)	(0.01)	(0.04)	(0.03)
National identity		0.06			
		(0.04)			
Opinion on import	0.03				
	(0.02)				
Issue salience					−0.34
					(0.20)
Trust in parliament				−0.34	
				(0.21)	
Female	0.00	−0.11**	0.17***	−0.09	−0.08
	(0.03)	(0.05)	(0.02)	(0.19)	(0.12)
Age	0.00***	−0.00	−0.01***	0.01	−0.00
	(0.00)	(0.00)	(0.00)	(0.01)	(0.00)
Education	−0.04***	−0.02	−0.29***	−0.18	0.12
	(0.01)	(0.02)	(0.03)	(0.13)	(0.08)
Political ideology (right)	0.03**	0.02	−0.06***	0.03	−0.03
	(0.02)	(0.02)	(0.01)	(0.03)	(0.02)
Number of political parties	0.03	0.11***	0.09***	0.00	0.02
	(0.02)	(0.03)	(0.01)	(0.07)	(0.05)

Continued

194 Appendix C

Table C.2 *Continued*

Data	(1)	(2)	(3)	(4)	(5)
	ISSP		EVS	EES	
Dependent variable	National identity	Opinion on import	National pride	Issue salience	Trust in parliament
Unemployment rate	−0.00	0.01	−0.00	−0.06	0.11***
	(0.01)	(0.01)	(0.00)	(0.08)	(0.04)
Immigration	−0.02	−0.06***	0.02***	0.21***	−0.11***
	(0.01)	(0.02)	(0.00)	(0.06)	(0.03)
Social spending	−0.00	−0.01	0.01***	−0.05	−0.05**
	(0.01)	(0.01)	(0.00)	(0.04)	(0.02)
Corporatism			−0.29***	−0.37**	0.35***
			(0.03)	(0.15)	(0.09)
Constant	1.81***	1.98***	0.46***	−2.07**	0.31
	(0.17)	(0.25)	(0.09)	(0.90)	(0.54)
Number of observations	1,120	1,120	30,755	1,676	1,676
R-squared	0.04	0.04			
−2 x Log likelihood			41,240.6	963.1	2,058.5

Note: Standard errors are in parentheses. ***p < 0.01, **p < 0.05, *p < 0.1.
Source: ISSP (2003), EVS (1990, 1999, 2008, 2017), and EES (2009, 2014).

Table C.3 Effects of EPL on mediators

Data	(1)	(2)	(3)	(4)	(5)
	ISSP		EVS	EES	
Dependent variable	National identity	Opinion on import	National pride	Issue salience	Trust in parliament
EPL	−0.06***	0.23***	−0.19***	−0.59***	0.66***
	(0.02)	(0.05)	(0.01)	(0.14)	(0.08)
National identity		−0.30***			
		(0.06)			
Opinion on import	−0.07***				
	(0.01)				
Issue salience					−0.60***
					(0.16)
Trust in parliament				−0.57***	
				(0.17)	
Female	−0.01	−0.04	0.01	−0.02	−0.32***
	(0.03)	(0.06)	(0.02)	(0.16)	(0.10)
Age	0.00***	−0.01***	0.00	−0.00	0.01***
	(0.00)	(0.00)	(0.00)	(0.01)	(0.00)

Appendix C   **195**

	(1)	(2)	(3)	(4)	(5)
Data	ISSP		EVS	EES	
Dependent variable	National identity	Opinion on import	National pride	Issue salience	Trust in parliament
Education	−0.04***	0.05*	0.09***	−0.36***	0.33***
	(0.01)	(0.03)	(0.03)	(0.12)	(0.07)
Political ideology (right)	0.03**	−0.05*	−0.06***	0.07**	0.04**
	(0.01)	(0.03)	(0.01)	(0.03)	(0.02)
Number of political parties	−0.03	0.09**	−0.02***	−0.03	0.12***
	(0.02)	(0.04)	(0.01)	(0.06)	(0.03)
Unemployment rate	−0.01**	0.04***	−0.05***	−0.11**	−0.05***
	(0.01)	(0.01)	(0.00)	(0.05)	(0.02)
Immigration	−0.02**	0.05***	−0.01**	0.10***	−0.02*
	(0.01)	(0.01)	(0.00)	(0.03)	(0.01)
Social spending	0.00	−0.01	0.06***	−0.06**	0.01
	(0.00)	(0.01)	(0.00)	(0.03)	(0.01)
Constant	2.50***	2.36***	0.10	1.28	−2.98***
	(0.23)	(0.51)	(0.09)	(0.90)	(0.58)
Number of observations	1,305	1,305	31,361	2,185	2,185
R-squared	0.07	0.08			
−2 x Log likelihood			42,076.2	1,233.0	2,871.1

Note: Standard errors are in parentheses. ***p < 0.01, **p < 0.05, *p < 0.1.
Source: ISSP (2003), EVS (1990, 1999, 2008, 2017), and EES (2009, 2014).

Table C.4 Effects of LMPs on mediators

	(1)	(2)	(3)	(4)	(5)
Data	ISSP		EVS	EES	
Dependent variable	National identity	Opinion on import	National pride	Issue salience	Trust in parliament
LMP	−0.10***	0.16**	−0.15***	−0.43***	0.48***
	(0.03)	(0.07)	(0.02)	(0.11)	(0.06)
National identity		−0.31***			
		(0.06)			
Opinion on import	−0.07***				
	(0.01)				
Issue salience					−0.59***
					(0.17)
Trust in parliament				−0.55***	
				(0.17)	

Continued

196 Appendix C

Table C.4 *Continued*

Data	(1)	(2)	(3)	(4)	(5)
	ISSP		EVS	EES	
Dependent variable	National identity	Opinion on import	National pride	Issue salience	Trust in parliament
Female	−0.00	−0.07	−0.21***	−0.03	−0.32***
	(0.03)	(0.06)	(0.04)	(0.17)	(0.10)
Age	0.00***	−0.01***	0.01***	−0.00	0.01***
	(0.00)	(0.00)	(0.00)	(0.01)	(0.00)
Education	−0.04***	0.03	−0.56***	−0.31**	0.33***
	(0.01)	(0.03)	(0.06)	(0.12)	(0.07)
Political ideology (right)	0.04***	−0.07**	0.11***	0.06*	0.03*
	(0.01)	(0.03)	(0.01)	(0.03)	(0.02)
Number of political parties	0.02	−0.04	0.10***	0.19**	−0.12***
	(0.02)	(0.03)	(0.01)	(0.08)	(0.04)
Unemployment rate	0.01	−0.01	−0.03***	−0.19***	0.01
	(0.01)	(0.01)	(0.01)	(0.06)	(0.02)
Immigration	−0.01	0.02	−0.04***	0.12***	−0.00
	(0.01)	(0.01)	(0.01)	(0.04)	(0.02)
Social spending	0.00	−0.02*	0.03***	−0.02	−0.06***
	(0.00)	(0.01)	(0.01)	(0.04)	(0.02)
Constant	2.03***	4.24***	−3.27***	−0.22	−0.51
	(0.15)	(0.31)	(0.13)	(0.81)	(0.50)
Number of observations	1,305	1,305	30,935	2,139	2,139
R-squared	0.07	0.07			
−2 x Log likelihood			22,986.3	1,210.1	2,811.2

Note: Standard errors are in parentheses. ***$p < 0.01$, **$p < 0.05$, *$p < 0.1$.
Source: ISSP (2003), EVS (1990, 1999, 2008, 2017), and EES (2009, 2014).

Table C.5 Effects of wage inequality on mediators

Data	(1)	(2)	(3)	(4)	(5)
	ISSP		EVS	EES	
Dependent variable	National identity	Opinion on import	National pride	Issue salience	Trust in parliament
Wage inequality	0.06***	−0.08*	1.85***	2.19**	1.49**
	(0.02)	(0.04)	(0.44)	(1.04)	(0.64)
National identity		−0.33***			
		(0.06)			
Opinion on import	−0.07***				
	(0.01)				

Appendix C **197**

	(1)	(2)	(3)	(4)	(5)
Data	ISSP		EVS	EES	
Dependent variable	National identity	Opinion on import	National pride	Issue salience	Trust in parliament
Issue salience					−0.25*
					(0.14)
Trust in parliament				−0.22	
				(0.14)	
Female	−0.01	−0.06	−0.10	−0.04	−0.14
	(0.03)	(0.06)	(0.09)	(0.14)	(0.10)
Age	0.00***	−0.01***	0.01**	−0.01**	0.01*
	(0.00)	(0.00)	(0.00)	(0.00)	(0.00)
Education	−0.04***	0.02	−0.44***	−0.40***	0.34***
	(0.01)	(0.03)	(0.13)	(0.10)	(0.07)
Political ideology (right)	0.04***	−0.06**	0.10***	0.06**	0.07***
	(0.01)	(0.03)	(0.02)	(0.03)	(0.02)
Number of political parties	−0.08**	0.06	0.02	0.05	0.14***
	(0.03)	(0.07)	(0.03)	(0.05)	(0.03)
Unemployment rate	−0.00	0.01	−0.03*	−0.11***	−0.11***
	(0.01)	(0.01)	(0.02)	(0.04)	(0.02)
Immigration	−0.02*	0.01	−0.02	0.07**	0.00
	(0.01)	(0.03)	(0.02)	(0.03)	(0.02)
Social spending	0.01	−0.02	−0.04***	−0.03	−0.00
	(0.01)	(0.01)	(0.01)	(0.02)	(0.01)
Constant	1.98***	4.48***	−3.55***	−1.61*	−1.80***
	(0.15)	(0.32)	(0.54)	(0.96)	(0.65)
Number of observations	1,280	1,280	6,804	2,119	2,119
R-squared	0.07	0.07			
−2 x Log likelihood			4,163.6	1,545.8	2,780.5

Note: Standard errors are in parentheses. ***p < 0.01, **p < 0.05, *p < 0.1.
Source: ISSP (2003), EVS (2008, 2017), and EES (2009, 2014).

Table C.6 Effects of unemployment inequality on mediators

	(1)	(2)	(3)	(4)	(5)
Data	ISSP		EVS	EES	
Dependent variable	National identity	Opinion on import	National pride	Issue salience	Trust in parliament
Unemployment inequality	0.07	−0.15	−0.02	0.85***	0.24
	(0.05)	(0.10)	(0.03)	(0.22)	(0.16)

Continued

Appendix C

Table C.6 *Continued*

Data Dependent variable	(1) ISSP National identity	(2) Opinion on import	(3) EVS National pride	(4) EES Issue salience	(5) Trust in parliament
National identity		−0.35*** (0.06)			
Opinion on import	−0.08*** (0.01)				
Issue salience					−0.25* (0.14)
Trust in parliament				−0.22 (0.14)	
Female	0.01 (0.03)	−0.04 (0.06)	−0.25*** (0.04)	−0.04 (0.14)	−0.14 (0.10)
Age	0.00*** (0.00)	−0.01*** (0.00)	0.02*** (0.00)	−0.01 (0.00)	0.01* (0.00)
Education	−0.03*** (0.01)	0.01 (0.03)	−0.63*** (0.07)	−0.43*** (0.10)	0.32*** (0.07)
Political ideology (right)	0.04*** (0.01)	−0.06** (0.03)	0.10*** (0.01)	0.05* (0.03)	0.07*** (0.02)
Number of political parties	−0.04* (0.02)	−0.05 (0.05)	0.16*** (0.01)	0.03 (0.05)	0.12*** (0.03)
Unemployment rate	−0.01** (0.01)	−0.02 (0.01)	−0.01 (0.01)	−0.06* (0.04)	−0.10*** (0.02)
Immigration	−0.00 (0.01)	0.04*** (0.01)	−0.04*** (0.01)	0.01 (0.03)	−0.00 (0.02)
Social spending	0.01** (0.00)	0.00 (0.01)	−0.03*** (0.01)	−0.05** (0.02)	−0.01 (0.01)
Constant	1.99*** (0.15)	4.28*** (0.31)	−3.02*** (0.19)	−0.75 (0.75)	−1.08** (0.53)
Number of observations	1,235	1,235	27,319	2,119	2,119
R-squared	0.06	0.08			
−2 x Log likelihood			17,516.2	1,535.3	2,783.6

Note: Standard errors are in parentheses. ***p < 0.01, **p < 0.05, *p < 0.1.
Source: ISSP (2003), EVS (1990, 1999, 2008, 2017), and EES (2009, 2014).

APPENDIX D

A Robustness Check with Excluding Country/Years without a PRRP

Table D.1 The macro context and working-class support for the populist radical right

	(1)	(2)	(3)	(4)	(5)	(6)
Policymaking process						
Social pact agreement	0.09*					
	(0.05)					
Social pact failure	0.90**					
	(0.43)					
Unilateral legislation		0.06				
		(0.22)				
Policy output						
EPL			−0.59***			
			(0.14)			
LMP				−0.60***		
				(0.21)		
Policy outcome						
Wage inequality					1.63	
					(1.64)	
Unemployment inequality						0.87***
						(0.30)
Control variables						
Female	−0.30***	−0.29**	−0.24**	−0.25**	−0.38***	−0.39***
	(0.09)	(0.12)	(0.10)	(0.11)	(0.12)	(0.12)
Age	−0.01***	−0.01***	−0.02***	−0.01***	−0.01*	−0.01**
	(0.00)	(0.00)	(0.00)	(0.00)	(0.00)	(0.00)
Education	−0.41**	−0.42*	−0.41**	−0.39*	−0.05	−0.43**
	(0.17)	(0.25)	(0.18)	(0.21)	(0.17)	(0.19)
Political ideology (right)	0.32***	0.30***	0.32***	0.31***	0.44***	0.40***
	(0.05)	(0.05)	(0.05)	(0.06)	(0.05)	(0.04)
Number of political parties	−0.07	−0.07	0.10*	0.08	0.05	0.19***
	(0.10)	(0.17)	(0.06)	(0.09)	(0.10)	(0.07)

Continued

200 Appendix D

Table D.1 *Continued*

	(1)	(2)	(3)	(4)	(5)	(6)
Unemployment rate	−0.15	−0.12	−0.07	−0.11*	−0.10	−0.07
	(0.11)	(0.09)	(0.06)	(0.06)	(0.11)	(0.06)
Immigration	0.09***	0.01	0.09***	0.09***	0.12***	0.16***
	(0.03)	(0.08)	(0.02)	(0.02)	(0.03)	(0.03)
Social spending	−0.04	0.12*	0.11***	0.16**	0.10*	0.15***
	(0.07)	(0.06)	(0.03)	(0.06)	(0.05)	(0.05)
Corporatism	0.13	0.13				
	(0.39)	(0.38)				
Constant	−2.23	−5.41**	−5.81***	−6.53***	−8.87***	−12.05***
	(1.87)	(2.13)	(0.97)	(1.73)	(2.32)	(1.69)
−2 x Log likelihood	9,891.7	9,568.9	9,597.6	9,745.4	3,360.1	6,186.4
Number of observations	17,540	17,152	17,540	17,540	4,908	13,260

Note: Logistic regression with clustered standard errors (by country/year) is used. Clustered standard errors are in parentheses. ***$p < 0.01$, **$p < 0.05$, *$p < 0.1$.

Source: EVS (1990, 1999, 2008, 2017).

APPENDIX E

A Robustness Check with a Country Fixed-Effect Model

Table E.1 The macro context and working-class support for the populist radical right

	(1)	(2)	(3)	(4)	(5)	(6)
Policymaking process						
Social pact agreement	0.10**					
	(0.04)					
Social pact failure	1.06***					
	(0.33)					
Unilateral legislation		0.34*				
		(0.18)				
Policy output						
EPL			−0.96***			
			(0.20)			
LMP				−1.26***		
				(0.31)		
Policy outcome						
Wage inequality						
					9.28***	
Unemployment inequality					(2.82)	0.07
						(0.41)
Control variables						
Female	−0.31***	−0.32***	−0.30***	−0.26***	−0.21*	−0.34***
	(0.10)	(0.10)	(0.09)	(0.09)	(0.12)	(0.12)
Age	−0.01***	−0.01***	−0.01***	−0.01***	−0.01**	−0.01**
	(0.00)	(0.00)	(0.00)	(0.00)	(0.00)	(0.00)
Education	−0.55***	−0.65***	−0.47**	−0.60***	−0.35**	−0.57***
	(0.18)	(0.20)	(0.19)	(0.16)	(0.16)	(0.18)
Political ideology (right)	0.32***	0.30***	0.32***	0.32***	0.41***	0.40***
	(0.05)	(0.05)	(0.05)	(0.05)	(0.04)	(0.04)
Number of political parties	0.38*	0.49*	0.23*	0.01	1.21**	0.72***
	(0.21)	(0.26)	(0.13)	(0.23)	(0.48)	(0.24)

Continued

202 Appendix E

Table E.1 *Continued*

	(1)	(2)	(3)	(4)	(5)	(6)
Unemployment rate	−0.16	−0.07	0.03	0.32**	0.15	−0.19*
	(0.11)	(0.09)	(0.10)	(0.14)	(0.14)	(0.11)
Immigration	0.13*	0.16	0.07	0.14*	0.04	0.27**
	(0.07)	(0.12)	(0.07)	(0.08)	(0.07)	(0.13)
Social spending	−0.16	0.10	−0.06	0.12	−0.33**	0.11
	(0.11)	(0.12)	(0.08)	(0.10)	(0.13)	(0.13)
Corporatism	0.02	−1.24				
	(1.13)	(1.18)				
Constant	−1.97	−8.54***	−1.56	−10.25***	−10.40***	−9.98***
	(2.29)	(2.32)	(1.59)	(2.23)	(1.35)	(3.05)
−2 x Log likelihood	9,805.3	9,535.6	9,674.4	9,800.8	3,213.6	6,336.6
Number of observations	24,020	23,632	24,020	24,020	5,728	19,740

Note: Logistic regression with clustered standard errors (by country/year) is used. Clustered standard errors are in parentheses. ***$p < 0.01$, **$p < 0.05$, *$p < 0.1$.

Source: EVS (1990, 1999, 2008, 2017).

References

Abedi, Amir. 2014. *Anti-Political Establishment Parties: A Comparative Analysis*. London: Routledge.

Abou-Chadi, Tarik. 2016. 'Niche Party Success and Mainstream Party Policy Shifts: How Green and Radical Right Parties Differ in Their Impact', *British Journal of Political Science* 46 (2): 417–36.

Abou-Chadi, Tarik and Markus Wagner. 2019. 'The Electoral Appeal of Party Strategies in Post-Industrial Societies: When Can the Mainstream Left Succeed?', *Journal of Politics* 81 (4): 1405–19.

Acemoglu, Daron and David Autor. 2011. 'Skills, Tasks and Technologies: Implications for Employment and Earnings', *Handbook of Labor Economics* 4 (B): 1043–71.

Achen, Christopher H. and Larry M. Bartels. 2016. *Democracy for Realists: Why Elections Do Not Produce Responsive Government*. Princeton, New Jersey: Princeton University Press.

Adams, James, Samuel Merrill III, and Bernard Grofman. 2005. *A United Theory of Party Competition: A Cross-National Analysis Integrating Spatial and Behavioral Factors*. Cambridge: Cambridge University Press.

Ahlquist, John S. 2010. 'Policy by Contract: Electoral Cycles, Parties and Social Pacts, 1974–2000', *Journal of Politics* 72 (2): 572–87.

Ahlquist, John S. 2017. 'Labor Unions, Political Representation, and Economic Inequality', *Annual Review of Political Science* 20: 409–32.

Ahrens, Leo. 2022. 'Unfair Inequality and the Demand for Redistribution: Why Not All Inequality is Equal', *Socio-Economic Review* 20 (2): 463–87.

Akkerman, Tjitske. 2015. 'Immigration Policy and Electoral Competition in Western Europe: A Fine-Grained Analysis of Party Positions over the Past Two Decades', *Party Politics* 21 (1): 54–67.

Akkerman, Tjitske, Sarah L. de Lange, and Matthijs Rooduijn. 2016. *Radical Rightwing Populist Parties in Western Europe: Into the Mainstream?* London: Routledge.

Alderson, Arthur S. and François Nielsen. 2002. 'Globalization and the Great U-Turn: Income Inequality Trends in 16 OECD Countries', *American Journal of Sociology* 107 (5): 1244–99.

Alesina, Alberto and Edward Glaeser. 2004. *Fighting Poverty in the U.S. and Europe: A World of Difference*. Oxford: Oxford University Press.

Alt, James and Torben Iversen. 2017. 'Inequality, Labor Market Segmentation, and Preferences for Redistribution', *American Journal of Political Science* 61 (1): 21–36.

Altemeyer, Bob. 1988. *Enemies of Freedom: Understanding Right-Wing Authoritarianism*. San Francisco, California: Jossey-Bass Publishers.

Alvarez, Maximiliano, Aude Bernard, and Scott N. Lieske. 2021. 'Understnding Internal Migration Trends in OECD Countries', *Population, Space and Place* 27 (7): 1–22.

Amengay, Abdelkarim and Daniel Stockemer. 2019. 'The Radical Right in Western Europe: A Meta-Analysis of Structural Forms', *Political Studies Review* 17 (1): 30–40.

Andersen, Patrick Lie and Marianne Nordli Hansen. 2012. 'Class and Cultural Capital—The Case of Class Inequality in Educational Performance', *European Sociological Review* 28 (5): 607–21.

Anderson, Christopher and Pablo Baramendi. 2012. 'Left Parties, Poor Voters, and Electoral Participation in Advanced Industrial Societies', *Comparative Political Studies* 45 (6): 714–46.

204 References

Anderson, Christopher J. and Jonas Pontusson. 2007. 'Workers, Worries and Welfare States: Social Protection and Job Insecurity in 15 OECD Countries', *European Journal of Political Research* 46 (2): 211–35.

Anderson, Christopher J. and Matthew M. Singer. 2008. 'The Sensitive Left and and the Impervious Right: Multilevel Models and the Politics of Inequality, Ideology, and Legitimacy in Europe', *Comparative Political Studies* 41 (4-5): 564–99.

Armingeon, Klaus and Kai Guthmann. 2014. 'Democracy in Crisis? The Declining Support for National Democracy in European Countries, 2007–2011', *European Journal of Political Research* 53 (3): 423–42.

Armingeon, Klaus and David Weisstanner. 2022. 'Objective Conditions Count, Political Beliefs Decide: The Conditional Effects of Self-Interest and Ideology on Redistribution Preferences', *Political Studies* 70 (4): 887–900.

Arter, David. 2010. 'The Breakthrough of Another West European Populist Radical Right Party? The Case of the True Finns', *Government and Opposition* 45 (4): 484–504.

Arzheimer, Kai. 2009. 'Contextual Factors and the Extreme Right Vote in Western Europe, 1980–2002', *American Journal of Political Science* 53 (2): 259–75.

Arzheimer, Kai and Elisabeth Carter. 2006. 'Political Opportunity Structure and Right-wing Extremist Party Success', *European Journal of Political Research* 45 (3): 419–33.

Attewell, David. 2021. 'Deservingness Perceptions, Welfare State Support and Vote Choice in Western Europe', *West European Politics* 44 (3): 611–34.

Attewell, David. 2022. 'Redistribution Attitudes and Vote Choice across the Educational Divide', *European Journal of Political Research* 61 (4): 1080–1101.

Avdagic, Sabina. 2010. 'When Are Concerted Reforms Feasible? Explaining the Emergence of Social Pacts in Western Europe', *Comparative Political Studies* 43 (5): 628–57.

Avdagic, Sabina. 2013. 'Partisanship, Political Constraints, and Employment Protection Reforms in an Era of Austerity', *European Political Science Review* 5 (3): 431–55.

Avdagic, Sabina. 2015. 'Does Deregulation Work? Reassessing the Unemployment Effect of Employment Protection', *British Journal of Industrial Relations* 53 (1): 6–26.

Avdagic, Sabina, Martin Rhodes, and Jelle Visser (eds). 2011. *Social Pacts in Europe: Emergence, Evolution, and Institutionalization*. Oxford: Oxford University Press.

Avdagic, Sabina and Paola Salardi. 2013. 'Tenuous Link: Labour Market Institutions and Unemployment in Advanced and New Market Economies', *Socio-Economic Review* 11 (4): 739–69.

Azzollini, Leo. 2021. 'The Scar Effects of Unemployment on Electoral Participation: Withdrawal and Mobilization across European Societies', *European Sociological Review* 37 (6): 1007–26.

Baccaro, Lucio. 2002. 'The Construction of "Democratic" Corporatism in Italy', *Politics and Society* 30 (2): 327–57.

Baccaro, Lucio and Sang-Hoon Lim. 2007. 'Social Pacts as Coalitions of the Weak and Moderate: Ireland, Italy, and South Korea in Comparative Perspective', *European Journal of Industrial Relations* 13 (1): 27–46.

Baccaro, Lucio and Diego Rei. 2007. 'Institutional Determinants of Unemployment in OECD Countries: Does the Deregulatory View Hold Water?', *International Organization* 61 (3): 527–69.

Baccaro, Lucio and Marco Simoni. 2008. 'Policy Conertation in Europe: Understanding Government Choice', *Comparative Political Studies* 41 (10): 1323–48.

Bail, Christopher A. 2008. 'The Configuration of Symbolic Boundaries against Immigrants in Europe', *American Sociological Review* 73 (1): 37–59.

Balbona, David Luque and Sergio González Begega. 2015. 'Austerity and Welfare Reform in South-Western Europe: A Farewell to Corporatism in Italy, Spain, and Portugal?', *European Journal of Social Security* 17 (2): 271–91.

Balch, George I. 1974. 'Multiple Indicators in Survey Research: The Concept "Sense of Political Efficacy"', *Political Methodology* 1 (2): 1–43.

Bale, Tim, Dan Hough, and Stijn van Kessel. 2013. 'In or Out of Proportion? Labour and Social Democratic Parties' Responses to the Radical Right', in Jens Rydgren (ed.), *Class Politics and the Radical Right*. London: Routledge, 91–106.

Bale, Tim, Christoffer Green-Pedersen, André Krouwel, Kurt Richard Luther, and Nick Sitter. 2010. 'If You Can't Beat Them, Join Them? Explaining Social Democratic Responses to the Challenge from the Populist Radical Right in Western Europe', *Political Studies* 58 (3): 410–26.

Balz, Anne. 2017. 'Cross-National Variations in the Security Gap: Perceived Job Insecurity among Temporary and Permanent Employees and Employment Protection Legislation', *European Sociological Review* 33 (5): 675–92.

Bandau, Frank and Leo Ahrens. 2020. 'The Impact of Partisanship in the Era of Retrenchment: Insights from Quantitative Welfare State Research', *Journal of European Social Policy* 30 (1): 34–47.

Barbieri, Paolo and Giorgio Cutuli. 2016. 'Employment Protection Legislation, Labour Market Dualism, and Inequality in Europe', *European Sociological Review* 32 (4): 501–16.

Barr, Robert R. 2009. 'Populists, Outsiders and Anti-establishment Politics', *Party Politics* 15 (1): 29–48.

Barrio, Astrid, Sonia Alonso Sáenz de Oger, and Bonnie N. Field. 2021. 'VOX Spain: The Organisational Challenges of a New Radical Right Party', *Politics and Governance* 9 (4): 240–51.

Bartel, Ann P. and Frank R. Lichtenberg. 1987. 'The Comparative Advantage of Educated Workers in Implementing New Technology', *The Review of Economics and Statistics* 69 (1): 1–11.

Bassanini, Andrea and Romain Duval 2009. 'Unemployment, Institutions, and Reform Complementarities: Re-Assessing the Aggregate Evidence for OECD Countries', *Oxford Review of Economic Policy* 25 (1): 40–59.

Becher, Michael and Jonas Pontusson. 2011. 'Whose Interests do Unions Represent? Unionization by Income in Western Europe', in David Brady (ed.), *Comparing European Workers Part B: Policies and Institutions (Research in the Sociology of Work, Volume 22)*. Bingley, UK: Emerald Group Publishing Ltd, 181–211.

Béland, Daniel, Bea Cantillon, Rod Hick, and Amílcar Moreira. 2021. 'Social Policy in the Face of a Global Pandemic: Policy Responses to the COVID-19 Crisis', *Social Policy and Administration* 55 (2): 249–60.

Bélanger, Eric and Kees Aarts. 2006. 'Explaining the Rise of the LPF: Issues, Discontent, and the 2002 Dutch Election', *Acta Politica* 41 (1): 4–20.

Bélanger, Eric and Bonnie M. Meguid. 2008. 'Issue Salience, Issue Ownership, and Issue-Based Vote Choice', *Electoral Studies* 27 (3): 477–91.

Beramendi, Pablo, Silja Häusermann, Herbert Kitschelt, and Hanspeter Kriesi (eds). 2015. *The Politics of Advanced Capitalism*. Cambridge: Cambridge University Press.

Bergh, Johannes. 2004. 'Protest Voting in Austria, Denmark, and Norway', *Scandinavian Political Studies* 27 (4): 367–89.

Berman, Eli, John Bound, and Stephen Machin. 1998. 'Implications of Skill-Biased Technological Chang: International Evidence', *The Quarterly Journal of Economics* 113 (4): 1245–79.

206 References

Berman, Eli and Stephen Machin. 2000. 'Skill-biased Technology Transfer around the World', *Oxford Review of Economic Policy* 16 (3): 12–22.

Bertola, Giuseppe. 1990. 'Job Security, Employment and Wages', *European Economic Review* 34 (4): 851–79.

Betz, Hans-George. 1993. 'The New Politics of Resentment: Radical Right-Wing Populist Parties in Western Europe', *Comparative Politics* 25 (4): 413–27.

Betz, Hans-George. 1994. *Radical Right-Wing Populism in Western Europe*. New York: St Martin's Press.

Betz, Hans-George. 2018. 'The Radical Right and Populism', in Jens Rydgren (ed.), *The Oxford Handbook of the Radical Right*. Oxford: Oxford University Press, 86–104.

Betz, Hans-George. 2019. 'Facets of Nativism: A Heuristic Exploration', *Patterns of Prejudice* 53 (2): 111–35.

Biegert, Thomas. 2017. 'Welfare Benefits and Unemployment in Affluence Democracies: The Moderating Role of the Institutional Insider/Outsider Divide', *American Sociological Review* 82 (5): 1037–64.

Biegert, Thomas. 2019. 'Labor Market Institutions, the Insider/Outsider Divide and Social Inequalities in Employment in Affluent Countries', *Socio-Economic Review* 17 (2): 255–81.

Blanchard, Olivier and Justin Wolfers. 2000. 'The Role of Shocks and Institutions in the Rise of European Unemployment: The Aggregate Evidence', *The Economic Journal* 110 (462): 1–33.

Blanz, Mathias and Birgit Aufderheide. 1999. 'Social Categorization and Category Attribution: The Effects of Comparative and Normative Fit on Memory and Social Judgment', *British Journal of Social Psychology* 38 (2): 157–79.

Blekesaune, Morten and Jill Quadagno 2003. 'Public Attitudes toward Welfare State Policies: A Comparative Analysis of 24 Nations', *European Sociological Review* 19 (5): 415–27.

Bluestone, Barry and Bennett Harrison. 1982. *The Deindustrialization of America*. New York: Basic Books.

Boeri, Tito, J. Ignacio Conde-Ruiz, and Vincenzo Galasso. 2003. 'Protecting against Labour Market Risk: Employment Protection or Unemployment Benefit?', *CEPR Discussion Paper Series* No. 3990.

Boeri, Tito and Pietro Garibaldi. 2009. 'Beyond Eurosclerosis', *Economic Policy* 24 (59): 409–61.

Bogliacino, Francesco and Matteo Lucchese. 2016. 'Endogenous Skill Biased Technical Change: Testing for Demand Pull Effect', *Industrial and Corporate Change* 25 (2): 227–43.

Boix, Carles. 1998. *Political Parties, Growth and Equality: Conservative and Social Democratic Economic Strategies in the World Economy*. Cambridge: Cambridge University Press.

Boninger, David S., Jon A. Krosnick, and Matthew K. Brent. 1995. 'Origins of Attitude Importance: Self-interest, Social Identification, and Value Relevance', *Journal of Personality and Social Psychology* 68 (1): 61–80.

Bornschier, Simon. 2012. 'Why a Right-wing Populist Party Emerged in France but Not in Germany: Cleavages and Actors in the Formation of a New Cultural Divide', *European Political Science Review* 4 (1): 121–45.

Bornschier, Simon and Hanspeter Kriesi. 2013. 'The Populist Right, the Working Class, and the Changing Face of Class Politics', in Jens Rydgren (ed.), *Class Politics and the Radical Right*. London: Routledge, 10–30.

Boulianne, Shelley. 2019. 'Building Faith in Democracy: Deliberative Events, Political Trust and Efficacy', *Political Studies* 67 (1): 4–30.

Bourdieu, Pierre. 1984. *Distinction: A Social Critique of the Judgement of Taste*. London: Routledge.

Bourdieu, Pierre. 1985. 'The Forms of Capital', in John G. Richardson (ed.), *Handbook of Theory and Research for the Sociology of Education*. New York: Greenwood Press, 241–58.

Bradley, David, Evelyne Huber, Stephanie Moller, Fraoncois Nielsen, and John D. Stephens. 2003. 'Distribution and Redistribution in Postindustrial Democracies', *World Politics* 55 (2): 193–228.

Brandl, Bernd. 2012. 'Successful Wage Concertation: The Economic Effects of Wage Pacts and Their Alternatives', *British Journal of Industrial Relations* 50 (3): 482–501.

Brandl, Bernd and Franz Traxler. 2005. 'Industrial Relations, Social Pacts and Welfare Expenditures: A Cross-national Comparison', *British Journal of Industrial Relations* 43 (4): 635–58.

Bronchetti, Erin. 2012. 'Workers' Compensation and Consumption Smoothing', *Journal of Public Economics* 96 (5–6): 495–508.

Broockman, David E., Joshua L. Kalla, and Sean J. Westwood. 2023. 'Does Affective Polarization Undermine Democratic Norms or Accountability? Maybe Not', *American Journal of Political Science* 67 (3): 808–28.

Browning, Martin and Thomas F. Crossley. 2001. 'Unemployment Insurance Benefit Levels and Consumption Changes', *Journal of Public Economics* 80 (1): 1–23.

Brunner, Eric and Ed Balsdon. 2004. 'Intergenerational Conflict and the Political Economy of School Spending', *Journal of Urban Economics* 56 (2): 369–88.

Burgoon, Brian. 2014. 'Immigration, Integration, and Support for Redistribution in Europe', *World Politics* 66 (3): 365–405.

Burgoon, Brian and Fabian Dekker. 2010. 'Flexible Employment, Economic Insecurity and Social Policy Preferences in Europe', *Journal of European Social Policy* 20 (2): 126–41.

Burgoon, Brian, Sam van Noort, Matthijs Rooduijn, and Geoffrey Underhill. 2019. 'Positional Deprivation and Support for Radical Right and Radical Left Parties', *Economic Policy* 34 (97): 51–93.

Burns, Peter and James G. Gimpel. 2000. 'Economic Insecurity, Prejudicial Stereotypes, and Public Opinion on Immigration Policy', *Political Science Quarterly* 115 (2): 201–25.

Burscher, Bjorn, Joost van Spanje, and Claes de Vreese. 2015. 'Owning the Issues of Crime and Immigration: The Relation between Immigration and Crime News and Anti-Immigrant Voting in 11 Countries', *Electoral Studies* 38: 59–69.

Busemeyer, Marius and Erik Neimanns. 2017. 'Conflictive Preferences toward Social Investments and Transfers in Mature Welfare States: The Cases of Unemployment Benefits and Childcare Provision', *Journal of European Social Policy* 27 (3): 229–46.

Busemeyer, Marius R., Mia Gandenberger, Carlo Knotz, and Tobias Tober. 2023. 'Preferred Policy Responses to Technological Change: Survey Evidence from OECD Countries', *Socio-Economic Review* 21 (1): 593–615.

Busemeyer, Marius R., Philip Rathgeb, and Alexander H. J. Sahm. 2022. 'Authoritarian Valus and the Welfare State: The Social Policy Preferences of Radical Right Voters', *West European Politics* 45 (1): 77–101.

Buss, Christopher. 2019. 'Public Opinion towards Workfare Policies in Europe: Polarisation of Attitudes in Times of Austerity?', *International Journal of Social Welfare* 28 (4): 431–41.

Bustikova, Lenka. 2014. 'Revenge of the Radical Right', *Comparative Political Studies* 47 (12): 1738–65.

Campos Lima, Maria da Paz, and Antonio Martin Artiles. 2011. 'Crisis and Trade Union Challenges in Portugal and Spain: Between General Strikes and Social Pacts', *Transfer: European Review of Labour and Research* 17 (3): 387–402.

Campos Lima, Maria da Paz, and Reinhard Naumann. 2011. 'Portugal: From Broad Strategic Pacts to Policy-Specific Agreements', in Sabina Avdagic, Martin Rhodes, and Jelle

Visser (eds), *Social Pacts in Europe: Emergence, Evolution, and Institutionalization*. Oxford: Oxford University Press, 174–202.

Calmfors, Lars and John Driffill. 1988. 'Bargaining Structure, Corporatism and Macroeconomic Performance', *Economic Policy* 3 (6): 13–61.

Camus, Jean-Yves and Nicolas Lebourg. 2017. *Far-Right Politics in Europe*. Cambridge, Massachusetts: Harvard University Press.

Canovan, Margaret. 1999. 'Trust the People! Populism and the Two Faces of Democracy', *Political Studies* 47 (1): 2–16.

Card, David. 2001. 'Immigrant Inflows, Native Outflows, and the Local Labor Market Impacts of Higher Immigration', *Journal of Labor Economics* 19 (1): 22–64.

Card, David and John E. DiNardo. 2002. 'Skill-Biased Technological Change and Rising Wage Inequality: Some Problems and Puzzles', *Journal of Labor Economics* 20 (4): 733–83.

Carreras, Miguel, Yasemin Lrepoglu Carreras, and Shaun Bowler. 2019. 'Long-Term Economic Distress, Cultural Backlash, and Support for Brexit', *Comparative Political Studies* 52 (9): 1396–1424.

Carvalho, João and Didier Ruedin. 2020. 'The Positions Mainstream Left Parties Adopt on Immigration: A Cross-Cutting Cleavage?', *Party Politics* 26 (4): 379–89.

Cassese, Erin C. and Tiffany D. Barnes. 2019. 'Intersectional Motherhood: Investigating Public Support for Child Care Subsidies', *Politics, Groups, and Identities* 7 (4): 775–93.

Castater, Eric G. 2015. 'Unionization and the Partisan Effect on Income Inequality', *Business and Politics* 17 (1): 1–40.

Castater, Eric G. and Kyung Joon Han. 2016. 'Deal or No Deal: Labor Union Fractionalization and Social Pact Agreement', *West European Politics* 39 (6): 1251–75.

Castater, Eric G. and Kyung Joon Han. 2018. 'Trying Not to Lose: The Electoral Consequences of Unilateral Reform Efforts and the Social Pact Formation Process', *European Journal of Political Research* 57 (1): 171–93.

Castels, Manuel. 2019. Rupture: *The Crisis of Liberal Democracy*. Cambridge: Polity Press.

Catterberg, Gabriela and Alejandro Moreno. 2006. 'The Individual Bases of Political Trust: Trends in New and Established Democracies', *Public Opinion Quarterly* 18 (1): 31–48.

Checchi, Daniele and Cecilia García-Peñalos. 2008. 'Labour Market Institutions and Income Inequality', *Economic Policy* 23 (56): 602–49.

Checchi, Daniele and Marco Leonardi. 2016. 'An Economic Perspective on Employment Protection Legislation and Labour Market Prospects', *European Sociological Review* 32 (4): 532–5.

Checchi, Daniele, Jelle Visser, and Herman G. Van De Werfhors. 2010. 'Inequality and Union Membership: The Impact of Relative Earnings Position and Inequality Attitudes', *British Journal of Industrial Relations* 48 (1): 84–108.

Chrisp, Joe and Nick Pearce. 2019. 'Grey Power: Towards a Political Economy of Older Voters in the UK', *Political Quarterly* 90 (4): 743–56.

Cinnirella, Marco. 1998. 'Exploring Temporal Aspects of Social Identity: The Concept of Possible Social Identities', *European Journal of Social Psychology* 28 (2): 227–48.

Claassen, Ryan L. and Benjamin Highton 2009. 'Policy Polarization among Party Elites and the Significance of Political Awareness in the Mass Public', *Political Research Quarterly* 62 (3): 538–51.

Clark, Andrew and Fabien Postel-Vinary. 2009. 'Job Security and Job Protection', *Oxford Economic Papers* 61 (2): 207–39.

Clark, Colin. 1957. *The Conditions of Economic Progress*. London: Macmillan.

Clifford, Scott. 2017. 'Individual Differences in Group Loyalty Predict Partisan Strength', *Political Behavior* 39 (3): 531–52.

Coenders, Marcel and Peer Scheepers. 1998. 'Support for Ethnic Discrimination in the Netherlands 1979–1993: Effects of Period, Cohort, and Individual Characteristics', *European Sociological Review* 14 (4): 405–22.

Coenders, Marcel and Peer Scheepers. 2003. 'The Effect of Education on Nationalism and Ethnic Exclusionism: An International Comparison', *Political Psychology* 23 (2): 313–43.

Colantone, Italo and Piero Stanig. 2018a. 'Global Competition and Brexit', *American Political Science Review* 112 (2): 201–18.

Colantone, Italo and Piero Stanig. 2018b. 'The Trade Origins of Economic Nationalism: Import Competition and Voting Behavior in Western Europe', *American Journal of Political Science* 62 (4): 936–53.

Colombo, Emilio, Patrizio Tirelli, and Jelle Visser. 2014. 'Reinterpreting Social Pacts: Theory and Evidence', *Journal of Comparative Economics* 42 (2): 358–74.

Copelovitch, Mark, Jeffrey Frieden, and Stefanie Walter. 2016. 'The Political Economy of the Euro Crisis', *Comparative Political Studies* 49 (7): 811–40.

Cordero, Guillermo and Pablo Simón. 2016. 'Economic Crisis and Support for Democracy in Europe', *West European Politics* 39 (2): 305–25.

Criscuolo, Chiara and Luis Garicano. 2010. 'Offshoring and Wage Inequality: Using Occupational Licensing as a Shifter of Offshoring Costs', *American Economic Review* 100 (2): 439–43.

Culpepper, Pepper D. 2002. 'Powering, Puzzling, and "Pacting": The Informational Logic of Negotiated Reforms', *Journal of European Public Policy* 9 (5): 774–90.

Culpepper, Pepper D. and Aidan Regan. 2014. 'Why Don't Governments Need Trade Unions Anymore? The Death of Social Pacts in Ireland and Italy', *Socio-Economic Review* 12 (4): 723–45.

Cummins, Jeff. 2009. 'Issue Voting and Crime in Gubernatorial Elections', *Social Science Quarterly* 90 (3): 632–51.

Curtis, K. Amber. 2016. 'Personality's Effect on European Identification', *European Union Politics* 17 (3): 429–56.

Cusack, Thomas, Torben Iversen, and Philipp Rehm. 2006. 'Risk at Work: The Demand and Supply Sides of Redistribution', *Oxford Review of Economic Policy* 22 (3): 365–89.

Cutts, David, Robert Ford, and Matthew J. Goodwin. 2010. 'Anti-Immigrant, Politically Disaffected or Still Racist after All? Examining the Attitudinal Drivers of Extreme Right Support in Britain in the 2009 European Elections', *European Journal of Political Research* 50 (3): 418–40.

Dassonneville, Ruth and Michael S. Lewis-Beck. 2013. 'Economic Policy Voting and Incumbency: Unemployment in Western Europe', *Political Science Research and Methods* 1 (1): 53–66.

Davis, Otto A., Melvin J. Hinich, and Peter C. Ordeshool. 1970. 'An Expository Development of a Mathematical Model of the Electoral Process', *American Political Science Review* 64 (2): 426–48.

Deaux, Kay, Anne Reid, Kim Mizrahi, and Kathleen A. Ethier. 1995. 'Parameters of Social Identity', *Journal of Personality and Social Psychology* 68 (2): 280–91.

De Beer, Paul. 2007. 'Why Work Is Not a Panacea: A Decomposition Analysis of EU-15 Countries', *Journal of European Social Policy* 17 (4): 375–88.

De Grauwe, Paul. 2017. *The Limits of the Market: The Pendulum between Government and Market*. Oxford: Oxford University Press.

Delwit, Pascal. 2013. 'The End of Voters in Europe? Electoral Turnout in Europe since WWII', *Open Journal of Political Science* 3 (1): 44–52.

De New, John P. and Klaus F. Zimmermann. 1994. 'Native Wage Impacts of Foreign Labor: A Random Effects Panel Analysis', *Journal of Population Economics* 7 (2): 177–92.

Dennison, James. 2019. 'A Review of Public Issue Salience: Concepts, Determinants and Effects on Voting,' *Political Studies Review* 17 (4): 436–46.

Dosi, Giovanni, Marcelo C. Pereira, Andrea Roventini, and Maria Enrica Virgillito. 2018. 'What If Supply-Side Policies Are Not Enough? The Perverse Interaction of Flexibility and Austerity,' *Journal of Economic Behavior and Organization* 162: 360–88.

Down, Ian and Kyung Joon Han. 2020. 'Marginalisation or Legitimation? Mainstream Party Positioning on Immigration and Support for Radical Right Parties,' *West European Politics* 43 (7): 1388–1414.

Duch, Raymond M. and Randolph T. Stevenson. 2008. *The Economic Vote: How Political and Economic Institutions Condition Electoral Results*. Cambridge: Cambridge University Press.

Duman, Anil and Achim Kemmerling. 2020. 'Do You Feel Like an Insider? Job Security and Preferences for Flexibilization across Europe,' *Social Policy Administration* 54 (5): 749–64.

Duncan, Lauren E. and Abigail J. Stewart. 2007. 'Personal Political Salience: The Role of Personality in Collective Identity and Action,' *Political Psychology* 28 (2): 143–64.

Dunn, Chris. 2015. 'Preference for Radical Right-Wing Populist Parties among Exclusive-Nationalists and Authoritarians,' *Party Politics* 21 (3): 367–80.

Dustmann, Christian and Ian P. Preston. 2007. 'Racial and Economic Factors in Attitudes to Immigration,' *The B.E. Journal of Economic Analysis and Policy* 7 (1): 1–39.

Easton, David. 1965. *A Systems Analysis of Political Life*. New York: John Wiley & Sons, Inc.

Eatwell, Roger. 2018. 'Charisma and the Radical Right,' in Jens Rydgren (ed.), *The Oxford Handbook of the Radical Right*. Oxford: Oxford University Press, 251–68.

Ebeid, Michael and Jonathan Rodden. 2006. 'Economic Geography and Economic Voting: Evidence from the US States,' *British Journal of Political Science* 36 (3): 527–47.

Ecker, Alejandro, Konstantin Glinitzer, and Thomas M. Meyer. 2016. 'Corruption Performance Voting and the Electoral Context,' *European Political Science Review* 8 (3): 333–54.

Eichengreen, Barry. 2018. *The Populist Temptation: Economic Grievance and Political Reaction in the Modern Era*. Oxford: Oxford University Press.

Ellemers, Naomi. 1993. 'The Influecne of Socio-structural Variables on Identity Management Strategies,' *European Review of Social Psychology* 4 (1): 27–57.

Ellemers, Naomi, Paulien Kortekaas, and Jaap W. Ouwerkerk. 1999. 'Self-categorisation, Commitment to the Group and Group Self-esteem as Related but Distinct Aspects of Social Identity,' *European Journal of Social Psychology* 29: 371–89.

Ellinas, Antonis A. 2013. 'Neo-Nazism in an Established Democracy: The Persistence of Golden Dawn in Greece,' *South European Society and Politics* 20 (1): 1–20.

Emmenegger, Patrick. 2014. *The Power to Dismiss: Trade Unions and the Regulation of Job Security in Western Europe*. Oxford: Oxford University Press.

Emmenegger, Patrick, Silja Häusermann, Bruno Palier, and Martin Seeleib-Kaiser. 2012. *The Age of Dualization: The Changing Face of Inequality in Deindustrializing Societies*. Oxford: Oxford University Press.

Emmenegger, Patrick, Paul Marx, and Dominik Schraff. 2015. 'Labour Market Disadvantage, Political Orientations and Voting: How Adverse Labour Market Experiences Translate into Electoral Behavior,' *Socio-Economic Review* 13 (2): 189–213.

Enggist, Matthias and Michael Pinggera. 2022. 'Radical Right Parties and Their Welfare State Stances—Not So Blurry after All?,' *West European Politics* 45 (1): 102–28.

Engler, Fabian and Reimut Zohlnhöfer. 2019. 'Left Parties, Voter Preferences, and Economic Policy-Making in Europe,' *Journal of European Public Policy* 26 (11): 1620–38.

Engler, Sarah and David Weisstanner. 2021. 'The Threat of Social Decline: Income Inequality and Radical Right Support,' *Journal of European Public Policy* 28 (2): 153–73.

Erikson, Robert and John Goldthorpe. 1992. 'Individual or Family? Results from Two Approaches to Class Assignment,' *Acta Sociologica* 35 (2): 95–105.

References 211

Esaiasson, Peter, Mikael Gilljam, and Mikael Persson. 2017. 'Responsiveness beyond Policy Satisfaction: Does It Matter to Citizens?', *Comparative Political Studies* 50 (6): 739–65.

Escudero, Verónica. 2018. 'Are Active Labour Market Policies Effective in Activating and Integrating Low-Skilled Individuals? An International Comparison', *IZA Journal of Labor Policy* 7 (4): 1–26.

Esping-Andersen, Gosta. 1990. *The Three Worlds of Welfare Capitalism.* Princeton, New Jersey: Princeton University Press.

Esping-Andersen, Gosta (ed.). 1996. *Welfare State in Transition: National Adaptations in Global Economies.* London: Sage Publication.

Esping-Andersen, Gosta and Sander Wagner. 2012. 'Asymmetries in the Opportunity Structure: Intergenerational Mobility Trends in Europe', *Research in Social Stratification and Mobility* 30 (4): 473–87.

Estevez-Abe, Margarita, Torben Iversen, and David Soskice. 2001. 'Social Protection and the Formation of Skills: A Reinterpretation of the Welfare State', in Peter A. Hall and David Soskice (eds), *Varieties of Capitalism: The Institutional Foundations of Comparative Advantage.* Oxford: Oxford University Press, 145–183.

Eurofound. 2015a. *Industrial Relations and Working Conditions Developments in Europe 2013.* Luxembourg: Publications Office of the European Union.

Eurofound. 2015b. *Developments in Working Life in Europe: EurWORK Annual Review 2014.* Luxembourg: Publications Office of the European Union.

Eurofound. 2016. *Developments in Working Life in Europe 2015: EurWORK Annual Review.* Luxembourg: Publications Office of the European Union.

Eurofound. 2017. *Developments in Working Life in Europe 2016: EurWORK Annual Review.* Luxembourg: Publications Office of the European Union.

Eurofound. 2020. *Industrial Relations: Developments 2015–2019.* Luxembourg: Publications Office of the European Union.

Evans, Geoffrey (ed.). 1999. *The End of Class Politics? Class Voting in Comparative Context.* Oxford: Oxford University Press.

Evans, Geoffrey. 2000. 'The Continued Significance of Class Voting', *Annual Review of Political Science* 3: 401–17.

Fenger, Menno. 2018. 'The Social Policy Agendas of Populist Radical Right Parties in Comparative Perspective', *Journal of International and Comparative Social Policy* 34 (3): 188–209.

Fernandez, Roberto M. 2001. 'Skill-Biased Technological Change and Wage Inequality: Evidence from a Plant Retooling', *American Journal of Sociology* 107 (2): 273–320.

Finkel, Steven E. 1985. 'Reciprocal Effects of Participation and Political Efficacy: A Panel Analysis', *American Journal of Political Science* 29 (4): 891–913.

Finseraas, Henning. 2010. 'What if Robin Hood is a Social Conservative? How the Political Response to Increasing Inequality Depends on Party Polarization', *Socio-Economic Review* 8 (2): 283–306.

Fligstein, Neil, Alina Polyakova, and Wayne Sandholtz. 2012. 'European Integration, Nationalism and European Identity', *Journal of Common Market Studies* 50 (S1): 106–22.

Flynn, Patricia M. 1988. *Facilitating Technological Change: The Human Resource Challenge.* Cambridge, Massachusetts: Ballinger.

Ford, Robert, Matthew J. Goodwin, and David Cutts. 2012. 'Strategic Eurosceptics and Polite Xenophobes: Support for the United Kingdom Independence Party (UKIP) in the 2009 European Parliament Elections', *European Journal of Political Research* 51 (2): 204–34.

Fowler, James H. and Cindy D. Kam. 2007. 'Beyond the Self: Social Identity, Altruism, and Political Participation', *Journal of Politics* 69 (3): 813–27.

Fröbel, Folker Jürgen Heinrichs, and Otto Kreye. 1980. *The New International Division of Labour: Structural Unemployment in Industrialised Countries and Industrialisation in Developing Countries*. Cambridge: Cambridge University Press.

Gabor, Daniela. 2014. 'Learning from Japan: The European Central Bank and the European Sovereign Debt Crisis', *Review of Political Economy* 26 (2): 190–209.

Gangl, Makus. 2003. 'The Only Way Is Up? Employment Protection and Job Mobility among Recent Entrants to European Labour Markets', *European Sociological Review* 19 (5): 429–49.

Garrett, Geoffrey and Deborah Mitchell. 2001. 'Globalization, Government Spending and Taxation in the OECD', *European Journal of Political Research* 39 (2): 145–77.

Garrett, Geoffrey and Christopher Way. 1999. 'Public Sector Unions, Corporatism, and Macroeconomic Performance', *Comparative Political Studies* 32 (4): 411–34.

Garrett, Kristin N. and Alexa Bankert. 2018. 'The Moral Roots of Partisan Division: How Moral Conviction Heightens Affective Polarization', *British Journal of Political Science* 50 (2): 621–40.

Gasper, John T. and Andrew Reeves. 2011. 'Make It Rain? Retrospection and the Attentive Electorate in the Context of Natural Disasters', *American Journal of Political Science* 55 (2): 340–55.

Gastil, John, Laura Black, and Kara Moscovitz. 2008. 'Ideology, Attitude Change, and Deliberation in Small Face-to-Face Groups', *Political Communication* 25 (1): 23–46.

Geishecker Ingo and Holger Görg. 2005. 'Do Unskilled Workers Always Lose from Fragmentation', *North American Journal of Economics and Finance* 16 (1): 81–92.

Gemenis, Kostas and Elias Dinas. 2010. 'Confrontation Still? Examining Parties' Policy Positions in Greece', *Comparative European Politics* 8 (2): 179-201.

Gest, Justin. 2016. *The New Minority: White Working Class Politics in an Age of Immigration and Inequality*. Oxford, Oxford University Press.

Gest, Justin, Tyler Reny, and Jeremy Mayer. 2018. 'Roots of the Radical Right: Nostalgic Deprivation in the United States and Britain', *Comparative Political Studies* 51 (13): 1694–1719.

Gidron, Noam, James Adams, and Will Horne. 2019. 'Toward a Comparative Research Agenda on Affective Polarization in Mass Public', *APSA Comparative Politics Newsletter* 29: 30–6.

Gidron, Noam, James Adams, and Will Horne. 2020. *American Affective Polarization in Comparative Perspective*. Cambridge: Cambridge University Press.

Gidron, Noam and Peter A. Hall. 2017. 'The Politics of Social Status: Economic and Cultural Roots of the Populist Right', *British Journal of Sociology* 68 (S1): 557–84.

Giersch, Herbert. 1985. 'Perspectives on the World Economy', *South African Journal of Economics* 53 (4): 215–25.

Giger, Nathalie, Jan Rosset, and Julian Bernauer. 2012. 'The Poor Political Representation of the Poor in a Comparative Perspective', *Representation* 48 (1): 47–61.

Gingrich, Jane and Ben Ansell. 2012. 'Preferences in Context: Micro Preferences, Macro Contexts, and the Demand for Social Policy', *Comparative Political Studies* 45 (12): 1624–54.

Gingrich, Jane and Silja Hausermann. 2015. 'The Decline of the Working-Class Vote, the Reconfiguration of the Welfare Support Coalition and Consequences for the Welfare State', *Journal of European Social Policy* 25 (1): 50–75.

Giugni, Marco, Ruud Koopmans, Florence Passy, and Paul Statham. 2005. 'Institutional and Discursive Opportunities for Extreme-Right Mobilization in Five Countries', *Mobilization: An International Quarterly* 10 (1): 145–62.

Glassner, Vera, Maarten Keune, and Paul Marginson. 2011. 'Collective Bargaining in a Time of Crisis: Developments in the Private Sector in Europe', *Transfer* 17 (3): 303–21.

Goedemé, Tim, Marii Paskov, David Weisstanner, and Brian Nolan. 2021. 'Between-Class Earnings Inequality in 30 European Countries', *Comparative Sociology* 20 (6): 741–78.

References   213

Golden, Miriam and Michael Wallerstein. 2011. 'Domestic and International Causes for the Rise of Pay Inequality in OECD Nations between 1980 and 2000', in David Brady (ed.), *Comparing European Workers Part A (Research in Sociology of Work, Vol. 22 Part 1)*. Bingley: Emerald Group Publishing Limited, 209–49.

Golder, Matt. 2003. 'Explaining Variation in the Success of Extreme Right Parties in Western Europe', *Comparative Political Studies* 36 (4): 432–66.

Golder, Matt. 2016. 'Far Right Parties in Europe', *Annual Review of Political Science* 19: 477–97.

Gomez, Raul and Luis Ramiro. 2019. 'The Limits of Organizational Innovation and Multi-Speed Membership: Podemos and Its New Forms of Party Membership', *Party Politics* 25 (4): 534–46.

Gómez-Reino, Margarita and Iván Llamazares. 2013. 'The Populist Radical Right and European Integration: A Comparative Analysis of Party-Voter Links', *West European Politics* 36 (4): 789–816.

Goos, Maarten, Alan Manning, and Anna Salomons. 2014. 'Explaining Job Polarization: Routine-Biased Technological Change and Offshoring', *The American Economic Review* 104 (8): 2509–26.

Gordon, Joshua. 2015. 'Protecting the Unemployed: Varieties of Unionism and the Evolution of Unemployment Benefits and Active Labor Market Policy in the Rich Democracies', *Socio-Economic Review* 13 (1): 79–99.

Goubin, Silke, Marc Hooghe, Martin Okolikj, and Dieter Stiers. 2020. 'Economic Inequality and Electoral Accountability: Inequality and Differences in Economic Voting across Western Democracies', *Comparative European Politics* 18 (5): 793–818.

Graziano, Paolo R. and Matteo Jessoula. 2011. '"Eppur si muovera..." The Italian Trajectory of Recent Welfare Reforms: From "Rescued by Europe" to Euro-scepticism', in Paolo R. Graziano, Sophie Jacquot, and Bruno Palier (eds), *The EU and the Domestic Politics of Welfare State Reforms*. Hampshire, Palgrave Macmillan, 148–84.

Guillaud, Elvire and Paul Marx. 2014. 'Preferences for Employment Protection and the Insider-Outsider Divide: Evidence from France', *West European Politics* 37 (5): 1177–85.

Hagendoorn, Louk and Shervin Nekuee. 2018. *Education and Racism: A Cross National Inventory of Positive Effects of Education on Ethnic Tolerance*. London: Routledge.

Hainmueller, Jens and Michael J. Hiscox. 2007. 'Educated Preferences: Explaining Attitudes toward Immigration in Europe', *International Organization* 61 (2): 399–442.

Hainmueller, Jens and Michael J. Hiscox. 2010. 'Attitudes toward Highly Skilled and Low-skilled Immigration: Evidence from a Survey Experiment', *American Political Science Review* 104 (1): 61–84.

Halikiopoulou, Daphne and Tim Vlandas. 2016. 'Risks, Costs and Labour Markets: Explaining Cross-National Patterns of Far Right Party Success in European Parliament Elections', *Journal of Common Market Studies* 54 (3): 636–55.

Hall, Peter A. and Robert J. Franzese. 1998. 'Mixed Signals: Central Bank Independence, Coordinated Wage Bargaining, and European Monetary Union', *International Organization* 52 (3): 505–35.

Hall, Peter A. and David Soskice (eds). 2001. *Varieties of Capitalism: The Institutional Foundations of Comparative Advantage*. Oxford: Oxford University Press.

Hall, Peter A. and Kathleen Thelen. 2007. 'Institutional Change in Varieties of Capitalism', *Socioeconomic Review* 7 (1): 7–34.

Hamann, Kerstin, Alison Johnston, Alexia Katsanidou, John Kelly, and Philip Pollock. 2015. 'Sharing the Rewards, Dividing the Costs? The Electoral Consequences of Social Pacts and Legislative Reform in Western Europe', *West European Politics* 38 (1): 206–27.

214 References

Hamann, Kerstin, Alison Johnston, and John Kelly. 2013. 'Unions against Governments: Explaining General Strikes in Western Europe, 1980–2006', *Comparative Political Studies* 46 (9): 1030–57.

Hamann, Kerstin and John Kelly. 2007. 'Party Politics and the Reemergence of Social Pacts in Western Europe', *Comparative Political Studies* 40 (8): 971–94.

Hamann, Kerstin and John Kelly. 2010. *Parties, Elections, and Policy Reforms in Western Europe: Voting for Social Pacts.* London: Routledge.

Han, Kyung Joon. 2013a. 'Income Inequality, International Migration, and Nationalistic Pride: A Test of Social Identification Theory', *International Journal of Public Opinion Research* 25 (4): 502–21.

Han, Kyung Joon. 2013b. 'Political Use of Asylum Policies: The Effects of Partisanship and Election Timing on Government Policies Regarding Asylum Seekers' Welfare Benefits', *Comparative European Politics* 11 (4): 383–405.

Han, Kyung Joon. 2015a. 'The Impact of Radical Right-Wing Parties on the Positions of Mainstream Parties Regarding Multiculturalism', *West European Politics* 38 (3): 557–76.

Han, Kyung Joon. 2015b. 'When Will Left-Wing Governments Introduce Liberal Migration Policies? An Implication of Power Resources Theory', *International Studies Quarterly* 59 (3): 602–14.

Han, Kyung Joon. 2016. 'Income Inequality and Voting for Radical Right-Wing Parties', *Electoral Studies* 42: 54–64.

Han, Kyung Joon. 2020a. 'Reacting to Isolation: How the Political Exclusion of Extreme Right-wing Parties Change the Party Support', *Representation* 56 (1): 71–87.

Han, Kyung Joon. 2020b. 'Beclouding Party Position as an Electoral Strategy: Voter Polarization, Issue Priority, and Position Blurring', *British Journal of Political Science* 50 (2): 653–75.

Han, Kyung Joon. Forthcoming. 'Issue Salience and Affective Polarization', *Journal of Elections, Public Opinion and Parties* (https://doi.org/10.1080/17457289.2023.2277429).

Han, Kyung Joon and Eric G. Castater. 2016. 'They May Not Have the Skills but They Have the Desire: How a Compositional Aspect of Trade Unions Determines Wage Inequality', *Research in Social Stratification and Mobility* 45: 1–12.

Han, Kyung Joon and Eric G. Castater. 2023. 'It's Not Just Where You Stand, It's How You Got There: Social Pacts and Manual Worker Support for Radical Right-Wing Parties', *European Politics and Society* 24 (2): 188–212.

Harteveld, Eelco. 2016. 'Winning the "Losers" but Losing the "Winners"? The Electoral Consequences of the Radical Right Moving to the Economic Left', *Electoral Studies* 44: 225–34.

Harteveld, Eelco, Philipp Mendoza, and Matthijs Roodujin. 2021. 'Affective Polarization and the Populist Radical Right: Creating the Hating?', *Government and Opposition* 57 (S4): 703–27.

Haskel, Jonathan E. and Matthew J. Slaughter. 2002. 'Does the Sector Bias of Skill-based Technical Change Explain Changing Skill Premia?', *European Economic Review* 46 (10): 1757–83.

Hassel, Anke. 2009. 'Policies and Politics in Social Pacts in Europe', *European Journal of Industrial Relations* 15 (1): 7–26.

Häusermann, Silja, Achim Kemmerling, and David Rueda. 2020. 'How Labor Market Inequality Transforms Mass Politics', *Political Science Research and Methods* 8 (2): 344–55.

Häuusermann, Silja, Michael Pinggera, Macarena Ares, and Matthias Enggist. 2022. 'Class and Social Policy in the Knowledge Economy', *European Journal of Political Research* 61 (2): 462–84.

Healy, Andrew and Gabriel S. Lenz. 2014. 'Substituting the End for the Whole: Why Voters Respond Primarily to the Election-Year Economy', *American Journal of Political Science* 58 (1): 31–47.

Healy, Andrew and Neil Malhotra. 2010. 'Random Events, Economic Losses, and Retrospective Voting: Implications for Democratic Competence', *Quarterly Journal of Political Science* 5 (2): 193–208.

Heimberger, Philipp. 2021. 'Does Employment Protection Affect Unemployment? A Meta-Analysis', *Oxford Economic Papers* 73 (3): 982–1007.

Heizmann, Boris. 2015. 'Social Policy and Perceived Immigrant Labor Market Competition in Europe: Is Prevention Better than Cure?', *Social Forces* 93 (4): 1655–85.

Helgason, Agnar Freyr and Vittorio Mérola. 2017. 'Employment Insecurity, Incumbent Partisanship, and Voting Behavior in Comparative Perspective', *Comparative Political Studies* 50 (11): 1489–1523.

Hemerijck, Anton, Johannes Karremans, and Marc van der Meer. 2023. 'Responsive Corporatism without Political Credit: Social Concertation, Constructive Opposition and the Long Tenure of the Rutte II Cabinet in the Netherlands (2012–2017)', *Acta Politica* 58 (1): 161–80.

Hernández, Enrique and Hanspeter Kriesi. 2016. 'The Electoral Consequences of the Financial and Economic Crisis in Europe', *European Journal of Political Research* 55 (2): 203–24.

Heyes, Jason and Paul Lewis. 2014. 'Employment Protection under Fire: Labour Market Deregulation and Employment in the European Union', *Economic and Industrial Democracy* 35 (4): 587–607.

Hicks, Raymond and Dustin Tingley. 2011. 'Causal Mediation Analysis', *The Stata Journal* 11(4): 605–19.

Hildebrandt, Achim, Eva-Maria Trüdinger, and Dominik Wyss. 2019. 'The Missing Link? Modernization, Tolerance, and Legislation on Homosexuality', *Political Research Quarterly* 72 (3): 539–53.

Hogg, Michael A. and Dominic Abrams. 1988. *Social Identifications: A Social Psychology of Intergroup Relations and Group Processes.* London: Routledge.

Hooghe, Liesbet, Ryan Bakker, Anna Brigevich, Catherine de Vries, Erica Edwards, Gary Marks, Jan Rovny, Marco Steenbergen, and Milada Vachudova. 2010. 'Reliability and Validity of the 2002 and 2006 Chapel Hill Expert Surveys on Party Positioning', *European Journal of Politial Research* 49 (5): 687–703.

Hooghe, Liesbet, Tobias Lenz, and Gary Marks. 2019. 'Contested World Order: The Delegitimation of International Governance', *Review of International Organizations* 14 (4): 731–43.

Hooghe, Liesbet and Gary Marks. 2005. 'Calculation, Community and Cues', *European Union Politics* 6 (4): 419–43.

Hooghe, Liesbet, Gary Marks, and Carole J. Wilson. 2002. 'Does Left/Right Structure Party Positions on European Integration?', *Comparative Political Studies* 35 (8): 965–89.

Hooghe, Marc, Ruth Dassonneville, and Jeniffer Oser. 2019. 'Public Opinion, Turnout and Social Policy: A Comparative Analysis of Policy Congruence in European Liberal Democracies', *Political Studies* 67 (4): 992–1009.

Hootegem, Arno Van, Koen Abts, and Bart Meuleman. 2024. 'Weakly Institutionalized, Heavily Contested: Does Support for Contemporary Welfare Reforms Rely on Norms of Distributive Justice?', *Journal of Social Policy* 53 (4): 1033-51.

Hope, David and Angelo Martelli. 2019. 'The Transition to the Knowledge Economy, Labor Market Institutions, and Income Inequality in Advanced Democracies', *World Politics* 71 (2): 236–88.

Hopkin, Jonathan and Julia Lynch. 2016. 'Winner-Take-All Politics in Europe? European Inequality in Comparative Perspective', *Politics and Society* 44 (3): 335–43.

216 References

Hornsey, Matthew J. 2008. 'Social Identity Theory and Self-categorization Theory: A Historical Review', *Social and Personality Psychology Compass* 2 (1): 204–22.

Huber, Evelyne and John D. Stephens. 2001. *Development and Crisis of the Welfare State: Parties and Policies in Global Markets*. Chicago, Illinois: The University of Chicago Press.

Huber, Evelyne and John D. Stephens. 2014. 'Income Inequality and Redistribution in Post-Industrial Democracies: Demographic, Economic, and Political Determinants', *Socio-Economic Review* 12 (2): 245–67.

Huddy, Leonie. 2001. 'From Social to Political Identity: A Critical Examination of Social Identity Theory', *Political Psychology* 22 (1): 127–56.

Huici, Carmen, María Ros, Ignacio Cano, Nicholas Hopkins, Nicholas Emler, and Mercedes Carmona. 1997. 'Comparative Identity and Evaluation of Socio-political Change: Perceptions of the European Community as a Function of the Salience of Regional Identities', *European Journal of Social Psychology* 27 (1): 97–113.

Hummels, David, Jakob R. Munch, and Chong Xiang. 2018. 'Offshoring and Labor Markets', *Journal of Economic Literature* 56 (3): 981–1028.

Huo, Jingjing, Moira Nelson, and John D. Stephens. 2008. 'Decommodification and Activation in Social Democratic Policy: Resolving the Paradox', *Journal of European Social Policy* 18 (1): 5–20.

Hutchings, Vincent L. 2001. 'Political Context, Issue Salience, and Selective Attentiveness: Constituent Knowledge of the Clarence Thomas Confirmation Vote', *Journal of Politics* 63 (3): 846–68.

Hyman, Richard. 2001. *Understanding European Trade Unionism: Between Market, Class and Society*. London: Sage Publications.

Imai, Kosuke, Luke Keele, and Dustin Tingley. 2010. 'A General Approach to Causal Mediation Analysis', *Psychological Methods* 15 (4): 309–34.

Imai, Kosuke, Luke Keele, Dustin Tingley, and Teppei Yamamato. 2011. 'Unpacking the Black Box of Causality: Learning about Causal Mechanisms from Experimental and Observational Studies', *American Political Science Review* 105 (4): 765–89.

Immerzeel, Tim, Eva Jaspers, and Marcel Lubbers. 2013. 'Religion as Catalyst or Restraint of Radical Right Voting?', *West European Politics* 36 (5): 946–68.

Ireland, Patrick R. 2004. *Becoming Europe: Immigration, Integration, and the Welfare State*. Pittsburgh, Pennsylvania: University of Pittsburgh Press.

Ivarsflaten, Elisabeth. 2005. 'The Vulnerable Populist Right Parties: No Economic Realignment Fuelling Their Electoral Success', *European Journal of Political Research* 44 (3): 465–92.

Ivarsflaten, Elisabeth. 2008. 'What Unites Right-Wing Populists in Western Europe? Re-Examing Grievance Mobilization Models in Seven Successful Cases', *Comparative Political Studies* 41 (1): 3–23.

Iversen, Torben and Thomas Cusack. 2000. 'The Causes of Welfare State Expansion: Deindustrialization or Globalization?', *World Politics* 52 (3): 313–49.

Iversen, Torben, and David Soskice. 2009. 'Distribution and Redistribution: The Shadow of the Nineteenth Century', *World Politics* 61 (3): 438–86.

Iversen, Torben, and David Soskice. 2010. 'Real Exchange Rates and Competitiveness: The Political Economy of Skill Formation, Wage Compression, and Electoral Systems', *American Political Science Review* 104 (3): 601–23.

Iversen, Torben, and John D. Stephens. 2008. 'Partisan Politics, the Welfare State, and Three Worlds of Human Capital Formation', *Comparative Political Studies* 41 (4–5): 600–37.

Iyengar, Shanto, Yphtach Lelkes, Matthew Levendusky, Neil Malhotra, and Sean J. Westwood. 2019. 'The Origins and Consequences of Affective Polarization in the United States', *Annual Review of Political Science* 22: 129–46.

Jackman, Robert W. and Karin Volpert. 1996. 'Conditions Favoring Parties of the Extreme Right in Western Europe', *British Journal of Political Science* 26 (4): 501–21.

Jagers, Jan and Stefan Walgrave. 2007. 'Populism as Political Communication Style: An Empirical Study of Political Parties' Discourse in Belgium', *European Journal of Political Research* 46 (3): 319–45.

Jahn, Detlef. 2016. 'Changing of the Guard: Trends in Corporatist Arrangements in 42 Highly Industrialized Societies from 1960 to 2010', *Socio-Economic Review* 14 (1): 47–71.

Jarness, Vegard, Magne Paalgard Flemmen, and Lennart Rosenlund. 2019. 'From Class Politics to Classed Politics', *Sociology* 53 (5): 879–99.

Jay, Sarah, Anatolia Batruch, Jolanda Jetten, Craig McGarty, Orla T. Muldoon. 2019. 'Economic Inequality and the Rise of Far-right Populism: A Social Psychological Analysis', *Journal of Community & Applied Social Psychology* 29 (5): 418–28.

Jennings, Will, Nick Clarke, Jonathan Moss, and Gerry Stokes. 2017. 'The Decline in Diffuse Support for National Politics: The Long View of Political Discontent in Britain', *Public Opinion Quarterly* 81 (3): 748–58.

Jensen, Carsten. 2011. 'Catching Up by Transition: Globalization as a Generator of Convergence in Social Spending', *Journal of European Public Policy* 18 (1): 106–21.

Jensen, Carsten and Georg Wenzelburger. 2021. 'Welfare State Reforms and Mass Media Attention: Evidence from Three Democracies', *European Journal of Political Research* 60 (4): 914–33.

Johnston, Ron, Carol Propper, Simon Burgess, Rebecca Sarker, Anne Bolster, and Kelvyn Jones. 2005. 'Spatial Scale and the Neighborhood Effect: Multinomial Models of Voting at Two Recent British General Elections', *British Journal of Political Science* 35 (3): 487–514.

Jones, Philip Edward. 2023. 'Political Awareness and the Identity-to-Politics Link in Public Opinion', *Journal of Politics* 85 (2): 510–23.

Jones, Philip Edward and Paul R. Brewer. 2020. 'Elite Cues and Public Polarization on Transgender Rights', *Politics, Groups, and Identities* 8 (1): 71–85.

Joppke, Christian. 1998. 'Why Liberal States Accept Unwanted Immigration', *World Politics* 50 (2): 266–93.

Jungar, Ann-Cathrine and Anders Ravik Jupskås. 2014. 'Populist Radical Right Parties in the Nordic Region: A New and Distinct Party Family?', *Scandinavian Political Studies* 37 (3): 215–38.

Kaase, Max. 1999. 'Interpersonal Trust, Political Trust and Non-Institutionalised Political Participation in Western Europe', *West European Politics* 22 (3): 1–21.

Kahne, Joseph and Joel Westheimer. 2006. 'The Limits of Political Efficacy: Educating Citizens for a Democratic Society', *PS: Political Science and Politics* 39 (2): 289–96.

Karol, David and Edward Miguel. 2007. 'The Electoral Cost of War: Iraq Casualties and the 2004 U.S. Presidential Election', *Journal of Politics* 69 (3): 633–48.

Karp, Jeffrey and Susan A. Banducci. 2008. 'Political Efficacy and Participation in Twenty-Seven Democracies: How Electoral Systems Shape Political Behaviour', *British Journal of Political Science* 38 (2): 311–34.

Karreth, Johannes, Jonathan Polk, and Christopher Allen. 2013. 'Catchall or Catch and Release? The Electoral Consequences of Social Democratic Parties' March to the Middle in Western Europe', *Comparative Political Studies* 46 (7): 791–822.

Katsambekis, Giorgos and Alexandros Kioupkiolis. 2019. *The Populist Radical Left in Europe.* London: Routledge.

Kelly, Nathan J. and Peter K. Enns. 2010. 'Inequality and the Dynamics of Public Opinion: The Self-Reinforcing Link between Economic Inequality and Mass Preferences', *American Journal of Political Science* 54 (4): 855–70.

218   References

Keman, Hans. 2011. 'Third Ways and Social Democracy: The Right Way to Go?', *British Journal of Political Science* 41 (3): 671–80.

Kenworthy, Lane. 2002. 'Corporatism and Unemployment in the 1980s and 1990s', *American Sociological Review* 67 (3): 367–88.

Kešić, Josip and Willem Duyvendak. 2019. 'The Nation under Threat: Secularist, Racial and Populist Nativism in the Netherlands', *Patterns of Prejudice* 53 (5): 441–63.

Kessler, Alan and Gary P. Freeman. 2005. 'Support for Extreme Right-Wing Parties in Western Europe: Individual Attitudes, Political Attitudes, and National Context', *Comparative European Politics* 3 (3): 261–88.

Kesternich, Iris, Heiner Schumacher, Bettina Siflinger, and Franziska Valder. 2022. 'Reservation Wages and Labor Supply', *Journal of Economic Behavior and Organization* 194: 583–607.

Ketola, Markus and Johan Nordensvard. 2018. 'Reviewing the Relationship between Social Policy and the Contemporary Populist Radical Right: Welfare Chauvinism, Welfare Nation State and Social Citizenship', *Journal of International and Comparative Social Policy* 34 (3): 172–87.

Keuschnigg, Christian and Evelyn Ribi. 2009. 'Outsourcing, Unemployment and Welfare Policy', *Journal of International Economics* 78 (1): 168–76.

Kim, Seongchul. Forthcoming. 'The Limits of Party Unionism: Far-Right Projects of Trade Union Building in Belgium, France, and Germany', *Journal of Contemporary European Studies* (https://doi.org/10.1080/14782804.2022.2118679).

King, Gary, Michael Tomz, and Jason Wittenberg. 2000. 'Making the Most of Statistical Analyses: Improving Interpretation and Presentation', *American Journal of Political Science* 44 (2): 341–55.

Kingzette, Jon, James N. Druckman, Samara Klar, Yanna Krupnikov, Matthew Levendusky, and John Barry Ryan. 2021. 'How Affective Polarization Undermines Support for Democratic Norms', *Public Opinion Quarterly* 85 (2): 663–77.

Kitschelt, Herbert. 1994. *The Transformation of European Social Democracy*. Cambridge: Cambridge University Press.

Kitschelt, Herbert. 1995. *The Radical Right in Western Europe: A Comparative Analysis*. Ann Arbor, Michigan: University of Michigan Press.

Kitschelt, Herbert. 1999. 'European Social Democracy between Political Economy and Electoral Competition', in Herbert Kitschelt, Peter Lange, Gary Marks, and John Stephens (eds), *Continuity and Change in Contemporary Capitalism*. Cambridge: Cambridge University Press, 317–45.

Klar, Samara. 2013. 'The Influence of Competing Identity Primes on Political Preferences', *Journal of Politics* 75 (4): 1108–24.

Klüver, Heike and Jae-Jae Spoon. 2016. 'Who Responds? Voters, Parties, and Issue Attention', *British Journal of Political Science* 46 (3): 633–54.

Knigge, Pia. 1998. 'The Ecological Correlates of Right-wing Extremism in Western Europe', *European Journal of Political Research* 34 (2): 249–79.

Knobloch, Katherine R., Michael Barthel, and John Gastil. 2020. 'Emanating Effects: The Impact of the Oregon Citizens' Initiative Review on Voters' Political Efficacy', *Political Studies* 68 (2): 426–45.

Ko, Hyejin and Eunchong Bae. 2020. 'Effects of Active Labour-Market Policies on Welfare State Finances', *Journal of International and Comparative Social Welfare* 36 (2): 200–16.

Kollmeyer, Christopher. 2009. 'Explaining Deindustrialization: How Affluence, Productivity Growth, and Globalization Diminish Manufacturing Employment', *American Journal of Sociology* 114 (6): 1644–74.

Kollmeyer, Christopher and John Peters. 2019. 'Financialization and the Decline of Organized Labor: A Study of 18 Advanced Capitalist Countries, 1970–2012', *Social Forces* 98 (1): 1–30.

Kopecky, Jonathan, Nathan Bos, and Ariel Greenberg. 2010. 'Social Identity Modeling: Past Work and Relevant Issues for Socio-cultural Modeling', *Proceedings of the 19th Conference on Behavior Representation in Modeling and Simulation*. Charleston, South Carolina.

Korpi, Walter. 1985. 'Power Resources Approach vs. Action and Conflict', *Sociological Theory* 3 (2): 31–45.

Korpi, Walter. 1991. 'Political and Economic Explanations for Unemployment: A Cross-National and Long-Term Analysis', *British Journal of Political Science* 21 (3): 315–48.

Korpi, Walter. 2002. 'The Great Trough in Unemployment: A Long-term View of Unemployment, Inflation, Strikes, and the Profit/Wage Ratio', *Politics and Society* 30 (3): 365–426.

Korpi, Walter. 2006. 'Power Resources and Employer-Centered Approaches in Explanations of Welfare States and Varieties of Capitalism: Protagonists, Consenters, and Antagonists', *World Politics* 58 (1): 167–206.

Korpi, Walter and Joakim Palme. 1998. 'The Paradox of Redistribution and Strategies of Equality: Welfare State Institutions, Inequality, and Poverty in the Western Countries', *American Sociological Review* 63 (5): 661–87.

Korpi, Walter and Joakim Palme. 2003. 'New Politics and Class Politics in the Context of Austerity and Globalization: Welfare State Regress in 18 Countries, 1975–95', *American Political Science Review* 97 (3): 425–46.

Kosterman, Rick and Seymour Feshbach. 1989. 'Toward a Measure of Patriotic and Nationalistic Attitudes', *Political Psychology* 10 (2): 257–74.

Krajnáková, Emília and Sergej Vojtovic. 2017. 'Struggles of Older Workers at the Labour Market', *Economics and Sociology* 10 (1): 319–33.

Kriesi, Hanspeter. 2020. 'Is There a Crisis of Democracy in Europe?', *Politische Vierteljahresschrift* 61: 237–60.

Kriesi, Hanspeter, Edgar Grande, Romain Lachat, Martin Dolezal, Simon Bornschier, and Timotheos Frey. 2006. 'Globalization and the Transformation of the National Political Space: Six European Countries Compared', *European Journal of Political Research* 45 (6): 921–56.

Kriner, Douglas L. and Andrew Reeves. 2012. 'The Influence of Federal Spending on Presidential Elections', *American Political Science Review* 106 (2): 348–66.

Krugman, Paul, and Robert Lawrence. 1993. 'Trade, Jobs, and Wages', *NBER Working Paper* 4478.

Kucera, David and William Milberg. 2003. 'Deindustrialization and Changes in Manufacturing Trade: Factor Content Calculations for 1978–1995', *Review of World Economics* 139 (4): 601–24.

Kweon, Yesola. 2018. 'Types of Labor Market Policy and the Electoral Behavior of Insecure Workers', *Electoral Studies* 55: 1–10.

Lahav, Gallya. 2004. *Immigration and Politics in the New Europe: Reinventing Borders*. Cambridge: Cambridge University Press.

Lamont, Michèle and Virág Molnár. 2002. 'The Study of Boundaries in the Social Sciences', *Annual Review of Sociology* 28: 167–95.

Landman, Todd and Marco Larizza 2009. 'Inequality and Human Rights: Who Controls What, When, and How', *International Studies Quarterly* 53 (3): 715–36.

Lauterbach, Fabian and Catherine E. De Vries. 2020. 'Europe Belongs to the Young? Generational Differences in Public Opinion towards the European Union during the Eurozone Crisis', *Journal of European Public Policy* 27 (2): 168–87.

Layard, Richard, Stephen Nickell, and Richard Jackman. 2005. *Unemployment: Macroeconomic Performance and the Labour Market*. Oxford: Oxford University Press.

220 References

Lazarus, Jeffrey and Shauna Reilly. 2010. 'The Electoral Benefits of Distributive Spending', *Political Research Quarterly* 63 (2): 343–55.

Lee, Cheol-Sung. 2005. 'International Migration, Deindustrialization and Union Decline in 16 Affluent OECD Countries, 1962–1997', *Social Forces* 84 (1): 71–88.

Lees, Charles. 2018. 'The "Alternative for Germany": The Rise of Right-wing Populism at the Heart of Europe', *Politics* 38 (3): 295–310.

Lehmbruch, Gerhard. 1979. 'Liberal Corporatism and Party Government', in Phipippe Schmitter and Gerhard Lehmbruch (eds), *Trends towards Corporatist Intermediation*. London: Sage, 147–83.

Levendusky, Matthew S. 2019. 'Americans, Not Partisans: Cam Priming American National Identity Reduce Affective Polarization', *Journal of Politics* 80 (1): 59–70.

Lewis-Beck, Michael S., Nicholas F. Martini, and D. Roderick Kiewiet. 2013. 'The Nature of Economic Perceptions in Mass Publics', *Electoral Studies* 32 (3): 524–28.

Lewis-Beck, Michael S. and Richard Nadeau. 2011. 'Economic Voting Theory: Testing New Dimensions', *Electoral Studies* 30 (2): 288–94.

Lewis-Beck, Michael S. and Mary Stegmaier. 2013. 'The VP-Function Revisited: A Survey of the Literature on Vote and Popularity Functions after over 40 Years', *Public Choice* 157: 367–85.

Lewis-Beck, Michael S. and Mary Stegmaier. 2018. 'Economic Voting', in Roger D. Congleton, Bernard Grofman, and Stefan Voigt (eds), *The Oxford Handbook of Public Choice, Volume 1*. Oxford: Oxford University Press, 247–65.

Lindvall, Johannes and David Rueda. 2014. 'The Insider–Outsider Dilemma', *British Journal of Political Science* 44 (2): 460–75.

Linos, Katerina and Martin West. 2003. 'Self-interest, Social Beliefs, and Attitudes to Redistribution: Re-addressing the Issue of Cross-nation Variation', *European Sociological Review* 19 (4): 393–409.

Lipset, Seymour Martin. 1960. *Political Man: The Social Bases of Politics*. Garden City, New York: Doubleday.

Lubbers, Marcel, Mérove Gijsberts, and Peer Scheepers. 2002. 'Extreme Right-wing Voting in Western Europe', *European Journal of Political Research* 41 (3): 345–78.

Luskin, Robert C. 1990. 'Explaining Political Sophistication', *Political Behavior* 12 (4): 331–61.

Luther, Kurt Richard. 2009. 'The Revival of the Radical Right: The Austrian Parliamentary Election of 2008', *West European Politics* 32 (5): 1049–61.

Macdonald, Stuart Elaine, George Rabinowitz, and Ola Lishthaug. 1995. 'Political Sophistication and Models of Issue Voting', *British Journal of Political Science* 25 (4): 453–83.

Malchow-Møller, Nikolaj, Jakob Roland Munch, Sanne Schroll, and Jan Rose Skaksen. 2009. 'Explaining Cross-Country Differences in Attitudes toward Immigration in the EU-15', *Social Indicators Research* 91 (3): 371–90.

Malhotra, Neil and Yotam Margalit. 2014. 'Expectation Setting and Retrospective Voting', *Journal of Politics* 76 (4): 1000–16.

March, Luke. 2012. *Radical Left Parties in Europe*. London: Routledge.

March, Luke and Cas Mudde. 2005. 'What's Left of the Radical Left? The European Radical Left after 1989: Decline and Mutation', *Comparative European Politics* 3 (1): 23–49.

Mares, Isabela. 2006. *Taxation, Wage Bargaining and Unemployment*. Cambridge: Cambridge University Press.

Mayda, Anna Maria. 2006. 'Who Is against Immigration? A Cross-Country Investigation of Individual Attitudes toward Immigrants', *Review of Economics and Statistics* 88 (3): 510–30.

McDonnell, Duncan and Annika Werner. 2018. 'Respectable Radicals: Why Some Radical Right Parties in the European Parliament Forsake Policy Congruence', *Journal of European Public Policy* 25 (5): 747–63.

References   221

Meijers, Maurits. 2017. 'Contagious Euroscepticism: The Impact of Eurosceptic Support on Mainstream Party Positions on European Integration', *Party Politics* 23 (4): 413–23.

Merkel, Wolfgang. 2014. 'Is Capitalism Compatible with Democracy?', *Zeitschrift für Vergleichende Politikwissenschaft* 8: 109–28.

Messina, Anthony M. 2007. *The Logics and Politics of Post-WWII Migration to Western Europe.* Cambridge: Cambridge University Press.

Mettler, Suzanne and Joe Soss. 2004. 'The Consequences of Public Policy for Democratic Citizenship: Bridging Policy Studies and Mass Politics', *Perspectives on Politics* 2 (1): 55–73.

Mijs, Jonathan J. B. 2021. 'The Paradox of Inequality: Income Inequality and Belief in Meritocracy Go Hand in Hand', *Socio-Economic Review* 19 (1): 7–35.

Mody, Ashoka and Milan Nedeljkovic. 2024. 'Central Bank Policies and Financial Markets: Lessons from the Euro Crisis', *Journal of Banking and Finance* 158: 107033.

Molina, Oscar and Martin Rhodes. 2002. 'Corporatism: The Past, Present, and Future of a Concept', *Annual Review of Political Science* 5: 305–31.

Mooi-Reci, Irma. 2012. 'Retrenchments in Unemployment Insurance Benefits and Wage Inequality: Longitudinal Evidence from the Netherlands, 1985–2000', *European Sociological Review* 28 (5): 594–606.

Morrell, Michael E. 2003. 'Survey and Experimental Evidence for a Reliable and Valid Measure of Internal Political Efficacy', *Public Opinion Quarterly* 67 (4): 589–602.

Mosimann, Nadja and Jonas Pontusson. 2017. 'Solidaristic Unionism and Support for Redistribution in Contemporary Europe', *World Politics* 69 (3): 448–92.

Mosimann, Nadja and Jonas Pontusson. 2022. 'Varieties of Trade Unions and Support for Redistribution', *West European Politics* 45 (6): 1310–1333.

Mosimann, Nadja, Line Rennwald, and Adrian Zimmermann. 2019. 'The Radical Right, the Labour Movement and the Competition for the Workers' Vote', *Economic and Industrial Democracy* 40 (1): 65–90.

Mudde, Cas. 1999. 'The Single-Issue Party Thesis: Extreme Right Parties and the Immigration Issue', *West European Politics* 22 (3): 182–97.

Mudde, Cas. 2004. 'The Populist Zeitgeist', *Government and Opposition* 39 (4): 541–63.

Mudde, Cas. 2007. *Populist Radical Right Parties in Europe.* Cambridge: Cambridge University Press.

Mudde, Cas. 2010. 'The Populist Radical Right: A Pathological Normalcy', *West European Politics* 33 (6): 1167–86.

Mudde, Cas. 2013. 'Three Decades of Populist Radical Right Parties in Western Europe: So What?', *European Journal of Political Research* 52 (1): 1–19.

Mudde, Cas. 2015. 'Populist Radical-right Parties in Europe Today', in John Abromeit, Gary Marotta, Bridget M. Chesterton, and York Norman (eds), *Transformations of Populism in Europe and the Americas: History and Recent Trends.* London: Bloomsbury Academic, 295–307.

Murtin, Fabrice and Jean-Marc Robin. 2018. 'Labor Market Reforms and Unemployment Dynamics', *Labour Economics* 50: 3–19.

Mutz, Diana C. and Byron Reeves. 2005. 'The New Videomalaise: Effects of Televised Incivility on Political Trust', *American Political Science Review* 99 (1): 1–15.

Myles, John and Paul Pierson. 2001. 'The Comparative Political Economy of Pension Reforms', in Paul Pierson (ed.), *The New Politics of the Welfare State.* Oxford: Oxford University Press, 305–33.

Nadeau, Richard and Michael S. Lewis-Beck. 2001. 'National Economic Voting in U.S. Presidential Elections', *Journal of Politics* 63 (1): 159–81.

Nadeau, Richard, Michael S. Lewis-Beck, and Éric Bélanger. 2013. 'Economics and Elections Revisited', *Comparative Political Studies* 46 (5): 551–73.

222 References

Nagayoshi, Kikuko, and Mikael Hjern. 2015. 'Anti-Immigration Attitudes in Different Welfare States: Do Types of Labor Market Policies Matter?', *International Journal of Comparative Sociology* 56 (2): 141–62.

Nagel, Joane. 1998. 'Masculinity and Nationalism: Gender and Sexuality in the Making of Nations', *Ethnic and Racial Studies* 21 (2): 242–69.

Natali, David, Maarten Keune, Emmanuele Pavolini, and Martin Seeleib-Kaiser. 2018. 'Sixty Years after Titmuss: New Findings on Occupational Welfare in Europe', *Social Policy Administration* 52 (2): 435–48.

Natali, David and Philippe Pochet. 2009. 'The Evolution of Social Pacts in the EMU Era: What Type of Institutionalization?', *European Journal of Industrial Relations* 15 (2): 147–66.

Natili, Marcello and Angelica Puricelli. 2023. 'Expanding Welfare State Borders: Trade Unions and the Introduction of Pro-Outsiders Social Policies in Italy and Argentina', *Journal of Social Policy* 52 (2): 339–57.

Nelson, Moira. 2009. 'An Application of the Estimated Dependent Variable Approach: Trade Union Members' Support for Active Labor Market Policies and Insider-Outsider Politics', *International Journal of Public Opinion Research* 21 (2): 224–34.

Nielsen, Julie H. 2018. 'The Effect of Affect: How Affective Style Determines Attitudes toward the EU', *European Union Politics* 19 (1): 75–96.

Nieuwbeerta, Paul and Wout Ultee. 1999. 'Class Voting in Western Industrialized Countries, 1945–1990: Systematizing and Testing Explanations', *European Journal of Political Research* 35 (1): 123–60.

Nijhuis, Dennie O. 2009. 'Revisiting the Role of Labor: Worker Solidarity, Employer Opposition, and the Development of Old-Age Pensions in the Netherlands and United Kingdom', *World Politics* 61 (2): 296–329.

Noël, Alain. 2020. 'Is Social Investment Inimical to the Poor?', *Socio-Economic Review* 18 (3): 857–80.

Norris, Pippa. 2005. *Radical Right: Voters and Parties in the Electoral Market.* Cambridge: Cambridge University Press.

Norris, Pippa. 2011. *Democratic Deficit: Critical Citizens Revisited.* Cambridge: Cambridge University Press.

Norris, Pippa and Ronald Inglehart. 2019. *Cultural Backlash: Trump, Brexit, and Authoritarian Populism.* Cambridge: Cambridge University Press.

O'Donnell, Rory, Maura Adshead, and Damian Thomas. 2011. 'Ireland: Two Trajectories of Institutionalization', in Sabina Avdagic, Martin Rhodes, and Jelle Visser (eds), *Social Pacts in Europe: Emergence, Evolution, and Institutionalization.* Oxford: Oxford University Press, 89–117.

O'Rourke, Kevin H. and Richard Sinnott. 2006. 'The Determinants of Individual Attitudes towards Immigration', *European Journal of Political Economy* 22 (4): 838–61.

Oakes, Penelope J. 1987. 'The Salience of Social Categories', in John. C. Turner, Michael A. Hogg, Penelope J. Oakes, Stephen D. Reicher, and Margaret S. Wetherell (eds), *Rediscovering the Social Group: A Self-Categorization Theory.* Oxford: Blackwell, 117–41.

Oakes, Penelope J., John C. Turner, and S. Alexander Haslam. 1991. 'Perceiving People as Group Members: The Role of Fit in the Salience of Social Categorizations', *British Journal of Social Psychology* 30 (2): 125–44.

Obinger, Herbert, Carina Schmitt, and Reimut Zohlnhöfer. 2014. 'Partisan Politics and Privatization in OECD Countries', *Comparative Political Studies* 47 (9): 1294–1323.

Obydenkova, Anastassia V. and Bruno Arpino. 2018. 'Corruption and Trust in the European Union and National Institutions: Changes over the Great Recession across European States', *Journal of Common Market Studies* 56 (3): 594–611.

Oesch, Daniel. 2006. 'Coming to Grips with a Changing Class Structure: An Analysis of Employment Stratification in Britain, Germany, Sweden and Switzerland', *International Sociology* 21 (2): 263–88.

Oesch, Daniel. 2008. 'Explaining Workers' Support for Right-Wing Populist Parties in Western Europe: Evidence from Austria, Belgium, France, Norway, and Switzerland', *International Political Science Review* 29 (3): 349–73.

Oesch, Daniel. 2013. 'The Cleavage between New Left and Radical Right', in Jens Rydgren (ed.), *Class Politics and the Radical Right*. London: Routledge, 31–51.

Öhberg, Patrik and Elin Naurin 2016. 'Party-constrained Policy Responsiveness: A Survey Experiment on Politicians' Response to Citizen-initiated Contacts', *British Journal of Political Science* 46 (4): 785–97.

Ove Moene, Karl and Michael Wallerstein. 2001. 'Inequality, Social Insurance, and Redistribution', *American Political Science Review* 95 (4): 859–74.

Pacek, Alexander C. and Benjamin Radcliff. 1995. 'Economic Voting and the Welfare State: A Cross-National Analysis', *Journal of Politics* 57 (1): 44–61.

Pateman, Carole. 1970. *Participation and Democratic Theory*. Cambridge: Cambridge University Press.

Patton, David. 2019. 'Protest Voting in Eastern Germany: Continuity and Change across Three Decades', *German Politics and Society* 37 (3): 72–88.

Peters, John. 2012. 'Neoliberal Convergence in North America and Western Europe: Fiscal Austerity, Privatization, and Public Sector Reform', *Review of International Political Economy* 19 (2): 208–35.

Petersen, Michael Bang, Rune Slothuus, Rune Stubager, and Lise Togeby. 2011. 'Deservingness versus Values in Public Opinion on Welfare: The Automaticity of the Deservingness Heuristic', *European Journal of Political Research* 50 (1): 24–52.

Pignatti, Clemente and Eva Van Belle. 2018. 'Better Together: Active and Passive Labor Market Policies in Developed and Developing Economies', *IZA Journal of Development and Migration* 12 (1): 1–27.

Pirro, Andrea L. P. Forthcoming. 'Performing (during) the Coronavirus Crisis: The Italian Populist Radical Right between National Opposition and Subnational Government', *Government and Opposition*.

Pitkin, Hanna F. 1967. *The Concept of Representation*. Berkeley, California: University of California Press.

Pontusson, Jonas. 2013. 'Unionization, Inequality, and Redistribution', *British Journal of Industrial Relations* 51 (4): 797–825.

Pontusson, Jonas and David Rueda. 2008. 'Inequality as a Source of Political Polarization: A Comparative Analysis of Twelve OECD Countries', in Pablo Beramendi and Christopher J. Anderson (eds), *Democracy, Inequality, and Representation: A Comparative Perspective*. New York: Russell Sage Foundation, 312–53.

Pontusson, Jonas, David Rueda, and Christopher Way. 2002. 'Comparative Political Economy of Wage Distribution: The Role of Partisanship and Labour Market Institutions', *British Journal of Political Science* 32 (2): 281–308.

Pontusson, Jonas and David Weisstanner 2018. 'Macroeconomic Conditions, Inequality Shocks and the Politics of Redistribution, 1990–2013', *Journal of European Social Policy* 25 (1): 31–58.

Powell, G. Bingham and Guy D. Whitten. 1993. 'A Cross-National Analysis of Economic Voting: Taking Account of the Political Context', *American Journal of Political Science* 30 (2): 315–46.

Putnam, Robert D. 1993. *Making Democracy Work: Civic Traditions in Modern Italy*. Princeton, New Jersey: Princeton University Press.

224 References

Rahn, Wendy M. and Thomas J. Rudolph. 2005. 'A Tale of Political Trust in American Cities', *Public Opinion Quarterly* 69 (4): 530–60.

Rathgeb, Philip and Michael B. Klitgaard. 2022. 'Protagonists or Consenters: Radical Right Parties and Attacks on Trade Unions', *Journal of European Public Policy* 29 (7): 1049–71.

Raven, Judith, Peter Achterberg, Romke van der Veen, and Mara Yerkes. 2011. 'An Institutional Embeddedness of Welfare Opinions? The Link between Public Opinion and Social Policy in the Netherlands (1979–2004)', *Journal of Social Policy* 40 (2): 369–86.

Reenock, Christopher, Michael Bernhard, and David Sobek 2007. 'Regressive Socioeconomic Distribution and Democratic Survival', *International Studies Quarterly* 51 (3): 677–99.

Regini, Marino. 2000. 'Between Deregulation and Social Pacts: The Responses of European Economies to Globalization', *Politics and Society* 28 (1): 5–33.

Regini, Marino. 2003. 'Tripartite Concertation and Varieties of Capitalism', *European Journal of Industrial Relations* 9 (3): 251–63.

Regini, Marino and Sabrina Colombo. 2011. 'Italy: The Rise and Decline of Social Pacts', in Sabina Avdagic, Martin Rhodes, and Jelle Visser (eds), *Social Pacts in Europe: Emergence, Evolution, and Institutionalization*. Oxford: Oxford University Press, 118–46.

Rehm, Philipp. 2009. 'Risks and Redistribution: An Individual-level Analysis', *Comparative Political Studies* 42 (7): 885–81.

Rehm, Philipp. 2016. *Risk Inequality and Welfare States: Social Policy Preferences, Development, and Dynamics*. Cambridge: Cambridge University Press.

Reiljan, Andres. 2020. 'Fear and Loathing across Party Lines' (also) in Europe: Affective Polarisation in European Party Systems', *European Journal of Political Research* 59 (2): 376–96.

Requena, Miguel. 2023. 'Class and Unemployment', *JRC Working Paper Series on Social Classes in the Digital Age* 2023/11.

Rhodes, Martin. 2005. 'Varieties of Capitalism' and the Political Economy of European Welfare States', *New Politial Economy* 10 (3): 363–70.

Rochat, Matthew. 2023. 'The Determinants of Growing Economic Inequality within Advanced Democracies', *International Review of Economics* 70 (4): 457–75.

Rooduijn, Matthijs. 2015. 'The Rise of the Populist Radical Right in Western Europe', *European View* 14 (1): 3–11.

Rooduijn, Matthijs and Tjitske Akkerman. 2017. 'Flank Attacks: Populism and Left-right Radicalism in Western Europe', *Party Politics* 23 (3): 193–204.

Rooduijn, Matthijs and Brian Burgoon. 2018. 'The Paradox of Well-being: Do Unfavorable Socioeconomic and Sociocultural Contexts Deepen or Dampen Radical Left and Right Voting among the Less Well-off?', *Comparative Political Studies* 51 (13): 1720–53.

Rooduijn, Matthijs, Brian Burgoon, Erika J. van Elsas, and Herman G. van de Werfhorst. 2017. 'Radical Distinction: Support for Radical Left and Radical Right Parties in Europe', *European Union Politics* 18 (4): 536–59.

Rooduijn, Matthijs, Sarah L. de Lange, and Wouter van der Brug. 2014. 'A Populist *Zeitgeist*? Programmatic Contagion by Populist Parties in Western Europe', *Party Politics* 20 (4): 563–75.

Rosenfeld, Bruce and Jake Western. 2012. 'Workers of the World Divide: The Decline of Labor and the Future of the Middle Class', *Foreign Affairs* 91 (3): 88–99.

Rosenstone, Steven J. 1982. 'Economic Adversity and Voter Turnout', *American Journal of Political Science* 26 (1): 25–46.

Rosset, Jan and Anna-Spohie Kurella. 2021. 'The Electoral Roots of Unequal Representation: A Spatial Modeling Approach to Party Systems and Voting in Western Europe', *European Journal of Political Research* 60 (4): 785–806.

Rothstein, Bo and Eric M. Uslaner. 2005. 'All of All: Equality, Corruption, and Social Trust', *World Politics* 58 (1): 41–72.

Rovny, Jan. 2013. 'Where Do Radical Right Parties Stand? Position Blurring in Multidimensional Competition', *European Political Science Review* 5 (1): 1–26.

Rovny, Jan and Jonathan Polk. 2019. 'New Wine in Old Bottles: Explaining the Dimensional Structure of European Party Systems', *Party Politics* 25 (1): 12–24.

Rowthorn, Robert and Ken Coutts. 2004. 'De-Industrialisation and the Balance of Payments in Advanced Economies', *Cambridge Journal of Economics* 28 (5): 767–90.

Rowthorn, Robert and Ramana Ramaswamy. 1999. 'Growth, Trade, and Deindustrialization', *IMF Staff Papers* 46 (1): 18–41

Rowthorn, Robert and John Wells. 1987. *Deindustrialisation and Foreign Trade.* Cambridge: Cambridge University Press.

Rueda, David. 2005. 'Insider-Outsider Politics in Industrialized Democracies: The Challenge to Social Democratic Parties', *American Political Science Review* 99 (1): 61–74.

Rueda, David. 2007. *Social Democracy Inside Out: Partisanship and Labor Market Policy in Industrialized Democracies.* Oxford: Oxford University Press.

Rueda, David. 2008. 'Left Government, Policy, and Corporatism: Explaining the Influence of Partisanship on Inequality', *World Politics* 60 (3): 349–89.

Rueda, David. 2014. 'Dualization, Crisis and Welfare State', *Socio-Economic Review* 12 (2): 381–407.

Rueda, David. 2015. 'The State of the Welfare State; Unemployment, Labor Market Policy, and Inequality in the Age of Workfare', *Comparative Politics* 47 (3): 296–314.

Rueda, David and Jonas Pontusson 2000. 'Wage Inequality and Varieties of Capitalism', *World Politics* 52 (3): 350–83.

Rydgren, Jens. 2007. 'The Sociology of the Radical Right', *Annual Review of Sociology* 33: 241–62.

Rydgren, Jens. 2008. 'Immigration Sceptics, Xenophobes or Racists? Radical Right-Wing Voting in Six West European Countries', *European Journal of Political Research* 47 (5): 737–65.

Rydgren, Jens. 2013. 'Introduction', in Jens Rydgren (ed.), *Class Politics and the Radical Right.* London: Routledge, 1–9.

Rydgren, Jens. 2018. 'The Radical Right: An Introduction', in Jens Rydgren (ed.), *The Oxford Handbook of the Radical Right.* Oxford: Oxford University Press, 1–16.

Rydgren, Jens and Sara van der Meiden. 2019. 'The Radical Right and the End of Swedish Exceptionalism', *European Political Science* 18 (3): 435–55.

Sachs, Jeffrey D. and Howard J. Shatz. 1996. 'U.S. Trade with Developing Countries and Wage Inequality', *American Economic Review* 86 (2): 234–39.

Salo, Sanna and Jens Rydgren. 2021. *The Battle over Working-Class Voters: How Social Democracy Has Responded to the Populist Radical Right in the Nordic Countries.* London: Routledge.

Sanders, Elizabeth. 1999. *Roots of Reform: Farmers, Workers, and the American State 1877-1917.* Chicago, Illinois: University of Chicago Press.

Saundry, Richard, Mark Stuart, and Valerie Antcliff. 2012. 'Social Capital and Union Revitalization: A Study of Worker Networks in the UK Audio-Visual Industries', *British Journal of Industrial Relations* 50 (2): 263–86.

Scheve, Kenneth F. and Matthew J. Salughter. 2001. *Globalization and the Perceptions of American Workers.* Washington, DC: Institute for International Economics.

Scheve, Kenneth F. and David Stasavage. 2009. 'Institutions, Partisanship, and Inequality in the Long Run', *World Politics* 61 (2): 215–53.

Schlenker, Eva and Kai D. Schmid. 2015. 'Capital Income Shares and Income Inequality in 16 EU Member Countries', *Empirica* 42 (2): 241–68.

Schmidt, Vivien A. 2002. *The Futures of European Capitalism*. Oxford, Oxford University Press.

Schmieder, Johannes F. and Till von Waechter. 2016. 'The Effects of Unemployment Insurance Benefits: New Evidence and Interpretation', *Annual Review of Economics* 8: 547–81.

Schneider, Silke L. 2008. 'Anti-Immigrant Attitudes in Europe: Outgroup Size and Perceived Ethnic Threat', *European Sociological Review* 24 (1): 53–67.

Schumacher, Gijs and Kees van Kersbergen. 2016. 'Do Mainstream Parties Adapt to the Welfare Chauvinism of Populist Parties?', *Party Politics* 22 (3): 300–12.

Schumacher, Gijs, Barbara Vis, and Kees van Kersbergen. 2013. 'Political Parties' Welfare Image, Electoral Punishment and Welfare State Retrenchment', *Comparative European Politics* 11 (1): 1–21.

Schwander, Hanna. 2019. 'Labor Market Dualization and Insider–Outsider Divides: Why New Conflict Matters', *Political Studies Review* 17 (1): 14–29.

Shayo, Moses. 2009. 'A Model of Social Identity with an Application to Political Economy: Nation, Class, and Redistribution', *American Political Science Review* 103 (2): 147–74.

Sheets, Penelope, Linda Bos, and Hajo Boomgaarden. 2016. 'Media Cues and Citizen Support for Right-Wing Populist Parties', *International Journal of Public Opinion Research* 28 (3): 307–30.

Sibley, Chris G., Andrew Robertson, and Marc S. Wilson. 2006. 'Social Dominance Orientation and Right-Wing Authoritarianism: Additive and Interactive Effects', *Political Psychology* 27 (5): 755–68.

Siebert, Horst. 1997. 'Labor Market Rigidities: At the Root of Unemployment in Europe', *Journal of Economic Perspective* 11 (3): 37–54.

Siisiäinen, Martti. 2003. 'One Concept, Two Approaches: Bourdieu and Putnam on Social Capital', *International Journal of Contemporary Sociology* 40 (2): 183–203.

Simoni, Marco. 2010. 'Labour and Welfare Reforms: The Short Life of Labour Unity', in Andrea Mammone and Giuseppe A. Veltri (eds), *Italy Today: The Sick Man of Europe*. London: Routledge, 229–42.

Simoni, Marco. 2013. 'The Left and Organized Labor in Low-Inflation Times', *World Politics* 65 (2): 314–49.

Sipma, Take and Marcel Lubbers. 2020. 'Contextual-Level Unemployment and Support for Radical-Right Parties: A Meta-Analysis', *Acta Politica* 55 (3): 351–87.

Smets, Kaat and Carolien van Ham. 2013. 'The Embarrassment of Riches? A Meta-Analysis of Individual-Level Research on Voter Turnout', *Electoral Studies* 32 (2): 344–59.

Smith, Anthony D. 1991. *National Identity*. New York: Penguin Books.

Smith, James P. and Barry Edmonston (eds). 1997. *The New Americans: Economic, Demographic, and Fiscal Effects of Immigration*. Washington, DC: National Academy Press.

Smith, Jason Matthew. 2010. 'Does Crime Pay? Issue Ownership, Political Opportunity, and the Populist Right in Western Europe', *Comparative Political Studies* 43 (11): 1471–98.

Smith, Tom W. and Seokho Kim. 2006. 'National Pride in Comparative Perspective: 1995/6 and 2003/04', *International Journal of Public Opinion Research* 18 (1): 127–36.

Solt, Frederick. 2008. 'Economic Inequality and Democratic Political Engagement', *American Journal of Political Science* 52 (1): 48–60.

Sørensen, Rune Jørgen. 2016. 'After the Immigration Shock: The Causal Effect of Immigration on Electoral Preferences', *Electoral Studies* 44: 1–14.

Spruyt, Bram, Gil Keppens, and Filip Van Droogenbroeck. 2016. 'Who Supports Populism and What Attracts People to It?', *Politiacl Research Quarterly* 69 (2): 335–46.

Steenvoorden, Eefje and Eelco Harteveld. 2018. 'The Appeal of Nostalgia: The Influence of Societal Pessimism on Support for Populist Radical Right Parties', *West European Politics* 41 (1): 28–52.

Stiers, Dieter, Ruth Dassonneville, and Michael S. Lewis-Beck. 2020. 'The Abiding Voter: The Lengthy Horizon of Retrospective Evaluations', *European Journal of Political Research* 59 (3): 646–68.

Stockemer, Daniel, Tobias Lentz, and Danielle Mayer. 2018. 'Individual Predictors of the Radical Right-Wing Vote in Europe: A Meta-Analysis of Articles in Peer-Reviewed Journals (1995–2016)', *Government and Opposition* 53 (3): 569–93.

Strabac, Zan, Ola Listhaug, and Tor Georg Jakobsen. 2012. 'Patterns of Ethnic Intolerance in Europe', *International Migration and Integration* 13 (4): 459–79.

Strangleman, Tim, James Rhodes, and Sherry Linkon. 2013. 'Introduction to Crumbling Cultures: Deindustrialization, Class, and Memory', *International Labor and Working-Class History* 84: 7–22.

Sundström, Aksel and Daniel Stockemer. 2015. 'Regional Variation in Voter Turnout in Europe: The Impact of Corruption Perceptions', *Electoral Studies* 40: 158–69.

Swank, Duane. 2011. 'Activating Workers? The Political Economy of Active Social Policy in Postindustrial Democracies', in David Brady (ed.), *Comparing European Workers Part B: Policies and Institutions*. Bingley: Emerald, 9–51.

Swank, Duane and Hans-Georg Betz. 2003. 'Globalization, the Welfare State and Right-wing Populism in Western Europe', *Socio-Economic Review* 1 (2): 215–45.

Swyngedouw, Marc. 2001. 'The Subjective Cognitive and Affective Map of Extreme Right Voters: Using Open-Ended Questions in Exit Polls', *Electoral Studies* 20 (2): 217–41.

Tajfel, Henri. 1982. 'Social Psychology of Intergroup Relations', *Annual Review of Psychology* 33: 1–39.

Tajfel, Henri, Michael G. Billig, Robert P. Bundy, and Claude Flament. 1971. 'Social Categorization and Intergroup Behaviour', *European Journal of Social Psychology* 1 (2): 149–78.

Tajfel, Henri and John Turner. 1979. 'An Integrative Theory of Intergroup Conflict', in Stephen Worchel and William G. Austin (eds), *The Social Psychology of Intergroup Relations*. Pacific Grove, California: Brooks/Cole, 33–48.

Tavits, Margit. 2007. 'Principle vs. Pragmatism: Policy Shifts and Political Competition', *American Journal of Political Science* 51 (1): 151–65.

Tavits, Margit and Joshua D. Potter. 2015. 'The Effect of Inequality and Social Identity on Party Strategies', *American Journal of Political Science* 59 (3): 744–58.

Thelen, Kathleen and Cathy Jo Martin. 2007. 'The State and Coordinated Capitalism: Contributions of the Public Sector to Social Solidarity in Postindustrial Societies', *World Politics* 60 (1): 1–36.

Thurik, A. Roy, Martin A. Carree, André van Stel, and David B. Audretsch. 2008. 'Does Self-Employment Reduce Employment?', *Journal of Business Venturing* 23 (6): 673–86.

Tillman, Erik R. 2021. *Authoritarianism and the Evolution of West European Electoral Politics*. Oxford: Oxford University Press.

Traxler, Franz and Bernd Brandl. 2010. 'Preconditions for Pacts on Incomes Policy: Bringing Structures Back In', *European Journal of Industrial Relations* 16 (1): 73–90.

Traxler, Franz and Bernhard Kittel. 2000. 'The Bargaining System and Performance: A Comparison of 18 OECD Countries', *Comparative Political Studies* 33 (9): 1154–90.

Trump, Kris-Stella. 2018. 'Income Inequality Influences Perceptions of Legitimate Income Differences', *British Journal of Political Science* 48 (4): 929–52.

Turner, John C. 1975. 'Social Comparison and Social Identity: Some Prospects for Intergroup Behavior', *European Journal of Social Psychology* 5 (1): 5–34.

228 References

Turner, John C. and Rupert Brown. 1978. 'Social Status, Cognitive Alternatives and Intergroup Relations', in Henri Tajfel (ed.), *Differentiation between Social Groups: Studies in the Social Psychology of Intergroup Relations*. New York: Academic Press, 201–34.

van der Brug, Wouter and Meindert Fennema. 2003. 'Protest or Mainstream? How the European Anti-Immigrant Parties Have Developed into Two Separate Groups by 1999', *European Journal of Political Research* 42 (1): 55–76.

van der Brug, Wouter and Meindert Fennema. 2007. 'Forum: Causes of Voting for the Radical Right', *International Journal of Public Opinion Research* 19 (4): 474–87.

van der Brug, Wouter, Meindert Fennema, and Jean Tillie. 2000. 'Anti-immigrant Parties in Europe: Ideological or Protest Vote?', *European Journal of Political Research* 37 (1): 77–102.

van der Brug, Wouter, Meindert Fennema, Sarah de Lange, and Inger Baller. 2013. 'Radical Right Parties: Their Voters and Their Electoral Competitors', in Jens Rydgren (ed.), *Class Politics and the Radical Right*. London: Routledge, 52–74.

van der Waal, Jeroen and Willem de Koster. 2018. 'Populism and Support for Protectionsim: The Relevance of Opposition to Trade Openness for Leftist and Rightist Populist Voting in the Netherlands', *Political Studies* 66 (3): 560–76.

van Haute, Emilie, Teun Pauwels, and Dave Sinardet. 2018. 'Sub-state Nationalism and Populism: The Cases of Vlaams Belang, New Flemish Alliance and DéFI in Belgium', *Comparative European Politics* 16 (6): 954–75.

Vanhoudt, Patrick. 1997. 'Do Labor Market Policies and Growth Fundamentals Matter for Income Inequality in OECD Countries? Some Empirical Evidence', *Staff Papers* 44: 356–73.

van Kessel, Stijn and Remco Castelein. 2016. 'Shifting the Blame, Populist Politicians' Use of Twitter as a Tool of Opposition', *Journal of Contemporary European Research* 12 (2): 594–614.

van Klingeren, Marijn, Hajo G. Boomgaarden, and Claes H. de Vreese. 2013. 'Going Soft or Staying Soft: Have Identity Factors Become More Important than Economic Rationale when Explaining Euroscepticism?', *Journal of European Integration* 35 (6): 689–704.

van Spanje, Joost. 2010. 'Contagious Parties: Anti-Immigration Parties and Their Impact on Other Parties' Immigration Stances in Contemporary Western Europe', *Party Politics* 16 (5): 563–86.

Vasilopoulou, Sofia. 2018. *Far Right Parties and Euroscepticism: Patterns of Opposition*. London: Rowman and Littlefield.

Veiga, Linda Gonçalves and Henry W. Chappell Jr. 2002. 'Politics and Unemployment in Industrialized Democracies', *Public Choice* 110 (3–4): 261–82.

Veugelers, John and André Magnan. 2005. 'Conditions of Far-right Strength in Contemporary Western Europe: An Application of Kitschelt's Theory', *European Journal of Political Research* 44 (6): 837–60.

Viebrock, Elke and Jochen Clasen. 2009. 'Flexicurity and Welfare Reform: A Review', *Socio-Economic Review* 7 (2): 305–31.

Visser, Jelle. 2002. 'Why Fewer Workers Join Unions in Europe: A Social Custom Explanation of Membership Trends', *British Journal of Industrial Relations* 40 (3): 403–30.

Visser, Jelle. 2019. *ICTWSS Database, Version 6.1*. Amsterdam: Amsterdam Institute for Advanced Labour Studies (AIAS), University of Amsterdam.

Visser, Jelle and Marc van der Meer. 2011. 'The Netherlands: Social Pacts in a Concertation Economy', in Sabina Avdagic, Martin Rhodes, and Jelle Visser (eds), *Social Pacts in Europe: Emergence, Evolution, and Institutionalization*. Oxford: Oxford University Press, 203–31.

Visser, Jelle and Martin Rhodes. 2011. 'The Evolution of Social Pacts: Trajectories and Mechanisms of Institutionalization', in Sabina Avdagic, Martin Rhodes, and Jelle Visser (eds), *Social Pacts in Europe: Emergence, Evolution, and Institutionalization*. Oxford: Oxford University Press, 61–85.

References   229

Vlandas, Tim and Daphne Halikiopoulou. 2019. 'Does Unemployment Matter? Economic Insecurity, Labour Market Politics and the Far-right Vote in Europe', *European Political Science* 18 (3): 421–38.

Voigt, Linda and Reimut Zohlnhöfer. 2020. 'Quiet Politics of Employment Protection Legislation? Partisan Politics, Electoral Competition, and the Regulatory Welfare State', *The ANNALS of the American Academy of Political and Social Science* 691 (1): 206–22.

Volkens, Andrea. 2007. 'Strengths and Weaknesses of Approaches to Measuring Policy Positions of Parties', *Electoral Studies* 26 (1): 108–20.

Walczak, Agnieszka, Wouter van der Brug, and Catherine Eunice de Vries. 2012. 'Long- and Short-term Determinants of Party Preferences: Inter-generational Differences in Western and East Central Europe', *Electoral Studies* 31 (2): 273–84.

Walgrave, Stefaan, Jonas Lefevere, and Anke Tresch. 2012. 'The Associative Dimension of Issue Ownership', *Public Opinion Quarterly* 76 (4): 771–82.

Wallerstein, Michael. 1999. 'Wage-Setting Institutions and Pay Inequality in Advanced Industrial Societies', *American Journal of Political Science* 43 (3): 649–80.

Wallerstein, Michael and Bruce Western. 2000. 'Unions in Decline? What Has Changed and Why', *Annual Review of Political Science* 3: 355–77.

Wang, Austin Horng-En. 2017. 'Patience as the Rational Foundation of Sociotropic Voting', *Electoral Studies* 50: 15–25.

Warhurst, Chris, Chris Tilly, and Mary Gatta. 2017. 'A New Social Construction of Skill', in Chris Warhurst, Ken Mayhew, David Finegold, and John Buchanan (eds), *Oxford Handbook of Skills and Training*. Oxford: Oxford University Press, 72–91.

Wehl, Nadja. 2019. 'The (Ir)relevance of Unemployment for Labour Market Policy Attitudes and Welfare State Attitudes', *European Journal of Political Research* 58 (1): 141–62.

Werts, Han, Peer Scheepers, and Marcel Lubbers. 2013. 'Euro-scepticism and Radical Right-wing Voting in Europe, 2002–2008: Social Cleavages, Socio-political Attitudes and Contextual Characteristics Determining Voting for the Radical Right', *European Union Politics* 14 (2): 183–205.

Western, Bruce. 1997. *Between Class and Market: Postwar Unionization in the Capitalist Democracies. Princeton*, New Jersey: Princeton University Press.

Weyland, Kurt. 2018. 'Populism and Authoritarianism', in Carlos de la Torre (ed.), *Routledge Handbook of Global Populism*. London: Routledge, 319–33.

Williamson, Peter J. 1985. *Varieties of Corporatism: A Conceptual Discussion*. Cambridge: Cambridge University Press.

Wimpy, Cameron and Guy D. Whitten. 2017. 'What Is and What May Never Be: Economic Voting in Developing Democracies?', *Social Science Quarterly* 98 (3): 1099–1111.

Winlow, Simon, Steve Hall, and James Treadwell. 2017. *The Rise of the Right: English Nationalism and the Transformation of Working-Class Politics*. Bristol: Policy Press.

Wlezien, Christopher. 2005. 'On the Salience of Political Issues: The Problem with "Most Important Problem"', *Electoral Studies* 24 (4): 555–79.

Wodak, Ruth 2019. 'Analysing the Micropolitics of the Populist Far Right in the "Post-Shame Era"', in Peter Bevelander and Ruth Wodak (eds), *Europe at the Crossroads: Confronting Populist, Nationalist, and Global Challenges*. Lund: Nordic Academic Press, 63–92.

Wood, Adrian. 1995. 'How Trade Hurt Unskilled Workers', *Journal of Economic Perspectives* 9 (3): 57–80.

Yang, Jae-Jin and Hyeok Yong Kwon. 2019. 'Union Structure, Bounded Solidarity and Support for Redistribution: Implications for Building a Welfare State', *International Political Science Review* 42 (2): 277–93.

Zagórski, Piotr, Jose Rama, and Guillermo Cordero. 2021. 'Young and Temporary: Youth Employment Insecurity and Support for Right-Wing Populist Parties in Europe', *Government and Opposition* 56 (3): 405–26.

Zaslove, Andrej. 2008. 'Exclusion, Community, and a Populist Political Economy: The Radical Right as an Anti-Globalization Movement', *Comparative European Politics* 6 (2): 169–89.

Zhirkov, Kirill. 2014. 'Nativist but Not Alienated: A Comparative Perspective on the Radical Right Vote in Western Europe', *Party Politics* 20 (2): 286–96.

Zohlnhöfer, Reimut and Linda Voigt. 2021. 'The Partisan Politics of Employment Protection Legislation: Social Democrats, Christian Democrats, and the Conditioning Effect of Unemployment', *European Political Science Review* 13 (3): 331–50.

Zulianello, Mattia. 2020. 'Varieties of Populist Parties and Party Systems in Europe: From State-of-the-Art to the Application of a Novel Classification Scheme to 66 Parties in 33 Countries', *Government and Opposition* 55 (2): 327–47.

Index

For the benefit of digital users, indexed terms that span two pages (e.g., 52–53) may, on occasion, appear on only one of those pages.

Note: Tables and figures are indicated by an italic *t* and *f*.

A

active labour market policies (ALMPs)
 defined 12 n.17, 113–114
 effects on party support 130–133, 132*t*, 137–138
 in measurement of government spending 66
 unemployment and inequality influenced by 119
 variation across countries and over time 121–122
affective polarization 181–182
Alliance for the Future of Austria 43–44, 43–44 n.17
Alternative for Germany 1, 3–4, 183
authoritarian ideologies
 among the working class 6, 6 n.8
 components of 22 n.26
 nationalism linked to 55–56, 55–56 n.8
 in PRRPs 22, 29, 180–181
average causal mediation effects (ACMEs), defined 98
average direct effects (ADEs), defined 98
average treatment effects (ATEs), defined 98

B

Biden, Joe 177–178
blue-collar workers, defined 30–31. *See also* working class
Bourdieu, Pierre 34
Broockman, David E. 182
Brothers of Italy 183 n.5
Burgoon, Brian 170–171

C

Calmfors, Lars 151–152 n.18
causal mediation analysis models
 first-stage model results 192*t*, 193*t*, 194*t*, 195*t*, 196*t*, 197*t*

mechanics and interpretation of 97–98, 172
 overview 19–20
 policymaking process effects on party support 99–104, 101*t*, 102*t*
 policy outcomes effect on party support 156–160, 159*t*, 161*t*, 170–171
 policy output effects on party support 126–130, 127*t*, 129*t*, 137
centre-left parties. *See* mainstream left-wing parties
centre-right parties. *See* mainstream right-wing parties
class-based social identity
 economic issue salience linked to 2–3, 59–60
 ISSP data used for 17–18
 macro-context effect on 2–3, 11–13, 64–72, 69*t*, 71*f*, 91
 in the three-stage theory 2–3, 10–11, 55–59, 79
consumer preferences, economic development and 32–33
consumption-oriented policies. *See* passive labour market policies (PLMPs)
contextual level unemployment 147–148
COVID-19 pandemic 154 n.20
crisis of democracy
 indicators and causes of 21–23, 180–181
 recommendations for alleviating 22–23
 role of PRRPs in 180–182
cultural capital, role in economic class 34–35
cultural grievance theory
 empirical support for 3 n.4
 literature review on 5–6
 overview 1–2
 policy outcomes and outputs associated with 49
 shortcomings of 9, 20, 172

232 Index

cultural issue salience
  changing views of mainstream parties
    40–41
  economic issue salience *vs.* 2, 14
  EES data on 18
  nation-based social identity linked to 20,
    59–60, 74*t*, 74–75, 172
  recommendations for mainstream parties
    176–178
  in the three-stage theory 2–3, 10–11,
    13–14, 79
  vote choice influenced by 60–63, 62*f*

D

de-industrialization
  causes of 32–33
  consequences of 34, 38–39, 146–147
  as policy outcome 49
demand-side factors in party support 48
demand-side policies. *See* passive labour
    market policies (PLMPs)
democracy in crisis. *See* crisis of democracy
deregulatory approach to unemployment
    151–153
disincentive perspective on unemployment
    150–151, 153
Driffill, John 151–152 n.18

E

Easton, David 2–3, 11
economic class, multidimensionality of
    34–35
economic development, consumer
    preferences and 32–33
economic grievance theory
  literature review on 3–5
  overview 1–2
  policy outcomes and outputs associated
    with 49
  shortcomings of 8, 20, 172
economic growth
  labour market reforms spurred by
    weakening 116–118
  role in economic voting 140
economic inequality. *See also* income
    inequality; unemployment inequality;
    wage inequality
  EPL effects on 114–115
  LMP effects on 119

micro- and macro-level consequences of
    22–23, 55, 142–143, 180–181
  rising levels of 3–4
  role in working-class support for the
    populist radical right 2–3, 21, 26
  self-reinforcing nature of 23–24, 179–180
  skill level and impacts of 16, 21
  social identity influenced by 58
  support for radical left and right linked to
    170–171
  union effect on 38
economic insiders and outsiders. *See* labour
    market insiders and outsiders
economic issue salience
  class-based social identity linked to
    59–60, 74*t*, 74–75
  cultural issue salience *vs.* 2, 14
  EES data on 18
  lower PRRP support linked to 75–79, 77*t*
  recommendations for mainstream parties
    176–178
  in the three-stage theory 2–3, 10–11,
    13–14, 79
  vote choice influenced by 60–63, 62*f*
economic voting 139–140
education level
  nationalist and authoritarian ideologies
    related to 6
  political awareness and 16
  skill level correlated with 164–165
  support for EPL and 114 n.3
  unemployment inequality and 12–13,
    66–67, 149–154, 150*t*, 152*f*
  variations in 35 n.7
EES. *See* European Election Studies (EES)
egalitarian norms 144
Eichengreen, Barry 7
employment. *See also* industrial
    employment; security of employment
  issue salience of 59
  LMP effects on 119, 121
  support for redistribution linked to 37*t*,
    37–38
employment protection legislation (EPL)
  defined 113–114
  de-industrialization effects and 34
  measurement of 66
  micro- and macro-level consequences of
    114–115

Index **233**

preferences of labour market insiders *vs.* outsiders 15–16, 133–134

security of employment and 21

social identity influenced by 12, 66–72, 69*t*, 71*f*

unemployment influenced by 150–151

variation across countries and over time 115–118, 116*t*, 117*f*

employment protection legislation (EPL), effect on party support

causal mediation model results 25–26, 126–130, 127*t*

expected results 12, 111, 123

first-stage model results 194*t*

labour market insiders *vs.* outsiders 134–137, 135*t*, 136*f*, 137*f*

logistic regression model results 123–126, 124*t*, 175–176

robustness checks on model 199*t*, 201*t*

summary of findings 174

employment security. *See* security of employment

Engler, Fabian 11, 55, 58

EPL. *See* employment protection legislation (EPL)

EPL index 115–118, 116*t*, 117*f*

European Debt Crisis (2009–mid-2010s) 88–89, 116, 145, 153–154, 170

European Election Studies (EES) 18, 72–73

European Social Survey (ESS) 35*t*, 35–36

European Union membership

budgetary rules imposed by 122

cultural grievance theory views on 5

economic grievance theory views on 4–5

perceived threats from 1–2, 29

rules and obligations associated with 49–50

European Values Study (EVS) 18–19, 24, 27, 35*t*, 35–36

Eurosclerosis, as term 152–153

F

failed social pact completion. *See* social pact failures

Fain, Shawn 177–178

France

declining economic status of working class in 3–4

growing support for PRRPs 1, 183

liberalization efforts in 117–118

pension reform in 177

G

Germany

declining economic status of working class in 3–4

growing support for PRRPs 1, 183

Gidron, Noam 11, 55, 58

globalization

economic grievance theory views on 4–5

nationalism in response to 55–56

PRRP criticism of 9

vote choice influenced by 8

wage inequality influenced by 146–147

working class vulnerability to 57, 146–147, 163–164, 170

Goedemé, Tim 141–142

government spending on labour market policies

elements of 12 n.17

measurement of 66

micro- and macro-level consequences of 118–119

preferences of labour market insiders *vs.* outsiders 15–16, 133–134

security of employment and 21

social identity influenced by 12, 66–72, 69*t*, 71*f*

summary of findings 174

variation across countries and over time 119–122, 120*t*, 121*f*

government spending on labour market policies, effect on party support

causal mediation model results 25–26, 126–130, 129*t*

expected results 12, 111, 123

first-stage model results 195*t*

labour market insiders *vs.* outsiders 134–137, 135*t*, 136*f*, 137*f*

logistic regression model results 123–126, 125*t*, 175–176

robustness checks on model 199*t*, 201*t*

H

Halikiopoulou, Daphne 128–130 n.13

Hall, Teter A. 11, 55, 58

I

Imai, Kosuke 19–20, 97, 156–158, 172
immigration
  cultural grievance theory views on 5–6
  economic grievance theory views on 4–5,
    4–5 n.6
  issue ownership by PRRPs 14, 62–63, 172,
    174–175
  issue salience of 13 n.18, 60–63, 62*f*
  perceived threats from 1–2, 29
  political discontent theory views on 6–9
  wages affected by 4–5 n.7
imports, increases in 33, 99, 146–147. *See
  also* opinion on imports
inclusive policymaking
  benefits for governing parties 47, 49, 89,
    107–110
  democracy strengthened by 22–23
  measurement of 65–66
  recommendations for mainstream parties
    176–178
income inequality. *See also* economic
  inequality; wage inequality
  micro- and macro-level consequences of
    142–143
  as policy outcome 49
  social identity influenced by 55, 58
  support for radical left and right linked to
    171
income redistribution. *See* redistribution
  policies
industrial employment
  changes over time 31–33, 32*f*
  decline in 3–4
  defined 31–32 n.5
  share of union members in 39*f*, 39–40
inequality. *See* economic inequality
Inglehart, Ronald 6, 22 n.26
Insider-Outsider Model 21, 133, 149–150.
  See also labour market insiders and
  outsiders
institutional approach to unemployment
  151–153
International Survey Programme (ISSP)
  robustness checks using 190*t*, 191*t*
  social identity and national pride
    questions 72–73
  use in statistical model 17–18, 184*t*
interpersonal *vs.* intergroup relations 50–51
  n.1

investment-oriented policies. *See* active
  labour market policies (ALMPs)
issue ownership
  aspects of 62–63
  immigration 14, 62–63, 172, 174–175
issue salience. *See also* cultural issue
  salience; economic issue salience;
  social identity, effect on issue salience
  (model Stage 2)
  blue-collar worker and party positions
    61–63, 62*f*
  EES data on 18
  social identity influence on 10–11, 13
  vote choice influenced by 60
issue salience, effect on party support
  (model Stage 3)
  expected results 13–14, 173
  overview 54–55
  policymaking process mediation effect
    99–104, 101*t*, 102*t*, 192*t*, 193*t*
  policy outcome mediation effect 156–160,
    159*t*, 161*t*, 196*t*, 197*t*
  policy output mediation effect 126–130,
    127*t*, 129*t*, 194*t*, 195*t*
  preliminary tests on 25, 75–79, 77*t*
  survey datasets used 17–19
  theoretical argument for 60–63, 173

J

job search subsidy perspective on
  unemployment 150–151, 153
job security. *See* security of employment

K

Kalla, Joshua L. 182
Keele, Luke 19–20, 97, 156–158
King, Gary 98
Kingzette, Jon 182

L

labour market insiders and outsiders
  changes over time 35*t*, 35–36
  defined 133
  effects of EPL *vs.* LMPs 25–26, 130,
    133–136, 135*t*, 136*f*, 137–138, 174
  increased support for PRRPs by both
    136–137, 137*f*
  union engagement with 105 n.19

labour market policies (LMPs). *See also* government spending on labour market policies
  benefits of inclusive decision-making on 49
  changes in policy mix 122
  defined 113–114
  unemployment focus of 118
labour market segmentation. *See also* labour market insiders and outsiders
  EPL effects on 114–115
  labour market reforms spurred by 116–118
labour unions. *See also* union membership
  fragmentation among 85–86, 88, 94–95
  inequality reduced by 38, 151–152
  participation in social pact negotiations 11–12, 65–66, 87–89
  political awareness among 15
  recommendations for mainstream parties 21, 176–178
  in the US 177–178
labour unions, declining power of
  from de-industrialization 38–40, 39*f*
  PRRP views on 180
  social identity influenced by 58
  vulnerability of lower-skilled workers to 164
  wage inequality affected by 146–147
left-wing parties. *See* mainstream left-wing parties; populist radical left-wing parties (PRLPs)
Le Pen, Marine 3–4, 177
LMPs. *See* labour market policies (LMPs)

M

macro-context, defined 48. *See also* policymaking processes; policy outcomes; policy outputs
macro-context, effect on social identity (model Stage 1)
  expected results 11–13, 173
  factors in 21
  multinomial logistic regression analysis 70–72 n.32, 184*t*
  overview 54–55
  preliminary tests on 25, 64–72, 69*t*, 71*f*
  robustness checks on the model 67 n.30, 190*t*
  survey datasets used 17–19

theoretical argument for 55–59, 173
Macron, Emmanuel 117–118, 177
mainstream left-wing parties
  economic and cultural positions of 7–8 n.10, 40–41, 61, 62*f*
  electoral constituency of 149–150
  former support from the working class 1, 40
  vote share by decade 41*t*
mainstream parties
  economic and cultural positions of 7–8, 49–50, 174–175
  inclusive policymaking benefits for 47, 49, 89, 107–110
  lack of response to working class concerns 6–8
  policymaking process opportunities for 49–50, 176
  policy output opportunities for 138, 176
  recommendations for 21, 176–178
mainstream right-wing parties
  changing views on cultural issues 40–41
  leftward shift on economic issues 7–8
  tempered opposition to welfare state policies 40
  vote share by decade 41–42
manual workers, defined 30–31. *See also* working class
manufacturing employment. *See* industrial employment
Meloni, Giorgia 183 n.5
mobilization thesis 147–148 n.12
Mudde, Cas 29–30 n.2

N

nationalism
  among PRRPs 1, 28–29, 31
  among the working class 6
  aspects of 72–73 n.34
  authoritarian tendencies linked to 55–56, 55–56 n.8
  nativist 1 n.2, 28–29, 28–29 n.1, 31, 60
national pride
  as measure of nation-based social identity 18–19, 72–73 n.34, 191*t*
  policymaking process mediation effect 92, 99–104, 101*t*, 102*t*
  policy outcome mediation effect 156–160, 159*t*, 161*t*

236 Index

national pride (*Continued*)
  policy output mediation effect 126–130,
    127t, 129t
National Rally (France) 1, 3–4, 177, 180, 183
nation-based social identity
  cultural issue salience linked to 2–3, 20,
    59–60
  macro-context effect on 2–3, 11–13,
    22–23, 64–72, 69t, 71f, 91
  national pride as measure of 18–19, 72–73
    n.34, 191t
  policymaking process mediation effect
    91–92, 99–104, 101t, 102t, 192t, 193t
  policy outcome mediation effect 156–160,
    159t, 161t, 196t, 197t
  policy output mediation effect 126–130,
    127t, 129t, 194t, 195t
  political relevance of 2–3
  self-reinforcing nature of inequality
    influenced by 24, 180
  survey datasets used 17–19
  in the three-stage theory 2–3, 10–11,
    55–59, 79
nativist nationalism
  defined 1 n.2, 28–29 n.1
  issue salience of 60
  PRRP promotion of 28–29, 31
neo-corporatist countries, social pacts in
    85–86, 85–86 n.2
neoliberal policies
  contribution to the crisis of democracy
    22–23
  inequality influenced by 146–147, 170
  perceived necessity of 49–50, 109,
    117–118
  political discontent theory views on 7–8
  working-class support for PRRPs
    influenced by 2–3, 21
Netherlands, neoliberal reform in 88–89
Nolan, Brian 141–142
Norris, Pippa 6, 22 n.26

O

occupation
  ISSP data used for 17–18
  role in economic class 34–35
  support for PRRPs by 42–46, 44t, 45t
  wage inequality and 141–142
offshoring 33, 163–164
opinion on imports

policymaking process mediation effect
    99–104, 101t, 102t, 192t, 193t
  policy outcome mediation effect 156–160,
    159t, 161t, 196t, 197t
  policy output mediation effect 126–130,
    127t, 129t, 194t, 195t
organized labour. *See* labour unions

P

Paskov, Marii 141–142
passive labour market policies (PLMPs)
  defined 12 n.17, 113–114
  effects on party support 130–133, 132t,
    137–138
  in measurement of government spending
    66
  unemployment and inequality influenced
    by 119
  variation across countries and over time
    120, 122
permeability of social groups 53, 56–58
policymaking processes. *See also* inclusive
    policymaking; social pact formation
    process; unilateral reform legislation
  defined 2–3, 11, 48
  lack of scholarly focus on 47, 49–50
  literature review on 47–50
  measurement of 65–66
  opportunities for mainstream parties 47,
    176
  political efficacy influence on 82–83
  recommendations for future research
    178–179
  social identity influenced by 10–11,
    65–72, 69t, 71f
  in the three-stage theory 2–3, 11–12
policymaking processes, effect on party
    support. *See also* social pact
    agreements, effect on party support;
    social pact failures, effect on party
    support; unilateral reform legislation,
    effect on party support
  expected results 11–12, 81
  first-stage model results 192t, 193t
  literature review on 82–83
  robustness checks on model 92 n.11, 199t,
    201t
  summary of findings 25, 174–176
policy outcomes. *See also* unemployment
    inequality; wage inequality

defined 2–3, 11, 48, 139
difficulty of identifying causes of 112
literature review on 47–50
measurement of 66–67
skill level and impacts of 16
social identity influenced by 10–11, 66–72, 71*f*
in the three-stage theory 2–3, 11–13
policy outcomes, effect on party support. *See also* unemployment inequality, effect on party support; wage inequality, effect on party support
expected results 12–13, 139
first-stage model results 196*t*, 197*t*
literature review on 139–140
robustness checks on model 92 n.11, 199*t*, 201*t*
summary of findings 26, 174–176
policy outputs. *See also* employment protection legislation (EPL); government spending on labour market policies
defined 2–3, 11, 48
literature review on 47–50
measurement of 66
opportunities for mainstream parties 47, 176
social identity influenced by 10–11, 66–72, 69*t*, 71*f*
in the three-stage theory 2–3, 11–12
policy outputs, effect on party support. *See also* employment protection legislation (EPL), effect on party support; government spending on labour market policies, effect on party support
expected results 12, 111
first-stage model results 194*t*, 195*t*
literature review on 112–113
robustness checks on model 92 n.11, 199*t*, 201*t*
summary of findings 25–26, 174–176
political awareness
union membership influence on 21, 104
working-class support for PRRPs influenced by 14–16
political discontent theory
literature review on 6–8
overview 1–2
policy outputs associated with 49
shortcomings of 9, 20, 172

political efficacy 82–83, 104
political participation
factors influencing 22–23, 22–23 n.25
political efficacy and 82–83
unemployment effects on 147–148 n.12
populist movements
democracy threatened by 29
lengthy history of 7
populist radical left-wing parties (PRLPs)
clarity on issues 22 n.27
emphasis on leftist economic positions 40–41
inequality linked to support for 170–171
vote share by decade 41*t*
populist radical right-wing parties (PRRPs). *See also* working-class support for the populist radical right
authoritarian nature of 22, 29, 180–181
changing constituency of 3, 174–175
characteristics of 1, 24, 28–30
clarity on issues 22 n.27, 174–175
democracy threatened by 22, 180–182
economic and cultural positions of 8 n.11, 40–41, 60–63, 62*f*, 174–175
efforts to weaken unions 180
growing support for 1, 182–183
issue ownership of immigration 14, 62–63, 172, 174–175
label for 27–28
list of 29–30 n.2, n.3, 30*t*, 92 n.11
participation in governing coalitions 41–42 n.16, 182–183
supply-side *vs.* demand-side factors in strength of 48
vote share by decade 41*t*, 41–42
welfare state policies of 131, 133
Power Resource Theory (PRT)
assumption of uniform policy preferences 160–162
EPL views 115–116
LMP spending views 120, 122
unemployment inequality views 149–150
union membership and political awareness 21
wage inequality views 143
productive policies. *See* active labour market policies (ALMPs)
pro-regulatory approach to unemployment 151–152

238 Index

protective policies. *See* passive labour market policies (PLMPs)
protest voting 6–7, 6–7 n.9, 178–179
PRRPs. *See* populist radical right-wing parties (PRRPs)
PRRP Support Index 43
public trust, political efficacy and 82–83. *See also* trust in parliament
Tutnam, Robert 34 n.6

R
redistribution policies
  blue-collar worker and party positions 55 n.7, 61, 62*f*
  economic inequality effects on preferences 142
  support by working class subgroup 37*t*, 37–38
  unemployment effects on preferences 147–148
Republicans (Germany) 43–44, 43–44 n.17
reservation wages 118, 121, 131, 146–147, 150–151
right-wing parties. *See* mainstream right-wing parties; populist radical right-wing parties (PRRPs)
Rooduijn, Matthijs 170–171
Rueda, David 133
Rutte, Mark 88–89

S
security of employment
  de-industrialization effects on 34
  effects of EPL *vs.* LMP government spending 21, 25–26, 114, 118, 122, 133–134, 137–138, 174
  labour insiders *vs.* outsiders 15–16, 133
  skill level and 162–163
  welfare state policy preferences and 36–38, 163, 176–177
sequential ignorability assumption 97 n.13, 103–104
service employment
  changes over time 31–33, 32*f*
  defined 31–32 n.5
  share of union members in 39*f*, 39–40
  support for PRRPs and 42–46, 44*t*, 45*t*
Shayo, Moses 10–11, 55, 58–59
skill-biased technological change 34, 146–147, 163, 170

skill level
  changes over time 35*t*, 35–36
  defined 162–163 n.26
  de-industrialization effects according to 34
  education level correlated with 164–165
  impacts of economic inequality influenced by 16, 21, 26, 146–147
  inequality within the working class and 160–165, 165*f*, 166*f*
  policy preferences and 37*t*, 37–38, 160–163
skill level, effect on party support
  expected results 165
  logistic regression model 166–170, 168*t*, 169*f*
  summary of findings 174
small business owners
  LMP spending views 118
  support for PRRPs among 42–46, 44*t*, 45*t*
social capital
  multiple meanings of 34 n.6
  role in economic class 34–35
social categorization and identification 53 n.4
Social Catholicism Thesis 115–116
social group membership
  issue salience influenced by 59
  social identity *vs.* 50–54
social identity. *See also* class-based social identity; macro-context, effect on social identity (model Stage 1); nation-based social identity; social identity, effect on issue salience (model Stage 2)
  availability of 52, 58
  comparative *vs.* normative fit of 52
  defined 9, 50–51
  dynamic nature of 53–54, 173
  ISSP data used for 17–18
  literature review on 25, 47, 173
  multinomial logistic analysis on 184*t*
  political awareness and 14–15 n.19
  social group membership *vs.* 50–54
social identity, effect on issue salience (model Stage 2)
  expected results 13, 173
  overview 54–55
  preliminary tests on 25, 72–75, 73*t*, 74*t*
  survey datasets used 17–19
  theoretical argument for 59–60, 173

social identity approach, defined 51–52
social identity theory of working-class
      support for the populist radical right.
      See also issue salience, effect on party
      support (model Stage 3);
      macro-context, effect on social identity
      (model Stage 1); social identity, effect
      on issue salience (model Stage 2);
      working-class support for the populist
      radical right
   implications of findings 20–24, 176–182
   overview 2–3, 9–10
   preliminary tests on 48, 63–64, 79
   stages of the model 10*f*, 10–14, 47–48
   summary of findings 2–3, 174–176
   theoretical argument 2–3, 10–11, 54–55,
      79, 173
social pact agreements
   benefits for governing parties 89, 107–109
   data on 83–87, 84*t*, 86*f*
   measurement of 91
   social identity influenced by 65–72, 69*t*
   union interests reflected in 105
social pact agreements, effect on party
      support
   expected results 11–12, 81, 91
   logistic regression model results 92–96,
      93*t*
   robustness checks on model 199*t*, 201*t*
   union membership impacts 104–109, 106*t*
social pact failures
   electoral consequences of 89–90
   frequency of 84*t*, 84–85
   measurement of 91
   social identity influenced by 65–72, 69*t*,
      71*f*
social pact failures, effect on party support
   causal mediation model results 99–104,
      101*t*
   expected results 11–12, 81, 91
   first-stage model results 192*t*
   logistic regression model results 92–96,
      93*t*, 175–176
   robustness checks on model 199*t*, 201*t*
   summary of findings 174
   union membership impacts 104–109,
      106*t*, 108*f*
social pact formation process. *See also* social
      pact agreements; social pact failures;
      unilateral reform legislation

expected effects on working-class support
      for PRRPs 25, 81, 90–91
   measurement of 65–66, 91
   social identity influenced by 11–12, 15
   union membership and 15, 21, 25,
      104–109, 106*t*, 108*f*
   utilization by governments 83–87, 84*t*,
      86*f*
social pacts
   defined 83
   first *vs.* second generation of 88–89, 94–95
   history of 87–90
sociotropic voting 140
spending on labour market policies. *See*
      government spending on labour
      market policies
state corporatism 85–86 n.2
statistical methodology. *See* causal
      mediation analysis models
status
   economic inequality-based loss of 55
   role in social identity 9–10
   of social groups 53–54
   working class loss of 1–2, 3–4, 57–58
supply-side factors in party support 48
supply-side policies. *See* active labour
      market policies (ALMPs)
survey data. *See also* European Election
      Studies (EES); European Values Study
      (EVS); International Survey
      Programme (ISSP)
   lack of single survey with relevant
      questions 16–17
   use in statistical model 17–19
Sweden Democrats 1, 180
symbolic boundaries 54

T

technological advancements. *See* skill-biased
      technological change
Tingley, Dustin 19–20, 97, 156–158
Tomz, Michael 98
Trump, Donald 177–178
trust in parliament
   policymaking process mediation effect
      99–104, 101*t*, 102*t*, 192*t*, 193*t*
   policy outcome mediation effect 156–160,
      159*t*, 161*t*, 196*t*, 197*t*
   policy output mediation effect 126–130,
      127*t*, 129*t*, 194*t*, 195*t*

240 Index

U

Underhill, Geoffrey 170–171
unemployment
  economic grievance theory views on 4–5
  EPL effects on 114–115
  labour market reforms spurred by
    116–118
  LMPs focused on 118, 122
  occurrence among the working class 147
  as policy outcome 49
  role in economic voting 140
  support for PRRPs and 78
  varying explanations for 149–153
  welfare state policy effects on 150–151
unemployment inequality
  importance to the working class 147
  measurement of 66–67, 149
  micro- and macro-level consequences of
    147–148
  recommendations for mainstream parties
    176–177
  social identity influenced by 66–72, 71*f*
  variation across countries and over time
    140–141, 149–154, 150*t*, 152*f*, 170
  within the working class 12–13, 160–165,
    166*f*, 171
unemployment inequality, effect on party
    support
  causal mediation model results 156–160,
    161*t*, 170–171
  expected results 12–13, 139, 154
  first-stage model results 197*t*
  logistic regression model results 154, 156,
    157*t*, 175–176
  robustness checks on model 199*t*, 201*t*
  skill level interactions 166–170, 168*t*, 169*f*
  summary of findings 174
unilateral reform legislation
  measurement of 65–66, 91
  social identity influenced by 65–72, 69*t*,
    71*f*
  utilization by governments 83–87, 84*t*,
    86*f*
unilateral reform legislation, effect on party
    support
  causal mediation model results 99–104,
    101*t*
  expected results 11–12, 81, 90–91
  first-stage model results 193*t*

  logistic regression model results 91–96,
    96*t*, 108*f*, 175–176
  robustness checks on model 199*t*, 201*t*
  summary of findings 174
  union membership impacts 104–109,
    106*t*, 108*f*
union density, changes over time 38–40, 39*f*
union membership. *See also* labour unions
  decline in 38–40, 58, 107–109, 146–147
  de-industrialization effects and 34
  effect on party support 104–109, 106*t*,
    108*f*, 174
  income level influence on 23–24 n.28
  political awareness influenced by 21, 104
  social capital influenced by 35
  social pact formation process and 15, 21,
    25, 104–109, 106*t*, 108*f*
  support for redistribution linked to 37*t*,
    37–38
  two-way causality with inequality 23–24
unions. *See* labour unions
United States
  COVID-19 pandemic response 154 n.20
  crisis of democracy in 180–182
  organized labour in 177–178
  rural social identity in 57 n.11

V

van Noort, Sam 170–171
Varieties of Capitalism (VOC)
  EPL variations explained by 115–116
  LMP spending variations explained by
    120, 122
  skill level and response to inequality 21
  unemployment inequality views 150–152
  wage inequality variations explained by
    143–144
veto points, labour market spending reforms
    influenced by 122
Vlandas, Tim 128–130 n.13

W

wage inequality
  importance to the working class 141–142
  measurement of 66–67, 143, 145
  micro- and macro-level consequences of
    142–143
  recommendations for mainstream parties
    176–177
  social identity influenced by 66–72, 71*f*

variation across countries and over time 140–141, 143–147, 144*t*, 145*f*, 170
within the working class 12–13, 160–165, 165*f*
wage inequality, effect on party support
causal mediation model results 156–160, 159*t*, 170–171
expected results 12–13, 139, 154
first-stage model results 196*t*
logistic regression model results 154–156, 155*t*, 175–176
robustness checks on model 199*t*, 201*t*
skill level interactions 166–171, 168*t*, 169*f*
summary of findings 174
wages
effects of immigrants on 4–5 n.7
reservation wages 118, 121, 131, 146–147, 150–151
union effect on 38, 38 n.10
Weisstanner, David 11, 55, 58, 141–142
welfare state policies. *See also* neoliberal policies
changing views of mainstream parties 40
economic grievance theory views on 4–5
labour market insider *vs.* outsider views on 15–16, 133–134
need for collaboration with organized labour 21, 49, 138
of PRRPs 131, 133
recommendations for mainstream parties 138, 176–178
shift from demand to supply side 88
two-way causality with inequality 23–24, 147–151
varying opinions among working class 36–37, 75–76
Westwood, Sean J. 182
White, native blue-collar workers, empirical focus on 31. *See also* working class

Wilders, Geert 88–89 n.5
withdrawal thesis 147–148 n.12
Wittenberg, Jason 98
working class
as core constituency of PRRPs 3, 174–175
decline in status of 1–2, 3–4, 31, 57–58
defined 1 n.3
demographics of 35*t*, 35–36
economic challenges faced by 24, 27, 31–35, 32*f*
former support for the mainstream left 1, 40
heterogeneity of 27, 36–37, 58, 75–76
immigration views among 61, 62*f*
income redistribution support among 61, 62*f*
political landscape faced by 24, 27
support for union involvement in policymaking 90–91
vulnerability of 163–164
wage inequality importance to 141–142
working-class support for the populist radical right. *See also* social identity theory of working-class support for the populist radical right
demographic information 78
existing explanations for 1–2, 3–9, 172
literature review on 25
other occupations *vs.* 42–46, 44*t*
political awareness and 14–16
rise in 1, 182–183
shortcomings of existing theories on 8–9, 20
summary of argument 20–21, 173
supply side *vs.* demand side factors 48
variation across parties and over time 45*t*, 45–46

Y
Yamamoto, Teppei 19–20, 97, 156–158